DRIVING THE PACIFIC COAST

California

Help Us Keep This Guide Up to Date

Every effort has been made by the author and editors to make this guide as accurate and useful as possible. However, many things can change after a guide is published—establishments close, phone numbers change, hiking trails are rerouted, facilities come under new management, and so on.

We would love to hear from you concerning your experiences with this guide and how you feel it could be made better and be kept up to date. Although we may not be able to respond to all comments and suggestions, we'll take them to heart and we'll also make certain to share them with the author. Please send your comments and suggestions to the following address:

The Globe Pequot Press
Reader Response/Editorial Department
P.O. Box 480
Guilford, CT 06437

Or you may e-mail us at:

editorial@globe-pequot.com

Thanks for your input, and happy travels!

DRIVING THE PACIFIC COAST

California

Fifth Edition

Edited by Donna Peck

The
Globe
Pequot
Press

GUILFORD, CONNECTICUT

Text design by Lisa Reneson
Maps by Lisa Reneson © The Globe Pequot Press
Interior photography by Kenn Oberrecht except p. 95, by Nancy McKarney

ISBN 0-7627-2491-9
ISSN 1542-8605

Manufactured in the United States of America
Fifth Edition/First Printing

CONTENTS

NORTHERN CALIFORNIA

CONTENTS

INTRODUCTION

This is as much a tote-along companion as it is a book for reading, reference, and planning a trip to the California coast. Whether you're taking in all 1,100 miles of California's Pacific edge in a single trip or just looking for a place to relax and breathe some salt air for a couple of days, this is your getaway guide. You'll find it conveniently organized and easy to follow, regardless of which way you're traveling—up the coast, down the coast, or to a single destination.

Integral to the book, indeed its essence, is the idea of *getting away*, slipping off physically to a different place, perhaps mentally to a different time, and above all to a different pace. Often as important as getting to where you're going is getting away from where you are, especially if where you are is a throbbing megalopolis with crushing crowds and rushing freeways. *Getting away* means life in the slow lane.

That's one reason the largest city covered here is San Diego, and most others are considerably smaller. Another reason you won't find chapters on greater Los Angeles and the San Francisco Bay Area is that each would require another volume this size. Indeed, just a cursory coverage of San Francisco's restaurants would take a book as big as this. Besides, there are already plenty of books in print about those cities.

Instead of actual rates for lodging and campgrounds and prices for meals, you will find price ranges in this book expressed as *inexpensive*, *moderate*, *expensive*, and so on. Keep in mind that prices change and that these ranges are general. For example, if abalone is the only expensive entree on an otherwise moderately priced menu, prices are considered moderate.

Lodging rates are based on two-person occupancy. Room rates up to $125 are *inexpensive*, up to $185 *moderate*, up to $250 *expensive*, $251 to $500 *very expensive*, and over $500 *extremely expensive*.

Campground and RV-park rates are based on spaces for one vehicle with water and electrical hookups and either sewer hookup or tank dump available. Up to $15 a day is *inexpensive*, $16 to $28 *moderate*, $29 to $44 *expensive*, and over $44 *very expensive*.

Prices for meals are given per person. Breakfast up to $4.00, lunch to $8.00, and dinner to $12.00 qualify as *inexpensive*. Breakfasts from $4.01 to $8.00, lunches from $8.01 to $13.00, and dinners from $13.01 to $20.00 are *moderate*. Breakfasts from $8.01 to $13.00, lunches from $13.01 to $18.00, and dinners from $20.01 to $30.00 are *expensive*. Breakfasts over $13.00, lunches over $18.00, and dinners over $30.00 are *very expensive*.

The term *freeway* has become a metaphor to describe the hectic pace of modern life, and nowhere is the freeway more a part of life than in California. Although much of the coast route—Highway 1 and U.S. 101—is simple two-lane highway, those sections in the more populated areas are freeways. So it's impossible to drive the entire California coast without getting onto freeways from time to time.

California freeways are the butt of many jokes, and in some ways deservedly so. But the freeways in Portland, Seattle, Chicago, and New York are just as bad and just as good. They often get clogged, but they also move a lot of traffic. So don't be intimidated by California freeways; they're no different from freeways elsewhere. In fact, you'll find that California drivers have better freeway skills than most, and, believe it or not, they are among the most courteous drivers anywhere.

When traveling through the Los Angeles and San Francisco areas, try to avoid morning and evening rush hours on weekdays. Traffic is usually lightest in these cities early Saturday or Sunday morning, and very early or late on weekdays.

Coastal California is popular with bicyclists, but some narrow and winding portions of the Coast Highway pose hazards for bikers and drivers alike. On the North Coast, from Bodega Bay to Crescent City, beware of log trucks, which often carry timber. Remain alert, and exercise extra caution where the berm is narrow and bike lanes nonexistent.

It's still possible to rent bicycles in some communities, and rental agencies are listed in the following pages. Soaring insurance premiums, however, have forced many California bike shops out of the rental business. Those planning to augment their travels with bike tours should make sure rental equipment will be available or should take their own bicycles along.

Much of the California coast has a pleasant, Mediterranean climate with little variation between summer and winter temperatures. The northern California coast is seldom hot, even in summer. In fact, evenings and foggy or cloudy days can be chilly. Pack appropriate clothing, including a light parka or windbreaker. October to April is the rainy season on the north coast and stretches of the central coast, but that doesn't mean it rains every day. It means there's a chance it will rain or that a storm will come ashore anytime. So don't be put off by the idea of a rainy season. Just carry rainwear if you're traveling then, and take advantage of lower seasonal rates at many establishments and the uncrowded beaches and parks.

Above all, enjoy your visit to California's great Pacific Coast. If you plan to travel up the coast beyond California, be sure to pick up the companion volume—*Driving the Pacific Coast: Oregon and Washington.*

> *The information and rates listed in this guidebook were confirmed at press time. We recommend, however, that you call establishments before traveling to obtain current information.*

SOUTHERN CALIFORNIA

California Department of Fish and Game
1416 Ninth Street, Twelfth Floor
P.O. Box 944209
Sacramento, CA 94244
(916) 653–7664
www.dfg.ca.gov

California Department of Parks and Recreation
1416 Ninth Street
P.O. Box 942896
Sacramento, CA 94296
(916) 653–6995
www.cal-parks.ca.gov

California Trade and Commerce Agency
Division of Tourism
801 K Street, Suite 1600
Sacramento, CA 95814
(916) 322–2881
Tourist information packet: (800) 862–2543
www.gocalif.ca.gov

MONTEREY

Pacific Grove
Carmel
Pebble
Beach

Little Sur River

Big Sur

POINT SUR

Big Sur River

①

San Simeon

①

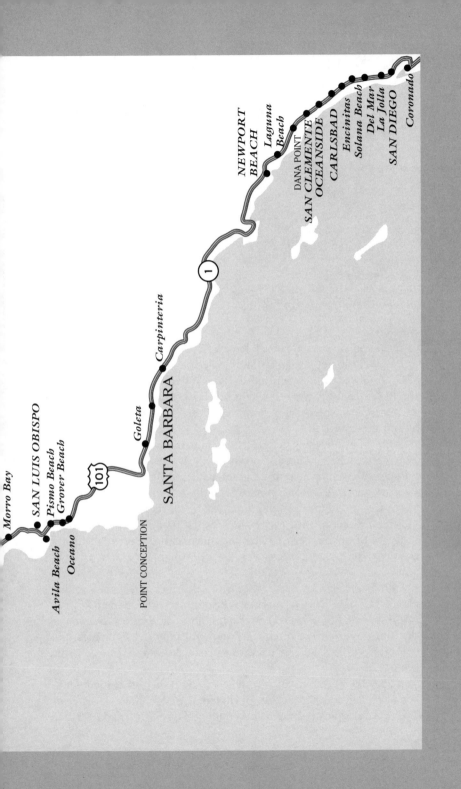

CORONADO

Population: 25,700

Location: *Less than 1 mile west of San Diego, via State Route 75 and the San Diego–Coronado Toll Bridge; 16 miles north of the U.S.–Mexico border; 120 miles south of Los Angeles.*

Coronado is sometimes referred to as an island, and it would be were it not for an isthmus called Silver Strand, which connects it to the mainland. Access to the peninsula is by way of the Route 75 loop, west off I–5 in San Diego, or south of San Diego at Palm City, where Palm Avenue (Route 75) leads west to Silver Strand Boulevard.

The most imposing yet graceful landmark on the peninsula is the famed Hotel del Coronado, known locally as The Del. It was for the purpose of building this magnificent structure that two men, Elisha Babcock and H. L. Story, purchased 4,100 acres of peninsula land in 1885. Construction began in March 1887, and the original five-story, 400-room hotel opened for business eleven months later. No doubt today, with our modern equipment and materials and more than a century of technological advances, the job would take at least twice as long.

From the start, a steady stream of celebrities and dignitaries has passed through The Del's portals, beginning with Thomas Edison, who supervised the lighting installation in the original building. Since that time, a dozen U.S. presidents, numerous foreign dignitaries, and countless movie stars and television personalities have stayed at the hotel.

The Del is a star in its own right, having been featured in a number of Hollywood productions, including the zany fifties classic *Some Like It Hot,* which starred Jack Lemmon, Tony Curtis, and Marilyn

Monroe. Part of *The Stunt Man*, starring Peter O'Toole, was filmed here, as were episodes of various television series, such as *Lifestyles of the Rich and Famous*, *Hart to Hart*, and *Simon and Simon*.

To maintain its stature as one of the world's finest waterfront resorts, the hotel has been continually renovated over the years, but without sacrificing any of its original beauty and appeal. Today its 680 rooms stand on thirty-three acres and constitute the largest beachfront hotel on the Pacific Coast of North America. It is also one of the largest wooden structures in the world.

Even those who haven't the inclination or the shekels to shell out for a stay at The Del ought to at least plan to visit the hotel for its historical value and to examine its elegance and its architecture. A self-guided audiocassette tour of the hotel is available to the public during business hours. The tour begins in the lobby and lasts about forty-five minutes.

The town of Coronado grew around this luxurious hotel into what it is today: a lovely year-round resort community flanked by San Diego Bay and the Pacific Ocean. Coronado's downtown is clustered along Orange Avenue, where visitors stroll and browse in the shops and galleries and enjoy a variety of foods at the area's restaurants and cafes. Ferries provide a pleasant way to travel from the San Diego waterfront, and trolleys serve the Coronado vicinity.

LODGING

Best Western Suites Hotel, 275 Orange Avenue, 92118; (619) 437–1666 or (800) 528–1234. On Orange at Third Avenue, near downtown shops and restaurants. Has 63 units, each with cable TV, refrigerator, microwave, and wet bar. View rooms available. Heated pool, whirlpool, and laundry facilities. Moderate to expensive.

Hotel del Coronado, 1500 Orange Avenue, 92118; (619) 435–6611; in California, (800) 468–3533. Southern California's only beachfront resort is on the ocean side of Orange Avenue, between Adella Avenue and Avenida del Sol. A National Historic Landmark with 680 rooms and every desirable accommodation and amenity, including ocean views, in-room bars, room service, health spa, tennis courts, Olympic-size pool, restaurants, lounges, shops, and opulent lobbies. Expensive to extremely expensive.

Villa Capri, 1417 Orange Avenue, 92118; (619) 435–4137; in California, (800) 231–3954. Overlooks historic Hotel del Coronado. Has 14 rooms and suites with cable TV. Kitchen units available. Heated pool. Near eighteen-hole golf course, tennis courts, health spa, restaurants, and shops. Moderate.

CAMPGROUNDS AND RV PARKS

Silver Strand State Beach, 5000 Highway 75, 92118; (619) 435–5184. On the Strand, southeast of town. En route campsites for overnight use by self-contained RVs only. Fire pits, showers, and facilities for handicapped. Entrance and parking fees. Inexpensive.

FOOD

The Brigantine, 1333 Orange Avenue, 92118; (619) 435–4166. Across from the Hotel del Coronado. Lunch Monday through Friday; dinner daily. Lunch includes seafood fettuccine, jalapeño shrimp, batter-fried seafood, steaks, chicken, and an assortment of hearty sandwiches. Lunch-size salads, such as crab Louis, and seafood-stuffed avocados and tomatoes. More than a dozen dinner appetizers, including jumbo shrimp and crab cocktails, oysters on the half shell, seviche, and steamed clams bordelaise. In addition to fresh catch-of-the-day dinners, such regular menu items as king crab legs, teriyaki shrimp, captain's platter, cioppino, jumbo shrimp, scallops, steaks, and chicken. Oyster bar. Full bar and wine list. Moderate.

Coronado Brewing Company, 170 Orange Avenue, 92118; (619) 437–4452. This microbrewery serves handcrafted beer, wood-fired pizza, salads, and grill specialties. Live entertainment Thursday, Friday, and Saturday nights from 9:30 to closing. Inexpensive to moderate.

Miguel's Cocina Restaurant, 1351 Orange Avenue, 92118; (619) 437–4237. In the courtyard of the El Cordova Hotel, across the street from the Hotel del Coronado. Monday through Saturday, lunch and dinner; Sunday, brunch and dinner. Fine Mexican cuisine. Choose from such appetizers as seviche, *taquitos,* and Mexican shrimp cocktail. Soups, salads, tacos, tostadas, burritos, enchiladas, *chile verde,* jumbo Gulf shrimp, calamari jalapeño, steak ranchero, and such house specialties as *carnitas* and fish tacos. Full bar, including Mexican beers. Inexpensive to moderate.

SHOPPING AND BROWSING

Ferry Landing Marketplace, 1201 First Street, 92118; (619) 435–8895; ferry information, (619) 234–4111. First Street and B Avenue, on the bayfront. Monday through Saturday, 10:00 A.M. to 9:00 P.M.; Sunday, 10:00 A.M. to 6:00 P.M. A shopping center containing specialty shops, galleries, restaurants, boardwalks, fishing piers, and bike rentals. Daily ferry service from the Broadway Pier in San Diego.

Historic Orange Avenue, from Eighth Street to the Hotel Del Coronado. Galleries, boutiques, and bookstores are housed in finely preserved historical buildings along this street.

BEACHES, PARKS, TRAILS, AND WAYSIDES

On the ocean side of Silver Strand Boulevard, south of Coronado, lies the broad, sandy Silver Strand State Beach, popular with swimmers and surfers. This is also an excellent beachcombing area, especially for shells, and a good spot for picnics.

Farther up the Strand, at Coronado, Coronado Shores Beach and Coronado City Beach offer swimming and surfing as their main activities. Avenida Lunar, Avenida de las Arenas, and Avenida del Sol lead west off Silver Strand Boulevard to a concrete promenade overlooking Coronado Shores Beach. City Beach lies north of the Strand and west of Ocean Boulevard. On the bay side of the Strand, across from Coronado Shores Beach, is Glorietta Bay Park, with a picnic area, playground, and municipal swimming pool.

WATER SPORTS AND ACTIVITIES

Anglers in this part of California enjoy some of the best saltwater fishing in the state, with a great variety of sport and food fishes available in good numbers. In the immediate vicinity of Coronado, surf fishing is popular along the ocean beaches, primarily for bass, croaker, corbina, and perch. Bay waters offer angling for bass, croaker, halibut, mackerel, perch, shark, and smelt, from shore, piers, and boats.

Offshore fishing is good all year for many species, including barracuda, bonito, halibut, kelp bass, rockfish, sheephead, yellowtail, and various bottom dwellers. Summer angling focuses on such game fishes as albacore, yellowfin tuna, shark, and dolphin (fish).

Those who tow boats to the area will find launching facilities at Glorietta Bay Park, off Silver Strand Boulevard, and at Glorietta Bay Marina, on Strand Way, east of Silver Strand Boulevard. Rental boats are also available at the marina.

RENTALS

Coronado Boat Rentals, 1715 Strand Way, 92118; (619) 437-1514. Rents a variety of watercraft seven days a week, weekdays from 8:00 A.M. to 7:30 P.M. and weekends from 7:00 A.M. to 7:30 P.M. Sailboats include Hobie Cats, Lidos, Victory 21s, Newports, and oceangoing sloops. Rents powerboats for cruising, fishing, and water-skiing as well as Kawasaki Tandem Sports and Wave Runners. Also rents canoes, rowboats, and pedal boats. Sailing and waterskiing lessons available.

Holland's Bicycles, 977 Orange Avenue, 92118; (619) 435–3153. Monday through Friday, 10:00 A.M. to 6:00 P.M.; Saturday, 9:00 A.M. to 6:00 P.M.; Sunday, 11:00 A.M. to 5:00 P.M. Rents, sells, and services Schwinn, Nishiki, and Trek-Klein bikes. Biking clothes available.

TOURS AND TRIPS

Coronado Walking Tour, (619) 435–5993 or 435–5444. Guided walking tours of Coronado depart from the Glorietta Bay Inn, across the street from the Hotel del Coronado, on Tuesday, Thursday, and Saturday at 11:00 A.M. Tours last about an hour and a half.

San Diego Bay Ferry, 1050 North Harbor Drive, San Diego 92101; (619) 234–4111, ext. 2. Ferry service between Coronado and San Diego. Ferry departs from Old Ferry Landing at Coronado every hour on the hour, Sunday through Thursday, 9:30 A.M. to 9:30 P.M.; Friday and Saturday, 9:30 A.M. to 10:30 P.M. Daily trackless-trolley service to the ferry landing. Also offers one- and two-hour harbor excursions.

GOLF

Coronado Municipal Golf Course, 2000 Visalia Row, 92118; (619) 435–3121. West of the San Diego–Coronado Toll Bridge, via Glorietta Boulevard. A municipal eighteen-hole, 6,466-yard, par-seventy-two course open to the public. Driving range and snack bar.

OTHER ATTRACTIONS

Coronado Playhouse, 1775 Strand Way, 92118; (619) 435–4856 (24-hour answering service). Just south of Coronado Boat Rental on Glorietta Bay. Thursday, Friday, and Saturday at 8:00 P.M.; Sunday at 2:00 P.M. Live theater and cocktails on the bay. Dinner shows on Saturday.

TRAVEL INFORMATION

Coronado Visitors Bureau, 1100 Orange Avenue, 92118; (619) 437–8788 or (800) 622–8300; www.coronadovisitors.com.

SAN DIEGO

Population: 2,600,000

Location: *In the southwest corner of the state, on I–5, I–8, and I–15; 16 miles north of the U.S.–Mexico border and 120 miles south of Los Angeles.*

How could San Diego be any better? By most standards, the climate is perfect. Mexico is only minutes away. Warm Pacific and bay waters lapping at the city's edges make surfing and swimming essential elements of the San Diego life-style. Scuba diving, snorkeling, and saltwater angling are unsurpassed anywhere in the state. The county is speckled with lakes and reservoirs offering excellent freshwater fishing and some of the biggest largemouth bass in the world. Golf courses galore, plenty of parks, and a myriad of museums, shops, galleries, and superb restaurants—what more could any traveler want?

The current estimate puts the population of greater San Diego at more than two million, making it one of the fastest-growing metropolitan areas and the seventh-largest city in the United States. But San Diego doesn't seem to suffer from those numbers. The city contradicts itself. It has crowds but isn't crowded. Despite all the vehicles, there's no sign of gridlock, and parking seems adequate everywhere. As big as the city is, it's easy to get around in, and it's not intimidating to visitors, who can avoid the freeways altogether if they wish.

So it's the contrasts that make San Diego such a pleasant surprise—the contrasts and the friendly natives. This is a busy, bustling boomtown full of laid-back people. Maybe it's the water—not something in the water that affects the people, but all that water the people spend so much time in, on, and near—that makes them so relaxed and hospitable. After all, there are 70 miles of beach, sprawling bays, and the Pacific Ocean, not to mention countless miles of trails, paths, boardwalks, sidewalks, and grassy parks. It's the joggers and bikers and skaters and hikers, anglers and sailors and surfers and swimmers, shoppers and browsers and theatergoers, picnic lovers and bird-watchers and Margarita sippers—everybody bent on the serious pursuit of fun.

How could San Diego be any better? What more could any traveler want?

LODGING

Andrea Villa Inn, 2402 Torrey Pines Road, La Jolla 92037; (858) 459–3311 or (800) 411–2141. West of I–5, via La Jolla Village Drive or Ardath Road. Cable TV in 50 rooms. Heated pool, sundeck, and exercise room. Near shops, restaurants, beaches, University of California–San Diego, Scripps Institution, and Torrey Pines Golf Course. Complimentary continental breakfast served poolside. Moderate to expensive.

Balboa Park Inn, 3402 Park Boulevard, 92103; (619) 298–0823 or (800) 938–8181. East of I–5, near Balboa Park. Has 26 suites with cable TV, cable movies, wet bars, some fireplaces, and some in-room whirlpools. Complimentary continental breakfast. Walk to the zoo. Moderate to expensive.

The Beach Cottages, 4255 Ocean Boulevard, 92019; (858) 483–7440. Located on the beach, west of I–5 and Mission Boulevard, in the Pacific Beach area. Cable TV in 78 units, including motel rooms, 1- and 2-bedroom apartments, and cottages. All but motel rooms have kitchens. Patios, balconies, barbecues, shuffleboard, and table tennis. Near restaurants and shops. Moderate to expensive.

Best Western Blue Sea Lodge, 707 Pacific Beach Drive, 92109; (858) 488–4700 or (800) 258–3732. West of I–5 and Mission Boulevard, in the Pacific Beach area. Queen and king beds in 100 rooms with cable TV. Standard and luxury oceanfront rooms with balconies and patios, suites with full kitchens. Skylights and sunken tubs in some rooms. Pool, whirlpool, and beach access. Expensive.

Dana Inn and Marina, 1710 West Mission Bay Drive, 92109; (619) 222–6440 or (800) 345–9995. West of I–5, in the Mission Bay area. Cable TV and coffeemakers in 196 rooms. Heated pool, whirlpool, tennis courts, and shuffleboard. Restaurant and private marina on premises. Paddleboat and bicycle rentals. Walk to Sea World. Expensive.

Holiday Inn San Diego Bayside, 4875 North Harbor Drive, 92106; (619) 224–3621 or (800) 345–9995. West of I–5 and south of I–8, via Rosecrans Street or Nimitz Boulevard, across the street from the marina and sportfishing docks. Cable TV, cable movies, and coffeemakers in 237 rooms. Balconies, bay view, and free newspapers. Pool, putting green, whirlpool, exercise room, volleyball, and shuffleboard. Bakers Square Restaurant and Seapoint Bottle Shop on premises. Expensive.

Humphrey's Half Moon Inn, 2303 Shelter Island Drive, 92106; (619) 224–3411 or (800) 345–9995. On Shelter Island, west of I–5 and south of I–8, via Rosecrans. Cable TV and cable movies in 182 rooms. Heated pool, whirlpool, bay view, private marina and yacht basin, putting green, gift shop, sight-seeing tours, airport and Amtrak limousine service. Humphrey's Restaurant on premises. Expensive.

The Sands of La Jolla, 5417 La Jolla Boulevard, La Jolla 92037; (858) 459–3336. North of Pacific Beach and west of I–5, in the village of La Jolla. Cable TV in 38 rooms with coffeemakers and mini-refrigerators. Kitchen suites available. Near shops, restaurants, tennis courts, golf course, and beaches. Heated pool. Ocean view. Inexpensive to moderate.

CAMPGROUNDS AND RV PARKS

Chula Vista RV Park, 460 Sandpiper Way, Chula Vista 92010; (619) 422–0111. West of I–5, south of San Diego. Has 237 full-hookup sites, showers, laundry, and pool. On San Diego Bay, adjacent to 550-slip marina. Tackle shop, cafe, boat ramp, RV supplies, and free shuttle to trolley. Expensive.

De Anza Harbor Resort, 2727 De Anza Road, 92109; (800) 924–7529. West of I–5, on the beach at Mission Bay, near Sea World. Has 245 sites with water and electricity hookups. Showers, tank dump, beach access, and boat ramps. Moderate to expensive.

San Diego Metro KOA Kampground, 111 North Second Avenue, Chula Vista 92010; (619) 427–3601. East of I–5 and west of I–805, between downtown San Diego and the Mexican border. Has 200 full-hookup and 45 tent sites. Pull-through sites and Kamping Kabins available. Tables, fire pits, firewood, showers, pool, whirlpool, recreation room, and horseshoe pits. Propane available. Expensive.

FOOD

Dakota Grill & Spirits, 901 Fifth Avenue, 92101; (619) 234–5554. At the Gaslamp Quarter. Lunch and dinner Monday through Friday; dinner Saturday and Sunday. Award-winning, upscale but casual restaurant with a menu featuring salads, pasta dishes, wood-fired pizzas, mesquite-grilled steaks, the freshest seafood, and house-made desserts. Full bar. Moderate.

Humphrey's Restaurant and Casablanca Lounge, 2241 Shelter Island Drive, 92106; (619) 224–3577. On Shelter Island, west of I–5 and south of I–8, via Rosecrans. Daily breakfast, lunch, and dinner; Sunday brunch. Sunday brunch features salads, omelets made to order, carved roasts, pasta, pizza, tacos, desserts, and free-flowing champagne. For dinner try such fresh seafood as salmon, halibut, swordfish, Cajun shrimp, or the lobster clambake: live Maine lobster steamed with oysters and crab, served with clarified butter, red potatoes, and an ear of corn. Full bar. Moderate.

Miguel's Cocina Restaurant, 2912 Shelter Island Drive, 92106; (619) 224–2401. In Point Loma, near Shelter Island and the sport-fishing docks. Monday through Friday, lunch and dinner; Saturday, dinner; Sunday, brunch and dinner. Mexican food. Brunch includes a variety of egg dishes—both Mexican and American. Soups, salads, tacos, tostadas, burritos, enchiladas, chimichangas, shrimp fajitas, and Mexican-style steaks. Full bar. Inexpensive to moderate.

Old Columbia Brewery & Grill, 1157 Columbia Street, 92101; (619) 234–2739. Between B and C Streets, downtown. Daily lunch and dinner. A working pub brewery producing and selling beverages brewed on the premises from the private recipes of Karl M. Strauss, a German-born, Bavarian-trained brewmaster. Sample the beers with a variety of snacks and appetizers or with such lunch and dinner entrees as half-pound hamburgers, grilled sausages and chicken, marinated short ribs, beer-batter fish-and-chips, and daily fresh-fish specials. Brewery tours available. Moderate.

SHOPPING AND BROWSING

Bazaar del Mundo, 2754 Calhoun Street, 92110; (619) 296–3161. Daily, 10:00 A.M. to 9:00 P.M. In Historic Old Town. Has fourteen shops and galleries offering crafts, gifts, collectibles, dinnerware, fabrics, artwork, jewelry, toys, and more. Also five restaurants.

Horton Plaza, Fourth and Broadway, 92101; (619) 238–1596. Between First and Fourth Avenues and Broadway and G Street, 3 blocks east of Harbor Drive, downtown. Enter from Fourth Avenue or G Street. Monday through Friday, 10:00 A.M. to 9:00 P.M.; Saturday, 10:00 A.M. to 9:00 P.M.; Sunday, 10:00 A.M. to 7:00 P.M. Restaurants, theaters, and some shops stay open later. A kaleidoscope of color and design, with several department stores and 140 specialty shops. Shop, browse, and dine inside or out. Fine restaurants and pushcart vendors. Mimes, jugglers, and street musicians. Seven-screen cinema. Live performances at the San Diego Repertory Theatre. Easy walk to and from the Embarcadero, Seaport Village, and other downtown attractions. Adjacent to the historic Gaslamp Quarter.

Seaport Village, 849 West Harbor Drive, 92101; (619) 235–6569. West of I–5, on the waterfront, downtown. June through August, 10:00 A.M. to 10:00 P.M. daily; September through May, 9:00 A.M. to 9:00 P.M. daily. More than seventy-five shops, galleries, and restaurants. Gifts, souvenirs, crystal, posters, nautical items, leather, silver, candles, decorative tiles, music boxes, mugs, clothing, toys and games, antiques, collectibles, candy, fudge, cookies, kites, and more.

MUSEUMS

For those who enjoy visiting museums, San Diego has more to offer than most other cities. Nearly two dozen museums exist here, half of them at Balboa Park. A brochure describing them is available at either of the city's two visitor centers.

Firehouse Museum, 1572 Columbia Street, 92101; (619) 232–3473. Thursday and Friday, 10:00 A.M. to 2:00 P.M.; Saturday and Sunday, 10:00 A.M. to 4:00 P.M. Interesting collection of antique fire-fighting equipment, engines, pictures, and memorabilia.

San Diego Aerospace Historical Center, 2001 Pan American Plaza, 92101; (619) 234–8291. At Balboa Park, east of I–5. Daily, 10:00 A.M. to 4:00 P.M. The San Diego Aerospace Museum displays vintage aircraft, aviation artifacts, and various aeronautical exhibits. The International Aerospace Hall of Fame pays tribute to pilots, inventors, and industrialists; displays their portraits; and provides biographical information.

San Diego Maritime Museum, 1306 North Harbor Drive, 92101; (619) 234–9153. West of I–5, downtown, at the Embarcadero. Daily, 9:00 A.M. to 8:00 P.M. Three beautifully preserved ships open for public tours: *Star of India,* an iron-hulled bark launched in

1863; *Medea*, a luxurious 1904 steam yacht; and the *Berkeley*, an 1898 San Francisco Bay steam ferry.

San Diego Natural History Museum, 1788 El Prado, 92101; (619) 232–3821. At Balboa Park, east of I–5. Daily in summer 9:30 A.M. to 5:30 P.M.; rest of the year 9:30 A.M. to 4:30 P.M. Plant and animal displays, gems and minerals, dinosaur skeletons, ecology exhibits, and special hands-on exhibits. Winter whale-watching trips to the Baja lagoons, classes, canyon hikes, and international expeditions.

Stephen Birch Aquarium-Museum, 2300 Expedition Way, Scripps Institution of Oceanography, UCSD, La Jolla 92093; recorded message, (858) 534–3474. West of North Torrey Pines Road. From I–5, take La Jolla Village Drive west about 1 mile; then follow the signs. Open 9:00 A.M. to 5:00 P.M. daily, except Christmas day. More than 3,000 species of fish and invertebrates from the Pacific Northwest to the tropical waters of Mexico and Indo-Pacific reside in thirty-three tanks and the tidepool plaza. The museum features the largest oceanographic exhibit in the United States. Book-and-gift shop and food concession on premises. Rated *must see* for anyone interested in sea life.

BEACHES, PARKS, TRAILS, AND WAYSIDES

At the entrance to San Diego Bay, west of North Island Naval Air Station, a finger of land known as Point Loma pokes southward into the Pacific. This is the site of the Cabrillo National Monument, which honors the Portuguese navigator Juan Rodriguez Cabrillo, who explored the California coast under the Spanish flag in 1542.

The lofty headland offers spectacular views of the ocean, bay, Coronado, and San Diego. From late December through February, this serves as an excellent place to watch gray whales as they pass the point on their 5,000-mile migration from their summer feeding grounds in Alaska to their winter calving grounds in the lagoons of Baja California, Mexico.

The west side of the point is a good place to explore tidepools. Here you'll find more than a hundred species of plants and animals specially adapted to this harsh environment, among them anemone, crabs, tiny sculpins, and even octopuses. You may watch and photograph them, but don't remove any; they're protected by law. The low tides of autumn, winter, and spring are best for studying the tidepools.

Lighthouse aficionados will delight in finding two here. The old Point Loma Lighthouse was built atop the point, 422 feet above sea

Old Point Loma Light in San Diego

level, making its light visible 25 miles out. Its lamp was first lighted on November 15, 1855, but was snuffed only thirty-six years later because fog and low clouds often obscured it. Another light station was erected on the west side of the point, 88 feet above the water, and began operating in March 1891, its light visible 15 miles out.

The monument is open daily from 9:00 A.M. to 5:15 P.M. A visitor center houses a gift shop and offers programs daily in the auditorium. Guided hikes and other activities are also scheduled.

To reach the monument from I–5, take the Rosecrans exit west. Turn right on Canon Street, then left on Catalina Boulevard to Point Loma. From I–8, take Nimitz Boulevard south and turn right on Chatsworth Boulevard, which leads to Catalina Boulevard.

Several beaches and picnic areas are on the bay, at Shelter Island, off North Harbor Drive; Spanish Landing Park, on North Harbor Drive, near Harbor Island; and Embarcadero Marina Park, on Harbor Drive, downtown. South of San Diego, Imperial Beach and Border Field State Park are on the ocean.

Old Town San Diego State Historic Park lies just east of I–5 and south of I–8, near the juncture of the two freeways. Here a number of buildings from San Diego's Mexican and early American periods— 1821 through 1872—stand in the shade of cork, eucalyptus, fig, and olive trees. Restaurants and shops are in the vicinity.

At the west end of town, north of Point Loma, is the crown jewel of San Diego's parks: Mission Bay City Park, the largest aquatic park on the West Coast. It encompasses the bay's entire shoreline, as well as Fiesta Island and Vacation Isle, and includes miles of beaches, trails, and sidewalks and plenty of shops and restaurants.

South of Mission Bay, on the ocean, are Ocean Beach Park, Ocean Beach City Beach, and Sunset Cliffs Park. North of Mission Bay is the La Jolla area, offering a number of beaches and parks on the ocean, tidepools, the La Jolla Caves, and the Coast Walk—a trail along the La Jolla Bluffs, a good vantage for viewing the caves and the abundant bird life.

WATER SPORTS AND ACTIVITIES

Life in San Diego is life on the water, with locals and visitors enjoying every form of water recreation imaginable. In addition to swimming and surfing, scuba diving and snorkeling are popular. Waterskiing is good in the protected waters of San Diego Bay and at Mission Bay.

Several yacht clubs and thousands of boat slips attest to the importance of powerboating and sailing. Opportunities exist here for every level of expertise, from the novice who can practice skills in the gentle bays and backwaters to the expert at navigation and offshore cruising who can set out from San Diego for any port in the world.

There are plenty of launch ramps and hoists for travelers who tow boats. For others, rental equipment of every kind and size is available—from kayaks to cruisers. Kayaking, sailboarding, sailing, and waterskiing instructors offer lessons at various levels, for neophytes looking for an introduction or veterans wanting to brush up on certain skills.

No other place in California offers greater opportunities to anglers than San Diego. Experts agree that the next world-record largemouth bass will come from one of San Diego County's reservoirs, which some years ago were stocked with the Florida strain of largemouth. These fish took well to local waters and have grown fast and large, approaching twenty pounds.

For saltwater angling, opportunities are boundless, with something to fit every angler's desires, from shore and pier fishing on the bay, to ocean surf fishing. Party boats and charter operators work out of Mission Bay and from the sportfishing docks near Shelter Island.

Those fishing from piers take a wide assortment of species, including surfperch, croaker, sea bass, halibut, mackerel, smelt, and shark. South of San Diego is a fishing pier at Imperial Beach, west of I–5, at the end of Palm Avenue. Downtown, fishing piers are west of Harbor

Drive at Embarcadero Marina Park and at the foot of G Street. Shelter Island also has an excellent pier.

Two piers on the west side of town, north of Point Loma, offer ocean fishing. The Ocean Beach Pier is a T-shaped structure, 2,150 feet long, west of Sunset Cliffs Boulevard, at the end of Niagra Avenue. Crystal Pier, in the Pacific Beach area, lies west of Ocean Boulevard at the end of Garnet Street. Although this is a private pier, it's open daily to the public, 7:00 A.M. to 5:00 P.M.

Popular surf-fishing areas south of San Diego are at Border Field State Park and Imperial Beach. Ocean Beach Park, west of Sunset Cliffs Boulevard, is also a good surf-fishing spot. Mission Bay City Park has plenty of shoreline for fishing. In the La Jolla area, Bird Rock, South Bird Rock, Sun Gold Point, and La Jolla Cove are favorite spots for rock and surf fishing.

Fisherman's Landing, 2838 Garrison Street, 92106; (619) 222–0391. Catch reports, (619) 224–1421; from Los Angeles, (213) 930–1015. At the sportfishing docks near Shelter Island. Large fleet of fully equipped short- and long-range sportfishing boats. Trips for albacore and yellowtail. Seasonal trips for rockfish. Trips from two and a half hours to nine days. Long-range trips to Mexico from three to twenty-three days. Also whale-watching excursions and private charters. Fisherman's Landing Tackle Shop stocks a full line of saltwater supplies and repairs tackle.

H & M Landing, 2803 Emerson Street, 92106; (619) 222–1144. Daily catch report, (619) 224–2800. At the sportfishing docks near Shelter Island. Books half-day, full-day, and long-range deep-sea fishing trips. Party trips and charter cruises. Scuba-diving and whale-watching trips. Skiff and tackle rental. Year-round half-day to four-day trips for marlin, yellowtail, sea bass, barracuda, bonito, and bottom fish, as well as albacore, bluefin, yellowfin, and bigeye tuna. Also four- to eight-day long-range trips.

Point Loma Sportfishing, 1403 Scott Street, 92106; (619) 223–1627. Daily catch report, (619) 223–1626 or (619) 224–3474; from Los Angeles, (213) 930–1013. At the sportfishing docks near Shelter Island. Half-day and longer trips to the Coronado Islands and Baja. Albacore trips, July to October; yellowtail trips, April to December. Two- to four-day long-range trips all year. Large fleet of boats from 48 to 90 feet. Also private charters, twilight trips, night shark-fishing trips, and dive trips.

Seaforth Sportfishing, 1641 Quivira Road, 92109; (619) 223–1681. Catch report, (619) 224–6695. Half-day, three-quarter-day, and twilight trips for rockfish, albacore, and other species. Night trips for shark fishing depart at 7:00 P.M. and return at 4:30 A.M. Whale-watching trips in season. Rental tackle available.

RENTALS

Seaforth Boat Rentals, 1641 Quivira Road, 92109; (619) 223–1681. On Mission Bay, west of I–5, north of I–8. Bike and boat rentals. Rents beach-cruiser bikes and tandems. Sailing fleet includes Hobie Cats, Lidos, Victory 21s, Newports, sailboards, and oceangoing sloops. Motor fleet includes cruise boats, speedboats, ski boats, Kawasaki Tandem Sports, Wave Runners, and fishing skiffs. Sailing and waterskiing lessons available.

TOURS AND TRIPS

Old Town Trolley Tours of San Diego, 2115 Kurtz Street, 92101; (619) 298–8687. Daily, 9:00 A.M. to nightfall. Comprehensive, narrated tours of San Diego, including more than one hundred points of interest. Take entire tour in two hours, or get off anywhere to explore and catch the next trolley. Trolleys arrive at stops every twenty to thirty minutes. Included in the route are Old Town, downtown, the Naval Training Center, Harbor Island, the Maritime Museum, San Diego Cruise Ship Terminal, Horton Plaza, Gaslamp Quarter, San Diego Zoo, Balboa Park museums, and the San Diego–Coronado Toll Bridge.

San Diego Harbor Excursions, 1050 North Harbor Drive, 92101; (619) 234–4111. At the Embarcadero. Ferry service to Coronado, dinner-and-dance cruises, and whale-watching excursions. One- and two-hour narrated harbor tours. Charter cruises and private parties. Bay Ferry departs Broadway Pier for Coronado approximately every hour. Sunday through Thursday, 10:00 A.M. to 10:00 P.M.; Friday and Saturday, 10:00 A.M. to 11:00 P.M.

GOLF

Balboa Park Municipal Golf Course, 2600 Golf Course Drive, 92102; pro shop, (619) 239–1660; reservations, (619) 570–1234. At Balboa Park, east of I–5, south of I–8. An eighteen-hole, par-seventy-two, 6,267-yard course and a nine-hole, par-thirty-two, 2,175-yard course. Driving range, putting greens, pro shop, clubhouse, showers, lockers, restaurant, and snack bar.

Carmel Mountain Ranch Country Club, 14050 Carmel Ridge Road, 92128; (858) 451–8353. With eighteen holes, this golf course is rated among the top thirty California courses.

Mission Bay Golf Course, 2702 North Mission Bay Drive, 92109; (858) 490–3370. With eighteen holes, driving range, restaurant, and lounge, this is San Diego's only night-lighted golf course.

Torrey Pines Golf Course, 11480 Torrey Pines Road, La Jolla 92037; office (858) 552–1784; golf shop (800) 985–4653; reservation system (619) 570–1234. An internationally famous municipal facility with two eighteen-hole courses offering superb ocean views. North course is par seventy-two and 6,647 yards; south course is par seventy-four and 7,055 yards. Driving range, pro shop, resident pro, club rental, restaurant, bar, and snack bar.

OTHER ATTRACTIONS

Reuben H. Fleet Space Theater and Science Center, 1875 El Prado, P.O. Box 33303, 92103; (619) 238–1233. At Balboa Park, east of I–5, south of I–8. Daily, 9:30 A.M. to 9:30 P.M. An IMAX/ OMNIMAX large-screen theater with six-channel sound lets you experience the thrills of mountain climbing, downhill skiing, and more. Shows almost hourly. Some shows may be sold out. Call for current schedule.

San Diego Zoo, 2920 Zoo Drive, P.O. Box 551, 92112; (858) 675–7900 or (800) 628–3066. At Balboa Park, east of I–5, south of I–8. July through Labor Day, 9:00 A.M. to 5:00 P.M. daily; post–Labor Day through June, 9:00 A.M. to 4:00 P.M. daily. World-renowned, hundred-acre botanical garden that's home to more than 4,000 rare and endangered animals and 6,500 varieties of exotic plants. Guided bus tour covers 80 percent of the zoo grounds. Aerial tram allows visitors to view animals from an altitude of 170 feet. Classified *must see.*

Sea World, 500 Sea World Drive, 92109; (619) 226–3901 or (800) 325–3150 for sales promotions; elsewhere, (800) 732–9675. At Mission Bay, west of I–5, north of I–8. Daily, 9:00 A.M. to dusk. Shark exhibit, killer-whale show, undersea theater, sea lions, penguins, and dolphins. A variety of entertainers perform daily. Guided tours. Stroller and wheelchair rentals.

TRAVEL INFORMATION

Cabrillo National Monument, National Park Service, 1800 Cabrillo Memorial Drive, 92106; (619) 557–5450; www.nps.gov/cabr

International Visitor Information Bureau, 11 Horton Plaza, 92101; (619) 236–1212; www.sandiego.org

Mission Bay Park Headquarters, Park and Recreation Department, 2581 Quivira Court, 92109; (619) 236–6652

Old Town San Diego State Historic Park, 4002 Wallace Street, 92110; (619) 237–6770

San Diego Convention and Visitors Bureau, 1200 Third Avenue, Suite 824, 92101; (619) 232–3101; recorded visitor information, (619) 239–9696; www.sandiego.org; e-mail: sdinfo@sandiego.org

Visitor Information Center, 2688 East Mission Bay Drive, 92109; (619) 276–8200; www.infosandiego.com

EVENTS

March	Mardi Gras in the Gaslamp Quarter, (619) 232–3101
April	San Diego Opera, (619) 236–1212
	San Diego Crew Classic, (619) 232–3101
June	Mainly Mozart Festival, (619) 236–1212
September	Cabrillo Festival, (619) 557–5450
October	San Diego Arts Festival, (800) 245–3378

DEL MAR

Population: 5,270

ENCINITAS

Population: 57,981

☆

Location: *Del Mar is 6 miles north of La Jolla and 16 miles south of Carlsbad, west of I–5, on Old Highway 101, now Route S21; Encinitas is 6 miles north of Del Mar and 10 miles south of Carlsbad, also on Route S21, as well as I–5.*

Remnants of the old coast highway, U.S. 101, between La Jolla and Carlsbad connect several small coastal communities, with Del Mar in the south, Encinitas in the north, and Solana Beach, a city of 13,000 people, between the two. Although each is distinctly different from the others, the communities share the main attractions of beautiful ocean beaches and a Mediterranean-type climate that moderates both summer and winter temperatures.

In its various incarnations since 1885, Del Mar has enjoyed booms and suffered busts. It has been rural ranchland, run-down beach community, home of Hollywood stars, and playground of the rich and famous. It seems now to have settled comfortably onto the coastal mesa as a charming seaside village, with sidewalk cafes and trendy little boutiques and galleries.

Del Mar is Spanish, meaning "by the sea." The main thoroughfare is the old coast highway, here called the Camino del Mar, or "road by the sea."

Maps and atlases printed before 1986 show the communities of Cardiff-by-the-Sea, Olivenhain, Leucadia, and Encinitas situated between Solana Beach and Carlsbad. But that year Encinitas was incorporated to include all four towns.

Supplying its own orchids and accolades, Encinitas bills itself as the "flower capital of the world." The pleasant climate here—rarely below forty degrees or above eighty-five degrees—is conducive to flower cultivation. Commercial florists of the vicinity produce millions of colorful roses, carnations, poinsettias, and other flowers annually. In addition to the usual activities associated with beaches and coastal communities, several more exotic pastimes are popular here. Watch the skies for sailplanes, hang gliders, and hot-air balloons. Although sailplaning and hang gliding aren't for everyone, anyone who wishes can take a ride in a balloon, and several local companies offer flights, usually with champagne and hors d'oeuvres afterward.

LODGING

Best Western Encinitas Inn at Moonlight Beach, 85 Encinitas Boulevard, Encinitas 92024; (760) 942–7455. West of I–5 via Encinitas Boulevard. Queen and king beds in 94 large rooms and suites, remote-control cable TV, and refrigerators. Kitchenettes, balconies, and in-room whirlpools available. Heated pool, whirlpool, and putting green. Terry robes furnished and daily newspapers delivered. Continental breakfast at poolside cabana. Only 3 blocks to the beach. The Boat House Restaurant on the premises. Moderate to expensive.

Best Western Stratford Inn of Del Mar, 710 Camino del Mar, Del Mar 92014; (858) 755–1501 or (800) 446–7229. South end of town, west of I–5 via Del Mar Heights Road. King beds in 93 rooms and suites with refrigerators, remote-control cable TV, and balcony or terrace. Some ocean views; two outdoor pools and spa. Bridal suite, executive rooms, and kitchenettes available. Walk to the beach, shops, and bistros. Cribs and roll-aways available. Moderate.

Country Inn by Ayres, 1661 Villa Cardiff Drive, Cardiff 92024; (760) 944–0427 or (800) 322–9993. East of I–5, via Birmingham exit. Queen and king beds and sleeper sofas in 105 rooms with refrigerators and Country French decor. Heated pool and whirlpool. Complimentary afternoon tea, happy hour, and full buffet breakfast. Moderate.

Del Mar Inn, 720 Camino del Mar, Del Mar 92014; (858) 755–9765 or (800) 451–4515. South end of town, west of I–5, via Del Mar Heights Road. Double, queen, and king beds in 81 rooms with satellite TV. Choice of oceanside or poolside rooms. Heated pool, whirlpool. Complimentary English tea and cakes each afternoon. Continental breakfast brought to your room. Walk to beach, shops, and restaurants. Moderate.

Del Mar Motel, 1702 Coast Boulevard, Del Mar 92014; (858) 755–1534 or (800) 223–8449. Refrigerators and cable TV in 44 rooms. Located right on the beach; walk to shopping and restaurants. Moderate to expensive.

L'Auberge Del Mar, 1540 Camino del Mar, P.O. Box 2889, Del Mar 92014; (858) 259–1515 or (800) 245–9757. Camino del Mar at Fifteenth Street. An elegant inn opened in the summer of 1989, with 120 rooms and suites with balconies or patios, marble baths, minirefrigerators, wet bars, and canopy beds. Some rooms have cathedral ceilings, fireplaces, and ocean views. European health spa with exercise equipment, steam room, Swiss shower, sauna, and underwater massage tubs. Beauty salon, bar, and Tourla's Restaurant on premises. Walk to shops, restaurants, and beach. Expensive to extremely expensive.

CAMPGROUNDS AND RV PARKS

San Elijo State Beach, (mailing address) 2680 Carlsbad Boulevard, Carlsbad 92008; (760) 753–5091 or (800) 444–7275. In Encinitas, west side of Old Highway 101 (Route S21), north of Chesterfield Drive. The southernmost developed state campground in California, with 171 full-hookup sites, each with table, stove, and cupboard. For RVs and trailers up to 35 feet. Showers, laundry, bait shop, convenience store, and beach access. Situated on a high bluff with stairway to the beach. Overflow camping in day-use area for self-contained units only. Moderate.

FOOD

En Feugo Cantina and Grill, 1342 Camino Del Mar, Del Mar 92014; (858) 792–6551. Downtown, open daily for lunch and dinner, weekend brunch. Offering authentic Mexican food, Southwestern specials, and a healthy selection of fresh fish in a charming atmosphere with an ocean view. Outdoor seating. Happy hour Wednesday through Sunday from 5:00 to 7:00 P.M.; full bar and great margaritas. Moderate.

Fish Market, 640 Via Del Valle, Del Mar 92014; (619) 858–2277. Lunch and dinner daily. Great fresh seafood in a vibrant, often crowded, and noisy dining room, specializing in family-style meals. Moderate.

Jake's Del Mar, 1660 Coast Boulevard, Del Mar 92014; (858) 755–2002. West of Route S21, on the beach, near the Amtrak depot. Lunch and dinner daily, Sunday brunch. Serves superb steaks, chicken,

San Elijo State Beach, Encinitas

and lamb. Specializes in fresh seafood, from swordfish to Maine lobster. Full bar. Moderate.

L'Affaire, 267 North El Camino Real, Encinitas 92024; (760) 436–4944. East of I–5, at the Village Encinitas Plaza. Lunch and dinner Tuesday through Sunday; closed Monday. Continental cuisine with such lunch specialties as duck pâté, French onion soup, various hot or cold sandwiches, omelets, green salad with feta, and California avocado and crab salad. Dinner appetizers include escargots, chicken liver Madeira, and jumbo shrimp cocktail. Among fifteen chicken specialties are coq au vin, chicken Bombay in light curry, chicken L'Affaire with pink peppercorns and whiskey sauce, and baked chicken Dijon. Seafood offerings include grilled rainbow trout and cheese tortellini with smoked mussels. Also veal, pork, and beef entrees. Desserts include caramel custard, New York cheesecake, apple strudel, and chocolate mousse cake. Inexpensive to moderate.

SHOPPING AND BROWSING

The Antique Warehouse, 212 South Cedros Avenue, Solana Beach 92075; (858) 755–5156. South end of town, just east of Route S21 and the railroad tracks. Wednesday through Monday, 10:00 A.M. to 5:00 P.M. Here are 101 shops selling American and European furniture, jewelry, and other antiques and collectibles.

Del Mar Plaza, 1555 Camino del Mar, Del Mar 92014; (858) 792-1555. Downtown, Fifteenth Street at Camino del Mar, across from the L'Auberge Del Mar. Five restaurants with open-air, ocean-view dining. More than thirty shops, galleries, and boutiques.

The Lumberyard Shopping Center, 765 First Street, Encinitas 92024. On Route S21 between E and F Streets. Monday through Saturday, 10:00 A.M. to 7:00 P.M.; Sunday, 10:00 A.M. to 6:00 P.M. A small, attractive shopping center with more than two dozen shops and restaurants.

BEACHES, PARKS, TRAILS, AND WAYSIDES

The beaches from the Del Mar area north to Encinitas are popular with swimmers and surfers, the former looking for the broad and gently sloping stretches where waves are small and water relatively calm, the latter favoring narrow beaches that slope steeply from the coastal bluffs and create the big waves better for riding. In addition to the predominant sandy beaches are rocky areas where tidepools are exposed as the tide wanes.

Beach access is good, all the way from Torrey Pines State Beach, just south of Del Mar and west of Torrey Pines Road via La Jolla Farms Road, to Leucadia State Beach, west of Old Highway 101, at the north end of Encinitas. Many east-west streets and avenues end at or near the beach. Where there are cliffs and bluffs, stairways and ramps provide beach access.

Torrey Pines State Reserve is south of Del Mar and west of North Torrey Pines Road, 2 miles north of Genesee Avenue, which exits I–5 near the University of California–San Diego campus and connects with Route S21. An extension of the reserve lies to the north, west of I–5, east of Route S21, between Carmel Valley Road and Del Mar Heights Road. Hiking and nature trails provide opportunities to view a variety of wildlife habitat and species, including such rare or endangered birds as the least tern, light-footed clapper rail, snowy plover, and white-tailed kite, as well as the rare Torrey pine.

WATER SPORTS AND ACTIVITIES

Scuba and skin divers like the area, as do clam diggers. Those fishing the surf take surfperch, flatfish, and other species with some regularity in both sandy and rock areas.

Grunion hunters take the night shift in summer, when the gravid, slender fish ride the surf ashore to spawn in the beach sands. The time to gather grunions is during the extremely high tides that coincide with the full and new moons and occur every two weeks. The runs continue for four or five nights following each of these high tides. Although good tides occur from March through September, current regulations prohibit harvesting the fish before June 1. Check the regulations synopsis, available at sport shops, for additional stipulations.

Beaches from Del Mar City Beach to Solana Beach County Park are good grunion beaches and popular surf-fishing areas. San Elijo and Leucadia State Beaches are other popular angling spots.

TOURS AND TRIPS

Skysurfer Balloon Company, 1221 Camino del Mar, Del Mar 92014; (858) 481–6800. Daily flights over Del Mar with champagne and hors d'oeuvres afterward. Flights last forty-five to sixty minutes. Balloons carry up to eighteen passengers. Call for reservations and information.

GOLF AND TENNIS

Encinitas Ranch Golf Course, 1275 Quail Gardens Drive, Encinitas 92024; (760) 944–1936. East of I–5 via Leucadia Boulevard (north of Encinitas Boulevard exit and south of La Costa Boulevard exit) 1 mile to Quail Gardens Drive. Owned by the City of Encinitas, this is an eighteen-hole, par-seventy-two, 6,821-yard course. Driving range, practice greens, clubhouse, and club and cart rental.

Lomas Santa Fe Executive Golf Course, 1580 Sun Valley Road, Solana Beach 92075; (858) 755–0195 or 578–0166. East of I–5 via Lomas Santa Fe Drive, then left on Sun Valley Road. An eighteen-hole, par-fifty-six, 2,317-yard executive course open to the public. Driving range, putting green, equipment rentals, restaurant, and cocktail lounge.

Surf and Turf Driving Range and Tennis Courts, 1555 Jimmy Durante Boulevard, Del Mar 92014; (858) 481–0363. Next to the Del Mar Hilton, across from the racetrack. Eight lighted tennis courts and a 59-tee lighted driving range. Call (858) 755–5435 to reserve a tennis court. Instructions available.

OTHER ATTRACTIONS

Del Mar Thoroughbred Club, Del Mar 92014; (858) 755–1141; reservations, (858) 481–1207. At the north end of town, east of Camino del Mar, west of I–5, south off Via de la Valle. Mid-July through mid-September; daily, except Tuesday; post time, 2:00 P.M. Nine races a day at this famous track founded in 1937 by Bing Crosby and Pat O'Brien. Unreserved and reserved clubhouse seats available. Dining room and lounge in clubhouse.

Quail Botanical Gardens, 230 Quail Gardens Drive, P.O. Box 5, Encinitas 92024; (760) 753–6041. Open seasonally; call the chamber of commerce for current hours of operation. Located ½-mile east of I–5 via Encinitas Boulevard, then north ¼-mile. Daily, 9:00 A.M. to 5:00 P.M.; gift shop, 10:00 A.M. to 4:00 P.M. A lovely twenty-five-acre reserve where exotic tropical and drought-resistant plants grow. Rare flowers, shrubs, and trees flourish in the ravines and on the hillsides, including the largest hibiscus collection on the West Coast and the greatest variety of bamboo plants in the United States.

TRAVEL INFORMATION

Cardiff by the Sea Chamber of Commerce, Cardiff Towne Centre, 2501 San Elijo Avenue, Cardiff 92007; (760) 436–0431; www.cardiffbythesea.org.

Del Mar Chamber of Commerce, 1104 Camino del Mar, Suite #1, Del Mar 92014; (858) 793–5291; www.delmarchamber.org

Encinitas Chamber of Commerce & Visitor's Center, 138 Encinitas Boulevard, Encinitas 92024; (760) 753–6041 or (800) 953–6041; www.encinitaschamber.org; e-mail: encchamb@encinitasca.org

Solana Beach Chamber of Commerce, 210 West Plaza Street, P.O. Box 623, Solana Beach 92075; (619) 755–4775; www.solanabeach.com

EVENTS

April	Del Mar National Horse Show, Del Mar, (858) 755–4844
	Fiesta del Sol, Solana Beach, (619) 755–4775
June	Annual Deep Pit BBQ, Encinitas, (760) 632–9711
July	Hot Air Balloon Classic, Del Mar, (858) 481–6800
August	Sunday Summer Concerts by the Sea, Encinitas, (760) 633–2740
September	Oktoberfest, Encinitas, (760) 753–6041
October	Cardiff Chili by the Sea Cookoff, (760) 436–0431

CARLSBAD
Population: 85,000

OCEANSIDE
Population: 166,000

Location: Carlsbad is 32 miles north of San Diego and 26 miles south of San Clemente, on I–5; Oceanside is immediately north of Carlsbad, 84 miles south of Los Angeles.

In the northwest corner of San Diego County, in an area locals call North County, lie the side-by-side cities of Carlsbad and Oceanside. Both are oceanfront communities with broad beaches and ocean-view resorts, but both also rise into the foothills and line the canyons east of the freeway.

Carlsbad has the lion's share of beaches, shops, restaurants, and lodging, but Oceanside has the beautiful harbor, a fine fishing pier, and one of the best stretches of surfing beach in the vicinity.

Locals claim to have the shortest thermometer in the nation, with average high temperatures of about sixty-five degrees in January and seventy-seven degrees in August, coupled with a mere 9 inches of rainfall a year. Naturally, hiking, biking, tennis, and golf are popular here, as are all water sports.

With more than 2,000 hotel and motel rooms available, some right on the ocean, the area is attractive to travelers in its own right but also serves as a good headquarters for visiting attractions north, south, and inland. From here it's an easy drive to Encinitas, Solana Beach, Del Mar, San Diego, and Coronado to the south, or north to San Clemente, Dana Point, Laguna Beach, and Newport Beach. Also within convenient range are Disneyland, Knott's Berry Farm, San Diego Wild Animal Park, and the Palomar Observatory.

Those so inclined can even park their wheels and visit communities north and south by rail. Amtrak makes eight scheduled runs a day between Los Angeles and San Diego, stopping at a number of towns, including Oceanside. Climb aboard the northbound train and be in San Clemente in fifteen minutes, or take a twenty-minute ride to Del Mar on the southbound. From Oceanside to San Diego takes about fifty minutes, and the San Diego station is only 4 blocks from the bay, near the Maritime Museum and Broadway Pier. Take trackless trolleys from there to other points of interest, or use the ferry or water taxi.

LODGING

Best Western Beach Terrace Inn, 2775 Ocean Street, Carlsbad 92008; (760) 729–5951 or (800) 433–5415. West off Carlsbad Boulevard, between Vista Way and Carlsbad Village Drive. From I-5, take Vista Way or Carlsbad Village Drive exit. Cable TV and cable movies in 49 rooms and suites, some with private balconies, fireplaces, and kitchenettes. Oceanfront honeymoon suite with in-room whirlpool. Pool, whirlpool, sauna, and ocean view. Near shops and restaurants. On the beach. Expensive.

Best Western Marty's Valley Inn, 3240 East Mission Avenue, Oceanside 92054; (760) 757–7700 or (800) 747–3529. East of I-5, 1¾ miles on Route 76. Cable TV and cable movies in 110 rooms and suites. Heated pool. Grove Restaurant and Lounge on premises. Live entertainment and dancing. Moderate.

Best Western Oceanside Inn, 1680 Oceanside Boulevard, Oceanside 92054; (760) 722–1821 or (800) 443–9995. West of I-5, east of Hill Street. Cable TV in 80 rooms, each with a hair dryer, iron, ironing board, and coffeemaker. Heated pool, whirlpool, sauna, laundry, and valet service. Complimentary morning newspaper, continental breakfast, tea, coffee, and evening refreshments. Moderate.

Carlsbad Inn Beach Resort, 3075 Carlsbad Boulevard, Carlsbad 92008; (760) 434–7020 or (800) 235–3939. West off I-5 via Carlsbad Village Drive exit. Cable TV in 132 units, some with kitchens. Pool, whirlpools, barbecue area, health club, tennis courts, and laundry facilities. Specialty shops, beauty salon, bakery, and restaurant on premises. Complimentary morning newspaper and continental breakfast. Expensive to very expensive.

La Costa Resort and Spa, Costa Del Mar Road, Carlsbad 92009; (760) 438–9111 or (800) 854–5000. East of I-5 via La Costa Avenue exit. Has 478 rooms and 1- and 2-bedroom suites. "La Costa" suites are adjacent to golf and tennis facilities. Also 2 3-bedroom presidential suites. Jogging trails, gardens, lakes, and heated pools throughout the 1,000-acre complex. Two PGA golf courses, 7 restaurants, 3 lounges, and a theater. Separate spas for men and women, and various spa plans available. Tennis anyone?—4 clay courts, 2 grass courts, and 17 composition courts, some lighted. Resident golf and tennis pros. Expensive to extremely expensive.

Olympic Resort Hotel and Spa, 6111 El Camino Real, Carlsbad 92009; (760) 438–8330 or (800) 522–8330. East of I–5 via Palomar Airport Road. Cable TV in 78 rooms and suites with queen and king beds. Fitness center, 5 lighted tennis courts, 2 Olympic-size pools, European spa, sauna, and large golf practice area. Restaurant and cocktail lounge on premises. Moderate to expensive.

Pelican Cove Inn, 320 Walnut Avenue, Carlsbad 92008; (760) 434–5995 or (888) 735–2683. West of I–5 via Carlsbad Village Drive, then south on Lincoln to Walnut. Twin, queen, and king beds in 8 guest rooms with private baths in this bed-and-breakfast inn. Only 200 yards from the ocean. Near shops and restaurants. Bicycles, beach chairs, and picnic baskets available. Full breakfast. Moderate to expensive.

Tamarack Beach Resort, 3200 Carlsbad Boulevard, Carlsbad 92008; (760) 729–3500 or (800) 334–2199. West of I–5 via Tamarack Avenue exit, then north on Carlsbad Boulevard. Cable TV in 77 rooms and 1- and 2-bedroom suites. Heated pool, two whirlpools, balconies, fitness center, outdoor barbecues, and ocean views. VCRs in suites. Across the street from the beach. Moderate to very expensive.

CAMPGROUNDS AND RV PARKS

Oceanside RV Park, 1510 South Coast Highway, Oceanside 92054; (760) 722–4404. West of I–5 via Oceanside Boulevard, then south on South Coast Highway, ½ block. Has 140 full-hookup sites with cable TV and privacy fences. Heated pool and shuffleboard. Two blocks to the ocean. Expensive.

South Carlsbad State Beach, 2680 Carlsbad Boulevard, Carlsbad 92008; (760) 438–3143 or (800) 444–7275. West of Carlsbad Boulevard at Ponto Drive. From I–5 take La Costa Avenue west, then Carlsbad Boulevard north. Campground situated on a bluff with stairway to beach. Has 226 campsites with water and electricity, tables, cupboards, and stoves. Showers, laundry, tank dump, convenience store, bait, and beach-equipment rentals. Moderate.

FOOD

Al's In-The-Village Cafe, 795 Carlsbad Village Drive, Carlsbad 92008; (760) 729-5448. At Carlsbad Village. Breakfast and lunch daily, dinner on Friday nights. A large breakfast menu with all the traditional egg dishes, pancakes, waffles, and Hawaiian-style French toast. Also house specialties, including Ben's Wild Man Eggs with bacon, onion, green chilies, and melted Jack cheese; Farm Breakfast, which includes three eggs, ham steak, biscuit and gravy, and home-fried red-skinned potatoes; and Hawaiian Loco Moco, ground sirloin on steamed rice, topped with gravy and a fried egg. Lunches include soups, salads, hot and cold deli-style sandwiches, a half-dozen chicken-breast specialty sandwiches, burgers, and fish-and-chips. Inexpensive.

Cafe 101, 631 South Coast Highway, Oceanside 92054; (760) 722-5220. On Old Highway 101. Breakfast, lunch, and dinner daily; breakfast served all day. Dine indoors or on the patio. The huge breakfast menu includes all the traditional favorites, including corned beef hash and eggs, sirloin steak and eggs, chicken-fried steak and eggs, biscuits and gravy, hot cakes, French toast, and a dozen different omelets. Lunch includes salads, soups, chili, more than a half-dozen different burgers, specialty sandwiches, burritos, and tacos. Among the dinner specialties are fish-and-chips, fried chicken, fried shrimp, meat loaf, beef liver and grilled onions, roast beef, pork chops, and turkey—all served with soup or salad, potato, vegetable, and dinner roll. Children's menu available. Inexpensive.

Chart House, 314 South Harbor Drive, Oceanside 92054; (760) 722-1345. On the harbor with a great view. Dinner daily. Start with seared peppered ahi tuna appetizer, clam chowder, or the restaurant's signature Caesar salad. Then choose one of the house specialties, such as filet mignon, Teriyaki beef medallions, slow-roasted prime rib, Hawaiian steak brochette, barbecued baby back ribs, glazed rack of lamb, peppercorn chicken, sesame-crusted salmon, grilled ahi tuna chop, whole New England lobster, or Alaskan king crab legs. If you have room for dessert, try the Chocolate Lava Cake. Full bar. Moderate.

Neimans Fine Dining & Entertainment, 300 Carlsbad Village Drive, Carlsbad 92008; (760) 729-4131. At Carlsbad Village. Daily lunch and dinner, Sunday champagne brunch. Choose from such appetizers as breaded chicken fingers, spicy chicken wings, chicken or shrimp quesadilla, breaded calamari, or garlic spiced shrimp. Check out the soup du jour, or try the vegetarian black bean soup

Oceanside Pier

or clam chowder. Specialty salads include Chinese chicken, smoked chicken, and California cobb salad, as well as Caesar salad, with or without chicken or shrimp. More than a half-dozen gourmet burgers and such specialty sandwiches as oak-fired chicken breast and southern California crab sandwich. Among the many dinner selections are pasta dishes, seafood, breast of duck, rack of lamb, grilled pork chops, New York pepper steak, and prime rib. Good selection of California wines by the glass or bottle. Nightly entertainment. Moderate to expensive.

Raintree Restaurant, 755 Raintree Drive, Carlsbad 92009; (760) 931–1122. West of I–5 via Poinsettia Lane, then right on Avenida Encinitas, and right on Raintree. Daily breakfast, lunch, and dinner; Sunday brunch. Specializes in fresh fish and shellfish, hickory-smoked and mesquite-broiled entrees—all with a Southwestern flair. Black-bean chili, mesquite-grilled pizza, Santa Fe green-chili stew, green-lip mussels, Cajun chicken sandwich, and tequila chicken fingers. Comfortable bar. Nice place to relax with good food and beverages. Moderate.

SHOPPING AND BROWSING

Carlsbad Village, the oldest shopping district in the city, has undergone a major redevelopment. This area, which lies between the beach and the freeway, several blocks each side of Carlsbad Village Drive, contains more than 600 business services, restaurants, specialty shops, antiques shops, and art galleries. Maps of the area are available at the Convention and Visitors Bureau, in the old train depot next to the railroad tracks, just north of Carlsbad Village Drive.

Other shops are scattered about Carlsbad and Oceanside. A major shopping area lies east of the freeway, on and near El Camino Real. The huge Plaza Camino Real mall is flanked by smaller shopping centers. Adjacent North County Plaza has forty stores and restaurants. To the east is Carlsbad Plaza, with sixty-one shops and restaurants.

Carlsbad Company Stores, 5620 Paseo Del Norte, Suite 100, Carlsbad 92008; (760) 804–9000 or (888) 790–7467. One block east of I–5, between Cannon and Palomar Airport Roads. Opens at 10:00 A.M. daily, closes at 8:00 P.M. Company outlet shopping center with more than 70 nationally renowned designers, manufacturers, specialty retailers, and restaurants represented. Men's and women's apparel, children's fashions, footwear, luggage, leather, home furnishings, jewelry, cosmetics, and more. Bellefleur Winery and Restaurant on premises.

Plaza Camino Real Shopping Center, 2525 El Camino Real, Carlsbad 92008; (760) 729–7927. East of I–5 via Carlsbad Village Drive in Carlsbad, or via Vista Way (Route 78) in Oceanside. The second-largest mall in the North County area, with 1.1 million square feet, 5 major department stores, 135 shops, and 4 movie theaters.

BEACHES, PARKS, TRAILS, AND WAYSIDES

About 10 miles of beaches border the cities of Carlsbad and Oceanside, beginning with South Carlsbad State Beach, on the west side of Carlsbad Boulevard, near Ponto Drive. Carlsbad State Beach and Carlsbad City Beach are west of Carlsbad Boulevard, in town, between Tamarack and Cypress avenues.

South Oceanside Beach is just north of Buena Vista Lagoon, west of Pacific Street, at the foot of Cassidy Street. Oceanside City Beach is spread north and south of the Oceanside Pier, along the Strand. Harbor Beach is at the north end of Pacific Street, west of the harbor.

All the beaches in the area are popular with swimmers, sunbathers, and surfers. Access is good and parking ample. At South Carlsbad State Beach, parking is tight in the day-use area, but space is usually available along Carlsbad Boulevard.

Buena Vista Lagoon, at the Carlsbad and Oceanside city limits, is a bird sanctuary where more than 225 species have been recorded. At the north end of Carlsbad Boulevard, turn east on Laguna Drive, then left on Jefferson Street. You can park along Jefferson east of I–5 to watch the reserve's wildlife.

During whale migrations, the bluffs above the beaches are good places for whale watching. Try the Whale Watcher's Walk between Elm and Tamarack in Carlsbad. The Oceanside Pier is another good spot, as is the Blufftop Walkway south of the pier.

WATER SPORTS AND ACTIVITIES

All the beach areas are popular surf-fishing spots and are enjoyed as well by scuba divers and snorkelers. South Carlsbad State Beach and the Oceanside Pier have bait shops.

South of Tamarack Avenue and Carlsbad State Beach is Agua Hedionda Lagoon. The calm lagoon waters make this a favorite angling spot and a popular waterskiing area.

The Oceanside Pier, once 1,900 feet long, was badly damaged during the 1982–83 winter storms, which reduced its length by about half. Nevertheless, this is a fine fishing pier that also offers a great view of Oceanside. This municipal pier is lighted at night and has fish-cleaning facilities.

The beautiful harbor in Oceanside has more than 900 slips up to 51 feet. This is a popular stopover for sailors traveling between San Diego and Newport Beach, and it's home to the Oceanside charter fleet. There is also access within the harbor for shore fishing. Even if you're not an angler or boater, you should visit the harbor to enjoy its beauty and serenity.

Helgren's Sportfishing Trips, 315 South Harbor Drive, Oceanside 92054; (760) 722–2133. At the harbor, near Cape Cod Village. Morning half-day; afternoon half-day; full-day; and twilight fishing trips. Long-range trips to Mexico. Two- and three-day island albacore trips. Charters and group rates available. Rod rental, bait, fishing licenses, and full galley. Two-hour whale-watching trips daily, December 26 through March 15.

Snug Harbor Marina, 4215 Harrison Street, Carlsbad 92008; (760) 434–3089. East of I–5, on Agua Hedionda Lagoon. March through October, 8:00 A.M. to sunset daily; November through February, 8:00 A.M. to sunset Wednesday through Sunday. Concrete launch ramp, fuel dock, snack bar, and picnic area. Also rents waterskiing equipment, Jet Skis, and Wave Runners.

RENTALS

Boat Rentals of America, 256 Harbor Drive South, Oceanside 92054; (760) 722–0028. Rents motorboats, sailboats, and kayaks.

GOLF

Emerald Isle Golf Course, 660 South El Camino Real, Oceanside 92054; (760) 721–4700. South off Mission Avenue, then left at the first traffic light (Vista Oceana). An eighteen-hole, par-three, executive course with pro shop, equipment and cart rental, driving range, and snack bar.

Oceanside Center City Golf Course, 2323 Greenbrier, Box 1088, 92051; (760) 433–8590. South on Barnes off Mission Avenue, east on Maxson, south on Grace, then east on Greenbrier. An eighteen-hole, par-sixty-six, 4,726-yard course. Putting green, pro shop, resident pro, equipment rentals, and restaurant.

Oceanside Golf Course, 825 Douglas Drive, Oceanside 92054; (760) 433–1360. East of I–5 via Mission Avenue exit, 4½ miles to Douglas, then left. An eighteen-hole, par-seventy-two, 6,450-yard public course. Driving range, putting green, pro shop, equipment rentals, clubhouse, snack bar, restaurant, and cocktail lounge.

Olympic Resort, 6111 El Camino Real, Carlsbad 92008; (760) 438–8330. East of I–5 via Palomar Airport Road. A public practice area with nineteen green-size targets, ponds, sand traps, putting green, two fairways, pro shop, and resident pro.

Rancho Carlsbad Country Club, 5200 El Camino Real, Carlsbad 92008; (760) 438–1772. East of I–5 via Palomar Airport Road, then left on El Camino Real. An eighteen-hole, par-fifty-six, 2,396-yard public executive course. Pro shop, resident pro, driving range, putting green, equipment rentals, and snack bar.

OTHER ATTRACTIONS

California Surf Museum, 223 North Coast Highway, Oceanside 92054; (760) 721–6876. Open Monday through Thursday, 10:00 A.M. to 4:00 P.M. Internationally recognized world-class surf museum about the sport and lifestyle of surfers.

Heritage Park Village and Museum, 220 Peyri Road, Oceanside 92054; (760) 433–8297, Friends of Heritage Park. Located behind the Mission San Luis Rey, this park is open daily from 9:00 A.M. to 5:00 P.M. and displays a stable and blacksmith shop, city jail, and doctor's office from the 1800s.

Legoland, LEGO Drive, Carlsbad 92008; (760) 918–5346. East of I–5, via Cannon Road; just follow the signs to LEGO Drive. Open 10:00 A.M. to 5:00 P.M. daily, with extended hours during summer and on holidays. America's first Legoland, this 128-acre park is not the usual amusement or theme park, crowded with wild rides. Rather, it features nine distinct viewing and play areas, many with hands-on play activities: The Beginning, Imagination Zone, Castle Hill, Miniland, The Garden, The Lake, Fun Town, Village Green, and The Ridge. The park was designed specifically for kids ages three to twelve, but teens and parents will get a kick out of it too, especially those whose own childhood play included building projects with the ingenious LEGO bricks. Food and beverages are available, and there are more than twenty-five specialty shops, including The Big Shop, with the nation's largest selection of LEGO products. This is a *must stop* for every family with children.

Mission San Luis Rey, 4050 Mission Avenue, Oceanside 92068; (760) 757–3651. Four miles east of I–5 via Mission Avenue. Monday through Saturday, 9:00 A.M. to 4:00 P.M; Sunday, 9:30 A.M. to 4:00 P.M. Known as the "King of Missions," the largest of California's twenty-one missions. Beautifully restored and open to the public. Self-guided tours. Museum open 10:00 A.M. to 4:30 P.M. daily.

TRAVEL INFORMATION

Carlsbad Convention & Visitors Bureau, Old Santa Fe Train Depot, Carlsbad Village Drive and State, P.O. Box 1246, Carlsbad 92008; (760) 434–6093 or (800) 227–5722; www.carlsbadca.org

Oceanside Chamber of Commerce, 928 North Coast Highway, P.O. Box 1578, Oceanside 92054; (760) 722–1534 or (800) 350–7873; www.oceansidechamber.com; e-mail: info@oceanside chamber.com

January	San Diego Marathon, (760) 434–6093
March	Carlsbad 5000 (5K run), (760) 434–6093
May	Carlsbad Village Street Faire, (760) 931–8400
	Cinco de Mayo, Oceanside, (760) 722–1534
June	Oceanside Triathalon, (760) 471–6500
	NSSA Surf Contest, (714) 536–0445
July	Freedom Days Celebration, (760) 722–3824
August	Mission Fiesta, (760) 757–3651
September	Harbor Days, Oceanside, (760) 722–5751
	Seagaze Concert, Carlsbad, (760) 434–2920
October	Oktoberfest, Carlsbad, (760) 434–6093
November	Carlsbad Village Street Faire, (760) 931–8400
December	Mission Christmas Craft Sale, Oceanside, (760) 722–1534
	Parade of Lights, Oceanside, (760) 722–5751

SAN CLEMENTE
Population: 45,050

DANA POINT
Population: 36,000

☆

Location: *San Clemente is 23 miles north of Oceanside and 4 miles south of Dana Point, on I–5; Dana Point is 6 miles south of Laguna Beach on California Highway 1 and midway between (60 miles from) San Diego and Los Angeles.*

Relatively unknown outside southern California circles only a few decades ago, San Clemente stepped into the world arena in 1969 when Richard M. Nixon purchased property that once belonged to one of the city's founding fathers. The estate soon became known as the Western White House, and whenever the president and his family occupied it, the network news anchors were sure to mention San Clemente in every broadcast.

With much of that fame, if not notoriety, in its past, San Clemente today is mainly a community of contented retirees and summer vacationers. Rumors, rumblings, and nearby multimillion-dollar property deals, however, indicate that the "Spanish Village" is on its way to resort status and will no doubt begin attracting greater numbers of visitors all year to its pleasant climate and recreational opportunities.

If San Clemente is about to arrive, Dana Point is already there. Named after Richard Henry Dana, who first came to these shores in 1835 aboard the brig *Pilgrim* and later wrote the classic adventure romance *Two Years before the Mast*, Dana Point plays well its role of romantic seaport. Everywhere are reminders of the city's nautical heritage, from its fine little maritime museum to the exquisite sailing replica of the *Pilgrim* moored in the $20-million harbor.

Dana Point is a shipshape town, with sandy beaches and grassy parks shaded by fan palms and eucalyptus trees. Although malls, plazas, shops, and galleries stand here and there, the focal point of interest for most travelers is the beautiful harbor, where there is plenty to see and do, including picnicking, boating, shopping, dining, exploring tidepools, or just relaxing on the beach.

For anyone driving the Pacific Coast, Dana Point is significant as the starting place for California Highway 1, the state's premier coastal route. It hugs the Pacific shores for most of its length, skimming over coastal lowlands and along the edges of mesas, winding switchback by switchback up craggy mountains, descending into the canyons and valleys of rivers and creeks, twisting through forests, hanging precariously on cliff faces, and straightening out on the broad marine terraces and poppy-dotted meadows. This is the Pacific Coast Highway, famous or infamous, depending on your point of view and the hurry you're in. Those of us who enjoy its quirks and kinks say, "Welcome to it." Those who prefer the rush and crush of freeway driving say, "You're welcome to it."

LODGING

Best Western Casablanca Inn, 1601 North El Camino Real, San Clemente 92672; (949) 361–1644 or (800) 752–9726. West of I–5 via Avenida Pico, then left on El Camino Real. Queen and king beds in 40 large rooms and 2 suites with remote-control cable TV, cable movies, and VCRs. Some rooms have balconies and whirlpool tubs. Kitchen suites have wet bars, microwaves, refrigerators, and whirlpool tubs. Moderate to expensive.

Best Western Marina Inn, 24800 Dana Point Harbor Drive, Dana Point 92629; (949) 496–1203 or (800) 255–6843. West of Pacific Coast Highway, at the harbor. Queen and king beds in 136 rooms and suites with cable TV, some with kitchens. Ocean view and pool. Complimentary continental breakfast. Near shops and charter operators. Michael's Supper Club nearby. Moderate.

Marriott Laguna Cliffs Resort, 25135 Park Lantern, Dana Point 92629; (949) 661–5000 or (800) 533–9748. West of Pacific Coast Highway, on a bluff overlooking the harbor. A 346-room, 17-suite resort situated on 42 acres of park and lawn, with 2 lighted tennis courts, 2 pools, Jacuzzis, sauna, exercise equipment, steam room, aerobics, massage. Expensive to extremely expensive.

San Clemente Beach Travelodge, 2441 South El Camino Real, San Clemente 92672; (949) 498–5954 or (800) 843–1706. Adjacent to municipal eighteen-hole golf course, east of I–5 via Magdalena. Remote-control cable TV and cable movies in 23 rooms and suites with

SOUTHERN CALIFORNIA

queen beds and refrigerators. In-room Jacuzzi's available. Rooms overlooking golf course or with ocean-view balconies. Walk to beach. Complimentary continental breakfast. Inexpensive to moderate.

CAMPGROUNDS AND RV PARKS

Doheny State Beach, 25300 Harbor Drive, Dana Point 92629; (949) 496–6172 or (800) 444–7275. Pacific Coast Highway at Del Obispo, just south of the harbor. Has 115 sites with drinking water, tables, and fire rings. Tank dump. Trails and beach access. Moderate.

San Clemente State Beach, 3030 Avenida del Presidente, San Clemente 92672; (949) 492–3156 or (800) 444–7275. West of I–5 via Avenida Calafia exit, south end of town. Campsites on a bluff above the beach, each with table, stove, and cupboard: 85 general sites with water and 72 full-hookup RV sites. Showers and laundry tubs. Trails to beach. Moderate.

San Onofre State Beach, Pendleton Coast District, 3030 Avenida del Presidente, San Clemente 92672; (949) 492–4872 or (800) 444–7275. South of San Clemente, west off I–5 at Basilone Road exit, then 2½ miles south. Campgrounds are on a bluff above the beach, with 221 trailer spaces and 40 primitive tent sites. No hookups. Water, outside showers, and tank dump. Inexpensive.

FOOD

The Brig Restaurant, 34461 Golden Lantern, Dana Point 92629; (949) 496–9046. At Mariner's Village, on the harbor. Breakfast, lunch, and dinner daily. Traditional breakfast and Mexican food. Soups, salads, burgers, deli-style sandwiches, mesquite-broiled chicken, shrimp fajitas, fish-and-chips, and pasta dishes. Breakfast served all day. Beer and wine. Inexpensive to moderate.

New Mandarin Garden, 111 West Avenida Palizada, San Clemente 92672; (949) 492–7432. West of I–5 and South El Camino Real, in the Old City Plaza. Daily lunch and dinner, Sunday champagne brunch. Chinese restaurant and carryout. Daily lunch specials. Roast duck, barbecued pork and spare ribs, sweet-and-sour pork, Peking fried chicken, beef with broccoli, egg rolls, fried rice, chow mein, and more. Inexpensive.

Ristorante Ferrantelli, 25001 Dana Point Harbor Drive, Dana Point 92629; (949) 493–1401. West of Pacific Coast Highway, at the Pavilion Shopping Center, adjacent to the harbor. Lunch and dinner

Dana Point Harbor

daily. Superb antipasti, meal-size salads, calamari, and other fresh seafood. All the usual Italian pasta dishes served with seafood, meat, or vegetable sauces. Full cocktail bar. Inexpensive to moderate.

SHOPPING AND BROWSING

San Clemente and Dana Point have a number of small malls and shopping centers as well as specialty shops, boutiques, and galleries throughout both communities. Serious shoppers and browsers, however, will no doubt want to make the short trek north to Laguna Beach, where there are blocks of shops and galleries.

MUSEUM

Orange County Marine Institute, 24200 Dana Point Harbor Drive, Dana Point 92629; (949) 496–2274. At the north end of Dana Point Harbor. Daily, 10:00 A.M. to 4:30 P.M. Has a number of programs, lectures, and classes, as well as marine-life displays, aquariums, touch tank, and skeleton of a gray whale to examine. The square-rigged brig *Pilgrim* is moored here and is part of many institute programs.

BEACHES, PARKS, TRAILS, AND WAYSIDES

Beaches along this stretch of coast—from San Clemente State Beach, in the south, to Doheny State Beach, just south of the Dana Point Harbor—are popular with picnickers, sunbathers, and hikers. Swimmers, however, should not venture into the water without first checking on local conditions. At times, riptides, currents, and undertows can be dangerous.

San Clemente Beach lies west of I-5, off Avenida Calafia, at the south end of town. San Clemente City Beach stretches from the north end of town, south past the Municipal Pier to San Clemente State Beach. When hiking from bluffs to beaches here, stay on the established trails, as the steep terrain is unstable and dangerous.

Doheny State Beach has bike and horse trails and a popular picnic area with grass, trees, tables, and fire rings. At Dana Point Harbor, a small beach off Ensenada Place offers swimming in warm, protected waters. There's a picnic park adjacent to the beach and others rimming the harbor and on the island, reached via Island Way, off Dana Point Harbor Drive.

WATER SPORTS AND ACTIVITIES

The same high bluffs, narrow beaches, and underwater contours that sometimes create dangerous conditions for swimmers along this stretch of the coast often form the kinds of waves surfers live for. Surfing is allowed at the north ends of both San Clemente and Doheny state beaches. Salt Creek Beach Park, west of Pacific Coast Highway, north of Dana Point, is also popular with surfers.

The San Clemente Municipal Pier, west of I-5 and South El Camino Real, via Avenida Del Mar, is a favorite of local anglers. Pier concessions sell food, beverages, bait, and tackle.

In Dana Point, anglers usually head for the harbor. This is where the sportfishing fleet operates, where anglers can either launch and moor their own boats or rent skiffs for fishing in harbor waters. Shorebound anglers will also find opportunities here.

Those fishing offshore will catch bonito, albacore, white sea bass, barracuda, halibut, shark, and a variety of bottom dwellers. Near shore, surf, rock, jetty, and pier, the take will include barred surfperch in good numbers, as well as halibut, bonito, corbina, sargo, croaker, and even the occasional barracuda. Fishing is often good in the harbor and from the jetties, although the west jetty is a dangerous place when the surf's up. Rocky shoreline areas north of Dana Point are also productive.

Capo Beach Watercraft Rentals, 3412 Embarcadero Place #B, Dana Point 92629; (949) 661–1690. At Dana Point Harbor, west of Pacific Coast Highway. Open every day. Rents Sea-Doo, WaveRunner, and other personal watercraft models. All rentals include lockers, instruction, life vests, and wet suits in season. Only two minutes from the harbor to the riding area.

Dana Island Yacht Sales and Charters, 34551 Casitas Place, Dana Point 92629; (949) 248–7400. At the harbor, west of Pacific Coast Highway. Powerboats and sailboats for hire—bare-boat or with crew. Sportfishing, coastal cruises, cocktail cruises, and brunch cruises to Newport Beach.

Dana Point Jet Ski, 34671 Puerto Place, Dana Point 92629; (949) 661–4947 or (800) 865–3875. At Dana Point Harbor, west of Pacific Coast Highway. Rents, sells, and services Kawasaki personal watercraft, with the largest fleet of current-year models on the West Coast. Also rents kayaks, surfboards, and bicycles by the hour or day.

Dana Wharf Sportfishing Charter and Whale Watching, 34675 Golden Lantern, Dana Point 92629; (949) 496–5794 or 831–1850. West of Pacific Coast Highway, at the south end of the harbor. Half-day, three-quarter-day, twilight, full-day, and two-day fishing trips aboard a fleet of fine vessels ranging in size from 31 to 65 feet. Licenses and tackle available. Open party and private charters. Galleys serve hot and cold food and beverages. Whale-watching excursions November through April. Parasailing trips. Also twenty-five-passenger half-day trips, private charters, and whale-watching excursions aboard the beautiful 82-foot classic schooner yacht *Kelpie.*

OTHER ATTRACTIONS

Mission San Juan Capistrano, Ortega Highway and Camino Capistrano, San Juan Capistrano 92675; (949) 234–1300. Built in 1776, this historic mission, with gardens and museum, is open daily with guided tours by appointment.

GOLF

The Links at Monarch Beach, 33033 Niguel Road, Dana Point 92629; (949) 240–8247. North of Dana Point, east of Pacific Coast Highway, via Niguel Road. An eighteen-hole, par-seventy, 6,200-yard public course with pro shop, cart and club rentals, and lessons available.

San Clemente Municipal Golf Course, 150 East Magdalena, San Clemente 92672; (949) 361–8384. Great ocean views from this eighteen-hole, par-seventy-two, 6,114-yard course. Driving range, practice greens, club and cart rental, pro shop, resident pro, clubhouse, restaurant, and bar.

WEATHER AND TIDE INFORMATION

Marine weather report; recorded message, (949) 496–2210

TRAVEL INFORMATION

Dana Point Chamber of Commerce, 24681 La Plaza, Suite 120, P.O. Box 12, Dana Point 92629; (949) 496–1555; www.danapoint chamber.com

San Clemente Chamber of Commerce, 1100 North El Camino Real, San Clemente 92672; (949) 492–1131; www.scchamber.com; e-mail: scchamber@fia.net

EVENTS

March	Festival of the Whales Fair, Dana Point, (949) 496–1555
May	Cinco de Mayo Festival, San Clemente, (949) 361–8264
	Blues Festival, Dana Point, (949) 496–1555
July	Ocean Festival, San Clemente, (949) 492–1131
August	Fiesta Street Festival, San Clemente, (949) 492–1131
	Fiesta 5000 (5K run/stride), San Clemente, (949) 492–1131
September	Tall Ships Festival, Dana Point, (949) 496–1555
	Doheny Days Music Festival, Dana Point, (949) 496–1555
October	Sea Fest, San Clemente, (949) 492–1131
November	Thanksgiving Day Turkey Trot 10K Run, Dana Point, (949) 496–1555
December	Christmas Festival and Tree Lighting, Dana Point, (949) 496–1555
	Harbor of Lights, Dana Point, (949) 496–1555

LAGUNA BEACH

Population: 26,000

Location: *On California Highway 1, 4 miles south of Newport, 10 miles north of San Clemente, and 66 miles north of San Diego.*

In the heart of an area stretching from Corona Del Mar to Dana Point known as the "California Riviera," Laguna Beach is a spotless little town with nothing faintly resembling a slum or anything less than affluence. This is the home base of high culture on the Orange Coast, but without any signs of stuffiness, and with that California sense of humor and laid-back attitude retained.

More than a century ago, the area's natural beauty began attracting visitors who arrived by wagon and stagecoach to camp on the beaches and in the nearby canyons. Ironically, today's traveling camper must head south to Dana Point and San Clemente or north to Newport Beach to pitch a tent or hook up a motor home. Overnighting at Laguna Beach means putting up at one of the many fine motels, resorts, or bed-and-breakfast inns.

The same spectacular seascapes and landscapes that drew vacationers to the area also caught the attention of artists, who began depicting the coastal life and scenery in the 1890s. The tradition continues, and now galleries galore greet visitors to this lovely hamlet.

Those fortunate enough to be in town on the first Thursday of any month enjoy Laguna Gallery Night, during which the Laguna Museum of Art and seventy-five Laguna Beach galleries are open from 6:00 to 10:00 P.M. Galleries plan special showings, often with artists present to meet visitors. The chamber of commerce provides gallery maps and information, and free tram service is available.

The community also stages two art festivals each year, including the one by which all others should be judged—The Festival of Arts and Pageant of the Masters, which lasts seven weeks in July and August. More than 160 area artists display works in all media. The festival grounds are open daily from 10:00 A.M. to 11:30 P.M., and tram service is provided from outlying parking areas on Laguna Canyon Road.

LODGING

Aliso Creek Inn, 31106 Pacific Coast Highway, South Laguna 92651; (949) 499–2271 or (800) 223–3309. On Highway 1, south of Laguna Beach, across the highway from Aliso Beach and fishing pier. Queen beds in 62 studio, 1-bedroom, and 2-bedroom suites with fully equipped kitchens, cable TV, and cable movies. Restaurant and lounge on premises, with live entertainment and dancing nightly. Beautiful nine-hole golf course on premises, with pro shop. Winter, moderate to expensive; summer, expensive.

By the Sea Inn, 475 North Coast Highway, 92651; (949) 497–6645 or (800) 297–0007. On Highway 1, ½-block from Diver's Cove. Cable TV and cable movies in 36 rooms with skylights and balconies. Kitchenettes and in-room whirlpools available. Heated pool, whirlpool, wet and dry saunas, and steam room. Walk to beach and village. Moderate to expensive.

Casa Laguna Inn, 2510 South Coast Highway, 92651; (949) 494–2996 or (800) 233–0449. On Highway 1, between Upland Drive and Solana Way. Cable TV and cable movies in 20 rooms, suites, and cottages—16 with kitchens. Gardens and pathways, patios, decks, and balconies. Most rooms have refrigerators. Antique and contemporary furnishings. Private baths, heated pool, and ocean view. Complimentary tea, wine, and hors d'oeuvres served each afternoon in the library. Continental breakfast also served in the library. Expensive.

Eiler's Inn, 741 South Coast Highway, 92651; (949) 494–3004. On Highway 1, in town. Twin, double, queen, and king beds in 11 rooms and 1 suite—all with private baths. Antique furnishings. Sundeck with ocean view. Courtyard. Fresh flowers, fruit, and candies in rooms. Guests receive bottle of champagne on arrival. Coffee and sun tea available all day. Wine and cheese served in the courtyard each evening. Full breakfast. Steps leading to beach. Expensive; Sunday through Thursday, October through May, moderate to expensive.

Holiday Inn Laguna Beach, 696 South Coast Highway, 92651; (949) 494–1001 or (800) 228–5691. On Highway 1, in town. Cable TV in 54 rooms and 4 suites. Rooms overlook courtyard. Suites have whirlpool baths. Heated pool. Monte Carlo Restaurant and Lounge on premises, featuring California cuisine. Complimentary continental breakfast, Monday through Friday. Moderate to very expensive.

Laguna Brisas Spa Hotel, 1600 South Coast Highway, 92651; (949) 497–7272 or (877) 503–1461. On Highway 1, south end of town. Queen and king beds in 66 rooms with remote-control cable TV, refrigerators, hair dryers, and marble baths with whirlpools. Heated pool, whirlpool, and laundry facilities. Complimentary continental breakfast. Walk to beach and village. Moderate to expensive.

Laguna Riviera, 825 South Coast Highway, 92651; (949) 494–1196 or (800) 999–2089. On Highway 1, in town. Cable TV in 41 rooms and suites. Pavilion with pool, whirlpool, and sauna. Decks with ocean view. Beach access. Complimentary continental breakfast. Moderate to expensive.

FOOD

Cedar Creek Inn, 384 Forest Avenue, 92651; (949) 497–8696. In the Lumberyard Mall, on Highway 1, at the south end of town. Daily lunch and dinner. Large menu featuring contemporary American cuisine. Fresh and delicious salads, big tasty sandwiches, pasta dishes, chicken, beef, and seafood with a flair. Try the turkey and Swiss sandwich on grilled sourdough with bacon, lettuce, tomato, avocado, and mayonnaise. Order the rare roast beef sandwich served open-faced on rye with Brie, butter lettuce, tomato, onion, and Dijon-horseradish sauce. Enjoy salmon poached in spiced apple juice or grilled and topped with apple-pistachio butter. Or cut into a thick New York steak topped with Gorgonzola butter and served with onion rings. Dine indoors, next to a fireplace, or outdoors on one of the garden patios. Full bar. Moderate.

Las Brisas, 361 Cliff Drive 92651; (949) 497–5434. Breakfast, lunch, and dinner daily; Sunday brunch. Mexican food in an elegant setting. Dine on chicken, beef, and seafood dishes and sip margaritas while you watch the ocean waves crashing below. Full bar. Moderate.

Partner's Bistro and Terrace, 448 South Coast Highway, 92651; (949) 497–4441. On Highway 1, in town. Daily lunch and dinner, Sunday brunch. Continental cuisine featuring fresh seafood, veal, and vegetarian dishes. Full bar. Moderate.

The White House, 340 South Coast Highway, 92651; (949) 494–8088. On Highway 1, in town. Monday through Friday, 8:00 A.M. to 10:00 P.M.; weekends, 8:00 to 1:00 A.M. This is a nightclub/restaurant combination, serving health-conscious food, including a full breakfast menu plus a good assortment of salads, sandwiches, fresh seafood, pasta, crepes, and steaks. Food is served in attractive surroundings of warm woods, mirrors, and Tiffany-style light shades. Daily specials. Nightly entertainment. Full bar. Inexpensive to moderate.

SHOPPING AND BROWSING

Fawn Memories, 384 Forest Avenue, Suite 7, 92651; (949) 494–2071. On Highway 1, south end of town in the Lumberyard Mall, next to Cedar Creek Inn. Sunday through Thursday 10:00 A.M. to 7:00 P.M., 10:00 A.M. to 9:00 P.M. Friday and Saturday. Apparel, jewelry, and hats, as well as porcelain, glass, agate, and ceramic wind chimes.

Laguna Surf and Sport, 1088 South Coast Highway, 92651; (949) 497–7000. Highway 1 at Oak Street, 1 block north of the Pottery Shack. Daily, 9:00 A.M. to 9:00 P.M. Bills itself as a "hardcore surf shop." Skateboards, surfboards, boogieboards, wet suits, equipment rentals, T-shirts, and swimsuits.

Roberta Gauthey's Chateau Laguna Antique Center, 1166 Glenneyre, 92651; (949) 494–9925. One block east of Highway 1, between Oak and Brooks Streets. Tuesday through Saturday, 10:00 A.M. to 5:00 P.M., Sunday noon to 4:00 P.M. Antiques and collectibles. Specializes in early American and Victorian furniture, silver, toys, dolls, and linens.

Sherwood Gallery, 460 South Coast Highway, 92651; (949) 497–2668. Downtown, between Laguna Avenue and Legion Street. Daily, 11:00 A.M. to 7:00 P.M.; except Sunday, noon to 6:00 P.M. A fascinating gallery featuring ceramics, sculpture, soft sculpture, and neon originals. More than twenty artists represented, with works both serious and whimsical, progressive and eclectic.

MUSEUM

Laguna Art Museum, 307 Cliff Drive, 92651; (949) 494–6531. Cliff Drive at North Coast Highway, north of Broadway. Thursday through Tuesday, 11:00 A.M. to 5:00 P.M. Contemporary California art complements a fine collection of historical works. Also displays private collections. Stop here before beginning a tour of Laguna Beach galleries.

Crescent Bay, Laguna Beach

BEACHES, PARKS, TRAILS, AND WAYSIDES

What makes this stretch of the Orange Coast so beautiful is its varied terrain and shoreline. In addition to the long, broad expanse of surf-lined sand at Main Beach are a number of coves beneath cliffs and rocky bluffs, with sandy strands at water's edge known as pocket beaches. Main Beach is in town, on the west side of Highway 1. Pocket beaches and coves are north and south.

Access to Main Beach is via Laguna Avenue, Ocean Avenue, Broadway, and Cliff Drive. Near this fine beach is a grassy picnic area, boardwalk, and playground. This is a good swimming area, except when riptides make swimming dangerous. That's a good time to hike the beach, play volleyball, or just lie back and relax.

A number of trails, walks, and stairways lead to the pocket beaches and coves, most found at the west ends of streets running perpendicular to Highway 1. Off South Coast Highway, beach accesses are at the ends of Moss Street, Diamond Street, Pearl Street, Agate Street, Bluebird Canyon Road, Mountain Road, Cress Street, Brooks Street, Oak Street, Anita Street, Thalia Street, Saint Anne's Street, Cleo Street, and Sleepy Hollow.

Off North Coast Highway, accesses are along Cliff Drive at several places, including the ends of Jasamine Street, Myrtle Street, and Fairview Street. There are rocky coves here with tidepools to explore.

At the north end of Laguna Beach, Crescent Bay Point Park, west of Highway 1, at the end of Crescent Bay Drive, lies a small but lovely park overlooking the coastal bluffs and rocks. This is a good spot to watch sea lions and birds and to photograph the city.

WATER SPORTS AND ACTIVITIES

Surfers like Aliso Beach County Park, west of Highway 1, at South Laguna. There's good fishing here, as well, from a fine ¼-mile-long pier with a snack bar and tackle shop.

Surf and rock fishing is often good at the pocket beaches and coves at the north end of Laguna Beach. Divers enjoy Heisler Park Marine Life Refuge, which lies offshore from Heisler Park, west of the 400 block of Cliff Drive.

GOLF

Aliso Creek Golf Club, 31106 South Coast Highway, South Laguna 92677; (949) 499–1919. On Highway 1, south of Laguna Beach, across the highway from Aliso Beach and the fishing pier. A nine-hole, par-thirty-two, 2,500-yard course. Clubhouse, locker room, pro shop, club and cart rentals, restaurant, and cocktail lounge.

WEATHER AND TIDE INFORMATION

Weather, tide, surf, and diving report; recorded message, (949) 494–6573

TRAVEL INFORMATION

Laguna Beach Visitors Bureau, 252 Broadway, 92651; (949) 497–9229; www.lagunabeachinfo.org; e-mail: lbvb@lagunabeach info.org

April	Sawdust "Art Walk," (949) 494–3030
	Laguna Charm House Tour, (949) 497–4525
June	Sawdust Festival, (949) 494–3030
	Art–a-Fair, (949) 494–4514
July	Sawdust Festival continues
	Art-a-Fair continues
	Festival of Arts and Pageant of the Masters,
	(949) 494–1145 or (800) 487–3378
August	Festival of Arts and Pageant of the Masters
	continue
	Sawdust Festival continues
	Art-a-Fair continues
September	Festival of Arts and Pageant of the Masters
	continue
October	Festival of Arts continues
November	Sawdust Winter Fantasy, (949) 494–3030
December	Sawdust Winter Fantasy continues

NEWPORT BEACH

Population: 69,069

Location: *On California Highway 1, 4 miles north of Laguna Beach, 70 miles north of San Diego, and 49 miles south of Santa Monica.*

Newport Beach is startling to the southbound traveler who has just left the concrete, asphalt, and smog of Los Angeles. The first impression is of how green the city is. That's the color of money.

It's soon obvious to the newcomer why Newport Beach was nicknamed "the Gold Coast." Everywhere are signs of affluence, from the chic shops of Fashion Island to the gleaming yachts moored on Newport Bay.

The city's boundaries encompass a number of distinct communities and small villages that have retained much of their character and individuality. On the seaward side of Highway 1, for example, lie the Balboa Peninsula, Balboa Island, and Lido Island—each unique in some way. The islands are on Lower Newport Bay, and the peninsula lies northwest to southeast, reaching to the harbor entrance, across the channel from Corona del Mar.

Brothers James and Robert McFadden, who started the shipping and lumber business in 1873 that eventually grew into the city of Newport, began trading at a landing on the Santa Ana River. When the shoal-filled waters of the river mouth and lower bay proved too hazardous for seagoing vessels, the McFaddens moved their business to the beach and built the Newport Pier in 1888. Originally a commercial wharf, now a fishing pier, this is the longest-standing pier on the entire southern California coast.

The famous Newport Dory Fishing Fleet has been fishing here since 1891. Each morning, the dorymen launch their flat-bottomed boats in the surf at dawn and return to the pier to sell their catch about 9:30 A.M.

Newport Boulevard exits south off Highway 1 and leads past the Lido Peninsula and Lido Island toward Newport Pier. As the thoroughfare curves east, it becomes Balboa Boulevard and leads to Balboa and beyond, ending at the west jetty and harbor entrance.

The cupola surmounting the roof of the Balboa Pavilion rises above other nearby buildings, making this landmark easy to spot. Local promoters built the pavilion and Balboa Pier in the early 1900s to attract tourists and help establish Balboa as a beach resort. Balboa became part of Newport Beach in 1906. In the past, the pavilion served as a casino and a dance hall where all the big bands played—the Dorsey brothers, Glenn Miller, Benny Goodman—and such stars as Gene Krupa and Bing Crosby appeared. Restored in 1962, the building is now headquarters for sight-seeing and sportfishing trips and contains a tackle shop and restaurant.

The Balboa Ferry operates nearby, transporting vehicles and their passengers, as well as bikers and foot traffic, between Balboa and the south side of Balboa Island. A small bridge connects the mainland to the north side of the island.

The biggest festival of the year is the Sea Fest. It takes place in September and includes such activities and events as a bike tour, boat races, harbor sailing, fishing tournament, kite contest, marine-art festival, sand-castle contest, surfing championships, tall-ships festival, sailboarding, volleyball tournament, and wooden-boat festival. And, of course, there's plenty of grub and grog to go around.

LODGING

Balboa Inn, 105 Main Street, Balboa 92661; (949) 675–3412 or (877) 225–2629. On the Balboa Peninsula, south of Highway 1 via Newport and Balboa Boulevards, 1 block past Washington Street. Has 34 rooms and suites in a recently renovated historical landmark. Ocean and bay views. Fireplaces and in-room whirlpool spas available. Pool and whirlpool. Room service and complimentary continental breakfast. Walk to Balboa Pier, harbor, beach, restaurants, and shops. Expensive; reduced winter rates.

Best Western Bay Shores Inn, 1800 West Balboa Boulevard, 92663; (949) 675–3463 or (800) 222–6675. On the Balboa Peninsula, south of Highway 1 via Newport Boulevard. Queen and king

Balboa Pavilion, Newport Beach

beds in 21 rooms, suites, and 2-bedroom apartments that accommodate up to 8 persons. Cable TV and cable movies. Some rooms with bay or ocean views. Walk to beach, Newport Pier, harbor, public tennis courts, and biking/jogging trails. Moderate to expensive.

Doryman's Inn Bed & Breakfast, 2102 West Ocean Front, 92663; (949) 675–7300. South of Highway 1 via Newport Boulevard, then east on Balboa Boulevard to McFadden Place. Inn is on Ocean Front at McFadden, near the Newport Pier. Queen and king beds in 10 spacious, elegantly appointed rooms with private baths and sunken marble tubs. Fireplaces, ocean views, and in-room whirlpools available. Full breakfast. Near many restaurants, shops, and other attractions. Walk to the pier, harbor, and beach. Moderate to very expensive.

Newport Channel Inn, 6030 West Coast Highway, 92663; (949) 642–3030 or (800) 255–8614. On Highway 1, west of Newport Boulevard, opposite the beach. Queen beds and waterbeds in 30 rooms with local TV. Sundeck, ocean view. Continental breakfast and beach towels provided. Short walk to beach—just across the highway. Near shops, restaurants, and charter services. Adjacent shopping center with coin-operated laundry and minimarket. Inexpensive to moderate.

CAMPGROUNDS AND RV PARKS

Newport Dunes, 1131 Back Bay Drive, 92660; (949) 729–3863. Located ¼-mile northeast of Highway 1 via Jamboree Road. More than 400 double-wide sites with full hookups. Everything for the RV traveler, and built to order for boaters and anglers. Pool, whirlpool, cable TV, clubhouse, grocery store, snack bar, restaurant, coin-operated laundry, and video arcade. Complete marina services, launch ramp, marine sales and repairs, boat rentals, slips, and dry boat storage. Expensive to very expensive.

FOOD

Newport Landing, 503 East Edgewater, 92661; (949) 675–2373. South of Highway 1 via Newport and Balboa Boulevards, on the Balboa Peninsula, 1 block from the Balboa Ferry. Daily lunch and dinner; Sunday brunch. A Newport Beach fixture—enjoy it from the main dining room or the casual oyster bar and lounge, which overlooks the busy harbor. Specialties include prime rib, rack of lamb, grilled duck breast, fresh local swordfish, deepwater shrimp, and abalone. Full bar and live entertainment nightly; dancing on weekends. Moderate to expensive.

Ruby's Diner, #1 Balboa Pier, Balboa 92661; (949) 675–7829. On the Balboa Peninsula, south of Highway 1 via Newport and Balboa Boulevards. Sunday through Thursday, 7:00 A.M. to 10:00 P.M.; Friday and Saturday, 7:00 A.M. to 11:00 P.M. A 1940s-style diner at the end of the pier. Breakfast choices include an assortment of omelets and other egg dishes, French toast, hotcakes, biscuits and gravy, and Rubymuffins. Salads of all sizes and varieties, chowder, chili, hot dogs, chili dogs, and an assortment of burgers and other sandwiches. From the fountain—malts, shakes, ice-cream sodas, floats, sundaes, and banana splits. Various beverages, including beer and wine. Inexpensive.

SHOPPING AND BROWSING

Fashion Island, Newport Beach 92660; (949) 721–2000 or (800) 495–4753. North of Highway 1, between MacArthur Boulevard and Jamboree Road—follow the signs. Monday through Friday, 10:00 A.M. to 9:00 P.M.; Saturday, 10:00 A.M. to 6:00 P.M.; Sunday, noon to 5:00 P.M. Orange County's premier open-air shopping center, with more than 200 shops, boutiques, and department stores, including Amen Wardy, The Broadway, Buffums, Bullocks Wilshire, Neiman

Marcus, and J. W. Robinson's. Here you'll find the famous Farmers Market at the Atrium Court, forty restaurants, and many food kiosks offering pastries, hot dogs, candies, ice cream, frozen yogurt, sushi, coffee, fruits, salads, and deli delights. Browse and shop at more than sixty men's, women's, and children's apparel and shoe stores, as well as jewelry, leather, luggage, and gift shops.

Lido Marina Village, 3400 Via Oporto, Suite 104, 92663; (949) 675–8662. South of Highway 1 on Newport Boulevard, then left on Via Lido, and left to the parking structure at the village. A beautiful waterfront area with tree-lined cobblestone streets, restaurants, sidewalk cafes, more than thirty-five shops and boutiques, and galleries. Enjoy the sun and salt air while strolling the harbor boardwalk. Yacht brokers, charter services, and sailing clubs are headquartered here. Browse amid the beautiful watercraft.

BEACHES, PARKS, TRAILS, AND WAYSIDES

Near the entrance to Newport Bay, just east of the east jetty, lies the broad, sandy Corona del Mar State Beach. For swimmers there are changing rooms and outdoor showers.

Newport Beach stretches more than 5 miles from its narrow northwest end past the Newport Pier, where it is much wider. Access is via Newport Boulevard, south off Highway 1.

Six-mile-long Balboa Beach is a broad strand that extends from Newport Beach to the west jetty at the end of the Balboa Peninsula. Most of the streets running perpendicular to Balboa Boulevard provide beach access.

Balboa Island, reached by bridge south of Highway 1 or by ferry from Balboa, is rimmed by a boardwalk that makes a scenic hiking route and leads to several small beaches.

The upper end of the Newport Bay estuary is a wildlife reserve reached by way of Back Bay Drive off Jamboree Road. This 752-acre wetland habitat, consisting mainly of intertidal mudflats and salt marsh, harbors numerous species of waterfowl, shorebirds, and songbirds. During the winter, when the reserve is crowded with migratory species, an organization known as the Friends of Upper Newport Bay offers guided tours on Saturday mornings.

Friends of Upper Newport Bay, P.O. Box 2001, 92663; (949) 646–8009.

WATER SPORTS AND ACTIVITIES

Southeast of the city of Newport Beach, between Arch Rock and Irvine Cove, is Crystal Cove State Park, one of the newer parks in the system. The adjacent offshore area is an underwater park popular with divers. Divers, snorkelers, and surfers also like Corona del Mar State Beach, east of the east jetty.

West of the west jetty and reached by way of Balboa Boulevard are Jetty View Park and a beach area famous for bodysurfing. The water here, where the jetty joins the peninsula, is known as "the Wedge" and is renowned for its enormous waves. Big waves can be dangerous, so it's no place for beginners.

Several natural features, an abundance of man-made ones, and a good variety of inshore and offshore species make this an extraordinarily good and diverse angling area. Those who tow boats will want to get familiar with Newport Dunes Aquatic Park, just north of Highway 1 on Back Bay Drive off Jamboree Road. There's a full-service marina here and launching facilities open twenty-four hours a day. From here, anglers can set out for offshore fishing grounds or can find plenty of action in Newport Bay, where there are probably a dozen species in abundance, with halibut, bass, croaker, and sargo topping the list.

A submarine canyon lies offshore and comes closest to shore near the Newport Pier. This deepwater structure has a dampening effect on incoming waves, keeping them small along this stretch of the beach. It also brings species near shore that are usually found many more miles out to sea. A number of charter operators are specialists in finding and catching these gamesters, including marlin and tuna.

There are ample shore-fishing opportunities as well, and good fishing from Newport Pier and Balboa Pier.

Adventures at Sea, 3101 West Coast Highway, 92663; (949) 645–2628 or (888) 446–6365. Romantic sunset cruises of the Newport harbor aboard quiet, graceful, electric-powered gondolas. Some of the canopied craft are painted gleaming white and have cushioned seats covered with tapestry or velvet. Others are black-hulled, mahogany-decked beauties with glove-leather upholstery. All have CD players on board. Three harbor tours available: after-dinner cruise for two, champagne cruise for two, and gourmet dinner cruise for two. Gondolas accommodate an extra person or couple for an additional charge.

Bongos Sportfishing Charters, 2130 Newport Boulevard, 92663; (949) 673–2810. South off Highway 1. Fishing charters aboard a fleet of fast, powerful, tournament-rigged boats for fishing trips to local hot spots, deepwater banks, and Catalina Island for marlin, tuna, bonito, halibut, yellowtail, barracuda, and shark. All the latest electronics, as well as stereo and color TV.

Davey's Locker, 400 Main Street, Balboa 92661; (949) 673–1434. Fishing reports (949) 972–9818. South of Highway 1 via Newport and Balboa Boulevards, at Balboa Pavilion. Davey's 50- to 80-foot boats fish local waters and Catalina Island. Half-day, all-day, and overnight trips. Whale-watching excursions. Private charters. Tackle store with a complete line of tackle, rental gear, licenses, bait, and local fishing information. Boat rentals for fishing and harbor cruising.

Newport Landing, Sportfishing, and Fuel Service, 309 Palm Street, Balboa 92661; (949) 675–0550. On the Balboa Peninsula, near the Balboa Ferry terminal. Weekdays, 6:00 A.M. to 6:00 P.M.; weekends, 5:00 A.M. to 7:00 P.M. Sportfishing, whale-watching, and harbor cruises. Complete marine service. Gas and diesel fuel, live and frozen bait, fishing tackle, licenses, beer, soft drinks, and ice.

RENTALS

Balboa Boat Rentals, 510 East Edgewater, Balboa 92661; (949) 673–7200. At Edgewater Avenue and Palm Street, between Adams and Washington Streets, north of Balboa Boulevard. Rents powerboats, sailboats, and kayaks.

There are also boat rentals at Davey's Locker. See above.

TOURS AND TRIPS

Catalina Passenger Service, 400 Main Street, Balboa 92661; (949) 673–5245. At the Balboa Pavilion, south of Highway 1 via Newport and Balboa Boulevards or via ferry from Balboa Island. One round-trip daily departs Newport Beach at 9:00 A.M. and Catalina at 4:30 P.M.; December 26 to Easter, weekend service only. Travel to Catalina Island aboard the largest catamaran in the United States—only seventy-five minutes from Newport Beach to Avalon, Catalina Island. Only hand-carried luggage and backpacks permitted. No diving equipment.

GOLF

Newport Beach Golf Course, 3100 Irvine Avenue, 92660; (949) 852–8681. Southwest of Corona del Mar Freeway, between

Jamboree Road and Newport Boulevard, northeast of Pacific Coast Highway. An eighteen-hole, 3,216-yard public course. Pro shop with lessons available. Pull-cart and club rental. Lighted for night play. Driving range, restaurant, and cocktail lounge.

Pelican Hill Golf Club, 22653 Pelican Hill Road South, Newport Coast 92657; (949) 760–0707. East on Newport Coast Drive off Highway 1, between Corona del Mar and Laguna Beach. Two challenging eighteen-hole courses in spectacular coastal hills, canyons, and pine forests. Practice range with putting, pitching, and chipping greens. Pros, lessons, club and cart rentals, pro shop, and food-and-beverage service.

TRAVEL INFORMATION

Newport Beach Conference and Visitors Bureau, 366 San Miguel #200, 92660; (949) 644–1190 or (800) 942–6278; www.newport beach-cvb.com

Newport Beach Chamber of Commerce, 1470 Jamboree Road, 92660; (949) 729–4400; www.newportbeach.com; e-mail: info@new portbeach.com

EVENTS

February	Baroque Music Festival, Corona del Mar, (949) 760–7887
March	International Film Festival, Newport Beach, (949) 851–6555
	Grunion Run, Newport Beaches, (949) 590–5132
April	Newport Harbor Boat Show, Newport Dunes Resort, (949) 262–0543
May	"Back" Bay Classic, Back Bay, Newport Beach, (949) 776–7490
	Spring Wine & Food Festival, Balboa Island, (949) 723–6171
	Newport Beach Jazz Festival, Hyatt Newporter, (949) 650–5483
June	Ocean Discovery Day, Upper Newport Bay, (949) 640–6746
	Baroque Music Festival, Corona del Mar, (949) 760–7887
	Irrelevant Week, Newport Beach, (949) 263–0727
July	Fireworks Extravaganza, Newport Dunes Resort, (949) 729–3863
	Independence Day Celebration, Mariners Park, (949) 644–3151
	Flight of the Lasers, Newport Harbor, (949) 729–4400
	Old Glory Boat Parade, Newport Harbor, (949) 673–5070
	Summer Concert Series, Fashion Island, (949) 721–2000
	Summer Jazz Series, Hyatt Newporter, (949) 729–1234
August	Summer Concert Series continues
September	Sand Castle Contest, Corona del Mar, (949) 729–4400
	Balboa Arts and Music Festival, Balboa Pier, (949) 644–3151
	Wooden Boat Festival, Newport Harbor, (949) 642–5031
December	Christmas Boat Parade, Newport Harbor, (949) 729–4400

SANTA BARBARA

Population: 89,600

Location: *On U.S. 101, 89 miles south of Grover Beach, 90 miles northwest of Los Angeles.*

C oastal California serves up several superb entree cities, but sweet Santa Barbara is the gourmet dessert—as beautiful to look at as it is to savor. It's one of the few cities in the nation that's as stunning in reality as it is in the travel magazines and books.

The mild climate keeps flowers blooming and lush greenery thriving all year, with palms lining the boulevards and eucalyptus trees shading and scenting parks and neighborhoods. Houses, shops, government buildings, and historic landmarks—as white as the frosting on a wedding cake and capped with red tile roofs—stand amidst all this splendor, from the ocean's edge to the rolling foothills.

It's ironic that the tragedy and devastation of an earthquake should have led to the preservation of and adherence to the Spanish-style architecture employed here. Although most of the city's early structures were of Spanish-Moorish design, in the early 1900s other styles began to encroach. But following the widely destructive earthquake of 1925, the city established an Architectural Board of Review to ensure conformity to certain building standards. The result is an eye-pleasing landscape of Mediterranean grace and grandeur.

Santa Barbara's downtown area is compact and just right for walking. So park your vehicle and stroll along the shady sidewalks, through the courtyards, to the cafes, galleries, antiques shops, and boutiques. The self-guided "Red Tile Tour," with map and guide available at the

63

visitor center, is a good way to see the area and visit many of the historical structures along the way.

No matter what activities you enjoy, you're never far from the beach in Santa Barbara. In fact, State Street, the city's main thoroughfare, leads directly to the beach and historic Stearns Wharf, the oldest operating wharf on the West Coast.

In addition to a good many annual events that take place throughout the year, an ongoing exhibit of arts and crafts draws locals and visitors to the shoreline east of Stearns Wharf every Sunday and holiday. More than 200 local artists and artisans offer their works for sale from 10:00 A.M. to dusk.

Along most of the California coast, the ocean lies west of Highway 1 or U.S. 101, with the foothills and mountains to the east. In the vicinity of Santa Barbara, however, U.S. 101 runs east to west, with the ocean to the south and foothills in the north. Keep that in mind as you travel to the various attractions.

LODGING

Reservation Services: B&B Santa Barbara, (800) 557–7898; Coastal Escapes, (800) 565–2347; Santa Barbara Hot Spots, (800) 793–7666. Centralized reservation clearinghouses for Santa Barbara hotels, motels, and bed-and-breakfast inns. Summer and holidays, book four to six weeks in advance. No charge for service.

Best Western Pepper Tree Inn, 3850 State Street, 93105; (805) 687–5511 or (800) 338–0030. North of U.S. 101 via Las Positas Road, in Northside. Queen and king beds in 150 rooms with cable TV, cable movies, and coffeemakers. Private balconies, room service, limo service, pool, whirlpool, massage facilities, gym, hair salons, and gift shop. Near eighteen-hole golf course and shopping center. Fichera's Treehouse Restaurant on premises, featuring American cuisine, fresh seafood, and local wines. Cocktail lounge with nightly entertainment. Moderate to expensive.

Mason Beach Inn, 324 West Mason Street, 93101; (805) 962–3203 or (800) 446–0444. South of U.S. 101, 1 block north of Cabrillo Boulevard, between Castillo and Bath Streets. Queen and king beds in 45 rooms with cable TV. Pool, whirlpool, and continental breakfast. Walk to shops, restaurants, beach, Stearns Wharf, charter docks, and marina. Moderate to expensive.

Secret Garden Inn & Cottages, 1908 Bath Street, 93101; (805) 687–2300 or (800) 765–6255. About 2 blocks north of U.S. 101 via Mission Street. Queen and king beds in 11 rooms and suites decorated with antiques. Private and shared baths. Walk or bike to downtown shops, galleries, and restaurants. Full breakfast. Wine and hors d'oeuvres. Moderate to expensive.

Simpson House Inn, 121 East Arrellaga Street, 93101; (805) 963–7067 or (800) 676–1280. About 2½ blocks north of U.S. 101. Double, queen, and king beds in 15 rooms decorated with antiques, original artwork, English lace, Oriental rugs, and fresh flowers. Private baths in 5 rooms. Expensive to very expensive.

The Upham Victorian Hotel & Garden Cottages, 1404 De La Vina Street, 93101; (805) 962–0058 or (800) 727–0876. North of U.S. 101 via Mission Street or Arrellaga Street, downtown. Beautiful, cupola-topped Victorian hotel with great verandas and exquisite interiors, located on an acre of gardens. Private baths and cable TV in 50 rooms and suites in the hotel, carriage house, and 5 garden cottages. Some porches, patios, and gas fireplaces. Master suite with fireplace, whirlpool tub, wet bar, and private yard with hammock. Double, queen, and king beds. Valet laundry and dry cleaning. Continental breakfast served in the lobby and on the garden veranda. Complimentary wine and cheese each afternoon. Louie's Restaurant, off the main lobby, serves daily lunch and dinner, featuring seafood, pasta, and California cuisine. Walk to shops, galleries, restaurants, and theaters. Expensive to very expensive.

West Beach Inn, 306 West Cabrillo Boulevard, 93101; (805) 963–4277 or (800) 423–5991. South of U.S. 101, across from the marina, via Castillo Street or State Street. Cable TV and cable movies in 44 rooms and suites with ocean or garden views. Complimentary continental breakfast and afternoon wine and cheese. In-room refrigerators. Walk to beach, Stearns Wharf, charter docks, shops, and restaurants. Moderate to expensive.

CAMPGROUNDS AND RV PARKS

Carpinteria State Beach, 5361 Sixth Street, Carpinteria 93013; (805) 684–2811, (805) 968–3294, or (800) 444–7275. South of U.S. 101, 12 miles east of Santa Barbara. Has 101 tent and RV sites in Anacapa and Santa Cruz campgrounds that accommodate RVs to 33 feet, but no hookups. Santa Rosa and San Miguel campgrounds have 37 sites for RVs from 22 to 30 feet. Full hookups available at Santa Rosa campground. Sites have tables and fire rings. Showers and tank dump. Easy beach access. Moderate.

FOOD

The Harbor Restaurant, 210 Stearns Wharf, 93101; (805) 963–3311. South of U.S. 101, at Stearns Wharf. Daily lunch and dinner, Sunday brunch. Sunday buffet: carved lamb, roast beef, turkey, ham, freshly baked pastries, omelets, eggs Benedict, lox and bagels, assorted cheeses, fresh fruit, fresh fish, juices, salad bar, and unlimited champagne—all served from 10:30 A.M. to 2:30 P.M. Oak-grilled steaks, fish, and shellfish. Prime rib and chicken dinners. Full bar. Moderate.

Moby Dick Restaurant, 220 Stearns Wharf, 93101; (805) 965–0549. On Stearns Wharf, south of U.S. 101. Breakfast, lunch, and dinner daily. Breakfast includes hot and cold cereals, and egg dishes. Specialty is open-face crab Benedict. Lunch is burgers and traditional sandwiches, salads, fish-and-chips. Dinners are steaks, chicken, and fresh seafoods. Choose from such specialties as scallone (scallop and abalone patty), Maryland crab cakes, Cajun catfish, and Idaho trout. Full bar and cocktail patio. Moderate.

Woody's BBQ, 5112 Hollister Avenue, 93101; (805) 967–3775. Lunch and dinner daily. From the sawdust on the floor to the oak-smoked country cooking, this is a local favorite, featuring chili, beans, charbroiled burgers, charbroiled chicken sandwiches, barbecued ribs, slowly smoked chicken and duckling, shrimp kabobs, and combination dishes. Beer and wine. Inexpensive to moderate.

SHOPPING AND BROWSING

Santa Barbara's compact downtown area is a shopper's and browser's delight. In addition to all the shops and galleries are more than forty antiques dealers, most within 1 or 2 blocks on each side of State Street.

Scattered around Santa Barbara County are nearly two dozen wineries, most of which offer tasting and sales, many of which offer tours. Pick up a copy of the "Vintners' Association Wine Touring Map" at the visitor center.

Antique Market Place, 26 East Ortega Street, 93101; (805) 966–5655. Three blocks north of U.S. 101, between State and Anacapa Streets. Monday through Friday, 11:00 A.M. to 5:00 P.M.; Saturday, 11:00 A.M. to 4:00 P.M.; closed Sunday. Oriental, European, and American antiques. Oriental rugs, paintings, porcelain, clocks, artwork, furniture, silver, bronze, cut glass, and American Indian artifacts.

Mission Santa Barbara

MUSEUMS

Old Spanish Days Carriage Museum, 129 Castillo Street, 93101; (805) 962–2353. South of U.S. 101, next to Pershing Park. Open Monday through Friday 8:00 A.M. to 3:00 P.M.; Sunday 1:00 to 4:00 P.M. More than sixty restored antique horse-drawn vehicles, including fine carriages, stagecoaches, a hearse, and a pumper fire engine. Also on display are saddles and horse tack once owned by such notables as the Cisco Kid, Clark Gable, and Will Rogers.

Santa Barbara Museum of Art, 1130 State Street, 93101; (805) 963–4364. Northeast of U.S. 101. Tuesday, Wednesday, Friday, and Saturday, 11:00 A.M. to 5:00 P.M.; Thursday, 11:00 A.M. to 9:00 P.M.; Sunday, noon to 5:00 P.M. An exquisite collection that spans more than 4,000 years, from early Greek and Roman sculpture to modern acrylics and photographs. Paintings by O'Keeffe, Hopper, Monet, Matisse, and Chagall; bronzes, drawings, and antiquities. Special exhibits and guided tours.

Santa Barbara Museum of Natural History, 2559 Puesta del Sol Road, 93101; (805) 682–4711. North of U.S. 101, 2 blocks north of the Old Mission, via Mission Street and Mission Canyon Road. Monday through Saturday, 9:00 A.M. to 5:00 P.M.; Sundays and most holidays, 10:00 A.M. to 5:00 P.M.; closed Thanksgiving, Christmas, and New Year's Day. Exhibits of the flora, fauna, geology, and prehistoric Indians of the Pacific Coast and Channel Islands. Planetarium and museum store.

South Coast Railroad Museum, 300 North Los Carnero Road, Goleta 93117; (805) 964–3540. South of U.S. 101, west of Santa Barbara. Wednesday through Sunday, 1:00 to 4:00 P.M. Located in a restored Victorian-style depot built in 1901, the museum exhibits railroad memorabilia and photographs. Outside displays include a bay-window caboose. A 300-square-foot, HO-gauge model railroad exhibit is a recent addition to the museum.

BEACHES, PARKS, TRAILS, AND WAYSIDES

Most of the beaches in the Santa Barbara area are easy to reach. Carpinteria State Beach, located on the south side of the city of Carpinteria, lies about 12 miles east of Santa Barbara. This is a broad, sandy beach popular with sunbathers and swimmers. A shallow offshore shelf that prevents riptides makes this one of the safest swimming beaches on the coast.

In the Montecito area, there's good beach access south of U.S. 101 via the Olive Mill exit. In Santa Barbara, the beach parallels Cabrillo Boulevard, reached by a number of streets, including State Street, south off U.S. 101.

Cabrillo Boulevard becomes Shoreline Drive near the harbor. This street leads to Leadbetter Beach and Shoreline Park, west of the Harbor, both of which have picnic areas.

At the east end of Cabrillo Boulevard, between Cabrillo and U.S. 101, is forty-two-acre Andree Clark Bird Refuge. A bike path and grassy area along the south and east shores of the marsh provide areas for viewing the abundant bird life, including ducks, geese, herons, and egrets.

WATER SPORTS AND ACTIVITIES

The east-west orientation of the coastline makes some of the beaches near Santa Barbara among the best in the world for surfing. Particularly popular are those from Santa Barbara west to Gaviota. El Capitan Point at El Capitan State Beach, south of U.S. 101, about 12 miles west of Goleta, is famous among surfers.

Offshore fishing is good for rockfish, calico bass, lingcod, halibut, and other species. Charter operators at the Santa Barbara Harbor offer trips to local hot spots as well as to the Channel Islands.

The harbor has launching facilities, rental boats, bait, and tackle. Goleta Beach County Park, west of Santa Barbara, also has a boat hoist, boat and motor rentals, fishing tackle, bait, and licenses. There's also good pier fishing here and at Stearns Wharf.

Captain Don's Sportfishing, 219–G Stearns Wharf, Box 6, 93067; (805) 969–5217. Charter fishing trips and whale-watching cruises to the productive waters off the Santa Barbara coast.

Hook, Line & Sinker, 4010 Calle Real, 93110; (805) 687–5689. Just north of U.S. 101. Bait-and-tackle shop with a full line of freshwater and saltwater gear, custom rods, tackle repair, and fishing licenses. Good source of local fishing information.

Santa Barbara Sailing Center, 133 Harbor Way, 93101; (805) 962–2826 or (800) 350–9090. A fleet of forty power and sail craft from 14 to 50 feet for rent, skippered charters, harbor tours, island cruises, champagne cruises, and dinner cruises. Sailing instruction and certification offered.

Sea Landing Sport Fishing, 301 West Cabrillo Boulevard, 93101; (805) 963–3564. Cabrillo Boulevard at Bath Street, on the waterfront, south of U.S. 101. Half-day, three-quarter-day, and all-day coastal and island fishing trips. Twilight trips in season. Live bait available. Tackle rental. Also private charters and scuba-diving trips.

Sunset Kidd's Sailing, 125 Harbor Way #13, 93109; (805) 962–8222. On the waterfront, south of U.S. 101. Hour-long harbor cruises, sunset and evening cruises, and overnight island trips—all under sail. Private charters also available.

GOLF

Glen Annie Golf Club, 405 Glen Annie Road, Goleta 93117; (805) 968–6400. A half-mile east of U.S. 101, via Glen Annie Road. Spectacular coastal views with the Santa Ynez Mountains as a backdrop on this eighteen-hole, par-seventy-one, 6,420-yard course. Pro shop, resident pro, clubhouse, club and cart rental, driving range, practice greens, restaurant, and bar.

Sandpiper Golf Course, 7925 Hollister Avenue, Goleta 93117; (805) 968–1541. South of U.S. 101 in Goleta, west of Santa Barbara. An eighteen-hole, par-seventy-two, 7,068-yard golf course on a bluff overlooking the ocean. Snack bar, pro shop, and equipment rentals.

Santa Barbara Golf Club, Las Positas Road and McCaw Avenue, 93101; (805) 687–7087. Just north of U.S. 101 via Las Positas Road. An eighteen-hole public course, pro shop, resident pro, equipment and cart rentals, and snack bar.

OTHER ATTRACTIONS

Botanic Garden, 1212 Mission Canyon Road, 93101; (805) 682–4726. North of U.S. 101, 1½ miles past the mission, off Foothill Road. Tours: daily at 2:00 P.M.; also at 10:30 A.M. Thursday, Saturday, and Sunday. A sixty-five-acre garden along upper Mission Creek with native trees and shrubs, cacti, and wildflowers. Three miles of nature trails.

Mission Santa Barbara, Laguna Street, 93101; (805) 682–4713. North of U.S. 101 at the upper end of Laguna Street via Los Olivos Street off State Street. Daily, 9:00 A.M. to 5:00 P.M. Founded in 1786 and known as the "Queen of the Missions," this certainly ranks among the most beautiful of the twenty-one California missions. Museum, chapel, cemetery, garden, and gift shop. Tours by appointment.

TRAVEL INFORMATION

Santa Barbara Visitor Information Center, One Santa Barbara Street, P.O. Box 299, 93102; (805) 965–3021 or (800) 927–4688; www.sbchamber.org

EVENTS

April	Spring Arts Festival, Lompoc, (805) 735–8511
	Santa Barbara Vintner's Festival, (805) 688–0881
May	Cinco de Mayo, (805) 965–8581
June	Summer Solstice Parade, (805) 965–3396
July	Semana Nautica Swim Competition, (805) 969–4755
	Santa Barbara National Horse Show, (805) 687–0766
	Greek Festival, (805) 683–4492
August	Old Spanish Days, (805) 688–4815
	Santa Barbara Museum of Natural History Wine Festival, (805) 682–4711
September	Danish Days, (800) 468–1488
October	Harbor and Seafood Festival, (805) 967–8778
	Avocado Festival, Carpinteria, (805) 684–5479
December	Yuletide Boat Parade, (805) 564–5520

GROVER BEACH

Population: 12,230

PISMO BEACH

☆

Population: 8,000

Location: *Side by side along Highway 1 and U.S. 101, 89 miles north of Santa Barbara and 12 miles south of San Luis Obispo, about midway between Los Angeles and San Francisco.*

In the vicinity of Grover Beach and Pismo Beach, the foothills push westward and slope quickly to the ocean, forcing the highway seaward, within view of the resorts atop the bluffs overlooking the beach and surf. Miles of wide beach extend southward from the city of Pismo Beach to the Pismo Dunes and beyond. To the north, at the base of the cliffs are tiny pocket beaches and tidepools.

Pismo is a Chumash Indian word roughly translating to "tar" and referring to the natural asphalt that bubbles up through fissures in the ocean bottom and washes ashore along the beaches of central California. The Indians used it to caulk their plank canoes and waterproof their baskets. The same material has combined with the extremely fine sands here to create beaches hard enough to drive on.

Pismo Beach has been a resort town for the better part of a century, and Grover Beach has been attracting fun seekers and outdoor enthusiasts for nearly as long. Most of the resort motels and hotels are in Pismo Beach and Shell Beach along the bluffs, while the campgrounds and RV parks are at Grover Beach and Oceano.

LODGING

Best Western Shore Cliff Lodge, 2555 Price Street, Pismo Beach 93449; (805) 773–4671 or (800) 441–8885. West of U.S. 101

and Highway 1 on a bluff overlooking the ocean. Remote-control cable TV in 99 rooms and kitchen suites. Pool, whirlpool, sauna, and lighted tennis courts. Ocean view and stairs to beach. Restaurant and bar on premises. Moderate to very expensive.

The Cliffs at Shell Beach, 2757 Shell Beach Road, Shell Beach 93449; (805) 773–5000 or (800) 826–7827. West of U.S. 101, north of Pismo Beach, via Spyglass Road. Remote-control cable TV in 165 large rooms and 27 deluxe suites loaded with such amenities as marble bathrooms, whirlpool tubs, and private balconies. Heated pool with waterfalls, whirlpool, fitness center, and beach access. Restaurant on premises. Room service available. Moderate to very expensive.

Edgewater Inn and Suites, 280 Wadsworth Avenue, Pismo Beach 93449; (805) 773–4811 or (888) 248–1354. West of U.S. 101. Queen and king beds in 93 rooms and kitchen suites with refrigerators and remote-control cable TV. Pool, whirlpool, ocean view, and beach access. Continental breakfast. Moderate to expensive.

Holiday Inn, 775 North Oak Park Boulevard, Grover Beach 93433; (805) 481–4447. West of U.S. 101, south of Pismo Beach. Double and king beds in 35 rooms with cable TV and cable movies. Some fireplaces and in-room whirlpools. Continental breakfast. Restaurant and cocktail lounge on premises. Moderate.

Pismo Lighthouse Suites, 2411 Price Street, Pismo Beach 93449; (805) 773–2411 or (800) 245–2411. West of U.S. 101. Cable TV and cable movies in 70 suites, some with wet bars, microwave ovens, and fireplaces. Heated pool, whirlpool, ocean view, and beach access. Moderate to expensive.

Sea Crest Resort Motel, 2241 Price Street, Pismo Beach 93449; (805) 773–4608 or (800) 728–8400. West of U.S. 101 on a bluff overlooking the ocean. Queen and king beds in 160 large rooms and executive, family, and Jacuzzi suites. Heated pool, whirlpools, glass-enclosed Sundeck, barbecue area, and shuffleboard court. Ocean view. Moderate to expensive.

SeaVenture Resort, 100 Ocean View Avenue, Pismo Beach 93449; (805) 773–4994 or (800) 662–5545. West of U.S. 101, off Dolliver. Cable TV in 50 units, 43 with spas—all with fireplaces, wet bars, and refrigerators. Heated pool and barbecue area. Continental breakfast. Rooftop restaurant open for dinner only. Cocktail lounge. Moderate to expensive.

CAMPGROUNDS AND RV PARKS

Oceano Memorial Campground, Oceano 93445; (805) 781–5930. South of Grover Beach, west of U.S. 101, off Highway 1, south of Pier Avenue. Has 22 campsites with hookups available, fire pits, and showers. Picnic areas. Inexpensive.

Pismo Coast Village, 165 South Dolliver, Pismo Beach 93449; (805) 773–1811; in California, (888) 782–3224. Has 400 full-hookup, grassy sites with trees, tables, and fire rings. Showers, laundry, heated pool, ocean-view sites, beach access. Bicycle, barbecue-grill, umbrella, boogieboard, and beach-chair rentals. Restaurant, general store, arcade, basketball and volleyball courts, and horseshoe pits. Propane, firewood, and ice available. Moderate.

Pismo State Beach North Beach Campground, South Dolliver Street, Oceano 93445; (805) 489–2684 or (800) 444–7275. West of U.S. 101 and Highway 1, south of Pismo Beach. Has 103 campsites with tables and stoves, no hookups. Tank dump. Ocean view, beach access, dunes access. Inexpensive.

Pismo State Beach Oceano Campground, Pier Avenue, Oceano 93445; (805) 489–2684 or (800) 444–7275. West of U.S. 101, off Highway 1, south of Grover Beach. Has 124 campsites, 42 with full hookups. Each site has table and stove. Showers, ocean view, trail to the beach. Moderate.

FOOD

Golden Gong Chinese Restaurant, 1591 Grand Avenue, Grover Beach 93433; (805) 481–7368. West of U.S. 101. Lunch and dinner daily. Large menu includes wonton soup, seaweed soup, egg flower soup, fried wonton, egg rolls, sweet-and-sour dishes, skewered beef, barbecued pork, Hunan and Szechuan beef and seafood dinners, Chow mein, chop suey, egg foo yung, and more. Carryout service available. Beer. Inexpensive.

F. McLintock's Saloon & Dining House, 750 Mattie Road, Pismo Beach 93449; (805) 773–1892. Lunch and dinner daily. Historic old saloon and restaurant serving great oak-barbecued ribs, ten-ounce filet mignon, and T-bone steaks of twenty-eight and thirty ounces. Seafood includes rainbow trout, stuffed sole, and scampi. Live country-western music nightly. Full bar. Moderate.

Old West Cinnamon Rolls, 861 Dolliver Street, Pismo Beach 93449; (805) 773–1428. West of U.S. 101, downtown. Monday through Saturday, 6:30 A.M. to 5:30 P.M.; Sunday, 6:30 A.M. to 2:00

P.M. An assortment of huge, fresh, sticky cinnamon rolls—the best you've ever had. Moderate.

Steamer's, 1601 Price Street, Pismo Beach 93449; (805) 773–4711. Daily breakfast, lunch, and dinner; Sunday brunch. Specializes in California cuisine. Fresh seafood, steaks, and prime rib. Homemade cheesecake and other desserts. Beer, wine, and cocktails. Dancing and live entertainment nightly.

SHOPPING AND BROWSING

Art Mesquit, 1353 Shell Beach Road, Shell Beach 93449; (805) 773–1776. West of U.S. 101, north of Pismo Beach. Monday through Saturday, 10:30 A.M. to 5:30 P.M.; Sunday, noon to 4:30 P.M. Oriental antiques, Art Deco items, antique radios, lamps, chairs, small tables, and fine furniture.

BEACHES, PARKS, TRAILS, AND WAYSIDES

South of Oceano and west of Highway 1 are the Pismo Dunes, the highest dunes in the state. In the past, when Hollywood needed footage of the Sahara Desert, camera crews headed for Pismo Dunes. In fact, the desert scenes in the silent classic *The Sheik,* starring Rudolph Valentino, were filmed here. Even today, the area is used in commercials and feature films.

All kinds of four-wheel-drive and off-road vehicles regularly descend on the dunes, and ordinary highway vehicles are allowed on the beach in designated areas. Those so inclined can rent four-wheelers locally and enjoy cruising the surfline or the exhilarating experience of a full-throttle climb up the slipface of a dune. Parts of the dunes are off-limits to vehicular traffic of any kind, so be sure to pick up maps and regulations before roaring off.

Hiking provides a pleasant way to enjoy the resplendent beauty of the dunes and adjacent beach. Among the wildlife hikers might encounter are more than fifty species of songbirds, shorebirds, and migratory waterfowl, as well as dune mice, cottontail rabbits, jack rabbits, and black-tailed deer. A lucky few will catch a glimpse of a fox, coyote, or bobcat.

Beach access is good from the city of Pismo Beach southward. You can reach the beach from the end of Wilmar Avenue, west off Price Street, and from Cypress Street at the west end of several intersecting streets, such as Wadsworth Avenue, Main Avenue, Stimson

Pismo State Beach

Avenue, Ocean Avenue, Park Avenue, and Addie Street.

In Grover Beach, beach access is at the west end of Grand Avenue, near LeSage Riviera Golf Course, and off Strand Way at the west end of most intersecting streets. Auto ramps leading to the beach are at the west end of Grand and Pier avenues and at the Oceano Beach entrance.

In the Shell Beach area, off Shell Beach Road, several overlooks and small parks along Ocean Boulevard and Seacliff Drive offer excellent views of the ocean and offshore rocks and islets that harbor sea lions as well as nesting and roosting populations of several bird species, including pigeon guillemot and brown pelicans. Access to pocket beaches and tidepools is via paths or stairways along Ocean Boulevard at the end of Palomar Avenue, Morro Avenue, and Vista del Mar and at Spyglass City Park on Seacliff Drive.

To reach Avila State Beach and Port San Luis Beach, take the Avila Beach exit off U.S. 101, 3 miles north of Pismo Beach.

WATER SPORTS AND ACTIVITIES

The Pismo Beach area is another popular spot with surfers. The best surfing is south of the Pismo Beach Pier.

Three piers in the area serve anglers. Pismo Beach Pier is 950 feet long and lighted for night fishing. Concessions sell snacks, beverages, bait, and tackle. There's another pier at Avila Beach, with fish-cleaning facilities at the end of the pier. The 1,320-foot pier at Port San Luis is also lighted at night. It's equipped with boat hoists, and fuel docks and a boat-trailer parking area are nearby.

Although the pismo clam is still the most sought-after clam on the central coast, populations of this great bivalve are a fraction of what they once were. The large clams, with shells 7 inches or more across, fed the Chumash Indians for centuries. Early white settlers literally plowed the beaches to harvest the clams by the thousands to use as fertilizer and livestock feed. By 1911, the clams' numbers had sufficiently dwindled to require regulation of the harvest, yet an incredibly liberal limit of 200 clams per day was imposed. Commercial harvest continued until 1947, when it was finally prohibited.

The limit is now ten clams, 4½ inches or larger, per person per day, which is enough for anyone. The problem is that most legal-size clams are found beyond the low-tide line and are available only to those willing to wade into the surf for them. The fear now among some biologists is that the growing numbers of sea otters along the central coast will ultimately wipe out the remaining clam colonies.

RENTALS: SUMMER ONLY

Pismo Bike Rental and Beach Supplies, 519 Cypress Street, Pismo Beach 93449; (805) 773–0355. Cypress Street at Stimson Avenue, 1 block south of the pier. Rents Schwinn cruisers, boogieboards, wet suits, beach chairs, umbrellas, and ice chests by the hour, half-day, day, and two-day.

Sand Center, 307 Pier Avenue, Oceano 93445; (805) 489–0395. Rents ATVs; helmets and goggles provided. Free beach shuttle.

GOLF

Avila Beach Golf Resort, Avila Beach Road, P.O. Box 2140, Avila Beach 93424; (805) 595–4000. Located 2½ miles west of U.S. 101, via Avila Beach exit, 3 miles north of Pismo Beach. An eighteen-hole, par-seventy-one, 6,500-yard course open to the public. Clubhouse, pro shop, resident pro, cart and club rentals, driving range, coffee shop, snack bar, and restaurant.

Pismo State Beach Golf Course, 9 LeSage Drive, Grover Beach 93433; (805) 481–5215. West of U.S. 101, 1 block north of Grand

Avenue, 1 mile south of Pismo Beach. A nine-hole public course on the beach. Clubhouse, pro shop, handcart rentals, club rental, driving range, and restaurant.

TRAVEL INFORMATION

Grover Beach Chamber of Commerce, 177 South Eighth Street, Grover Beach 93433; (805) 489–9091; www.thegrid.net/gb.chamber

Pismo Beach Chamber of Commerce, 581 Dolliver Street, Pismo Beach 93449; (805) 773–4382 or (800) 443–7778; www.pismo chamber.com

EVENTS

June	Pismo Beach Car Show, Pismo Beach, (805) 773–4382
July	Old Fashioned Fourth of July and Fireworks on the Beach, Pismo Beach, (805) 773–4382
August	Saint Anthony's Celebration, Pismo Beach, (805) 481–8012
September	Western Days, Pismo Beach, (805) 773–4382
October	Clam Festival, Pismo Beach, (805) 773–4382
	Jubilee by the Sea Jazz Festival, Pismo Beach, (805) 773–2241
	Pumpkins on the Pier, Pismo Beach, (805) 773–4382
November	Marching Band Review, Pismo Beach, (805) 773–4382
	Christmas Tree Lighting, Pismo Beach, (805) 773–4382

SAN LUIS OBISPO

Population: 43,700

Location: *On U.S. 101 and California Highway 1, 16 miles southeast of Morro Bay, 12 miles north of Pismo Beach, 200 miles north of Los Angeles, and 230 miles south of San Francisco.*

San Luis Obispo is set among rolling hills and ancient volcanic outcroppings in a lush green valley a few miles east of the coast. Travelers are drawn to this spotless town by its picturesque setting, proximity to the coast, friendly natives, and comfortable climate.

The area is bathed in sunshine an average 315 days a year and gets most of its rain from November through March. Summer days are warm, evenings cool enough for a light jacket or sweater.

The city, which is the seat of government for San Luis Obispo County, grew up around its lovely mission in the mid-nineteenth century and became a major supply center for nearby ranches. Today it still serves in a similar capacity for rural residents and those residing in smaller ranch and coastal communities. It's also an active center of social, cultural, and recreational activities, staging numerous events every year.

Many of the city's houses and commercial buildings were erected in the 1800s and early 1900s and have been carefully preserved and restored. Much of the downtown area, in fact, owes its magnetic charm to the fine historic buildings that house the many shops and restaurants. You can take a self-guided tour of the historical buildings by following the map and information in the *San Luis Obispo Visitors Guide,* published annually by the Chamber of Commerce and available at the visitor center.

Anyone fortunate enough to be in town on any Thursday evening is in for quite an experience. Residents and visitors by the droves fill downtown San Luis Obispo to enjoy Thursday Night Activities and Farmers' Market. From the aromatic smoke rising from hardwood coals around racks of barbecued ribs on giant outdoor grills to the rows of stands displaying a great array of flowers to the sights and sounds of street entertainers, it's a treat for all the senses. Farmers sell the freshest produce from stands and pickup-truck beds at bargain prices. Peppers, tomatoes, cucumbers, eggplant, zucchini, plums, nectarines, berries, and other vegetables and fruits—if it's grown locally, it's for sale here.

With its dozens of motels and inns, hundreds of shops and galleries, and more than eighty-five restaurants and cafes, San Luis Obispo is a great place for a visit in its own right. The city is also a good headquarters for day trips to Pismo Beach and the dunes country, Morro Bay, Hearst Castle, and the nearby wine country.

LODGING

Apple Farm Inn and Trellis Court, 2015 Monterey Street, 93401; (805) 544–2040; in California, (800) 255–2040. Just east of U.S. 101 via the Monterey Street exit. A Victorian-style country inn with 69 rooms. Gas-log fireplaces with hearths and mantels in each room. Decorated with 50 different wallpapers, fabrics, and paints. More than 600 artworks displayed. Canopy, 4-poster, brass, and enameled beds. Cozy furnishings include love seats, wing-back chairs, window seats, wicker, and antiques. A working mill with waterwheel on premises is open for tours. Beautifully landscaped courtyards, creek, and waterfalls. Complimentary coffee delivered to room at wake-up call. The single-story Trellis Court has 35 rooms with many of the amenities found in the inn rooms, such as fireplaces, canopy beds, and brass beds. Heated pool. Restaurant on premises. Room service available. Moderate to expensive.

Best Western Royal Oak Motor Hotel, 214 Madonna Road, 93405; (805) 544–4410 or (800) 545–4410. West of U.S. 101 via Madonna Road exit, at south end of town. Queen beds in 99 rooms with cable TV and cable movies. Wet bars available. Heated pool and whirlpool. Laundry and valet service available. Restaurant and cocktail lounge on premises. Moderate.

La Cuesta Motor Inn, 2074 Monterey Street, 93401; (805) 543–2777 or (800) 543–2777. East of U.S. 101 via Monterey Street exit. Cable TV and cable movies in 72 rooms. Heated pool and whirlpool. Complimentary coffee, afternoon tea, and continental breakfast. Moderate to expensive.

Madonna Inn, 100 Madonna Road, 93405; (805) 543–3000 or (800) 543–9666. On Madonna Road, just west of U.S. 101, south end of town. Cable TV in 109 rooms and suites—no two alike. Room decor ranges from eccentric to posh. Not much here is subdued. This unique hot-pink inn is a local landmark. Coffee shop, bakery, restaurant, cocktail lounge, and shops on premises. Moderate to expensive.

Ramada Inn San Luis Obispo, 1000 Olive Street, 93405; (805) 544–2800 or (800) 777–5847. West of U.S. 101 via Santa Rosa (Highway 1); take Morro Bay exit. King beds in 48 rooms and suites with cable TV, irons, ironing boards, hair dryers, and in-room coffee. Creekside rooms and family suites with kitchen available. Patios and balconies. Pool, sauna, and laundry facilities. Complimentary continental breakfast. Moderate.

FOOD

Apple Farm Restaurant, 2015 Monterey Street, 93401; (805) 544–6100; in California, (800) 255–2040. Just east of U.S. 101 via the Monterey Street exit. Breakfast, lunch, and dinner daily. Country-style breakfasts include buttermilk pancakes with real maple and honey syrup, Belgian waffles with fruit toppings, eggs, thick-sliced bacon, ham, and fresh-baked rolls and muffins. Lunch offerings are homemade soups, steamed vegetable dishes, chili, salad bar, and hearty sandwiches of roast beef, meat loaf, and roast turkey. Dinner selections are such American favorites as turkey and dressing, chicken and dumplings, baked chicken, and smoked ribs. Special desserts are strawberry shortcake, fruit cobblers, hot apple dumplings, and fresh apple pie with hot cinnamon sauce. Moderate.

Old Country Deli, 600 Marsh Street, 93401; (805) 541–2968. East of U.S. 101, in town. Daily, 8:00 A.M. to 6:00 P.M. Open until 9:00 P.M. on Thursday. Award-winning barbecued ribs, jerky, home-cured hams, homemade sausages, pastrami, corned beef, and bacon. Salads and deli-style sandwiches. Good wine selection. Moderate.

The Rib Line, 2121 Santa Barbara Street, 93401; (805) 543–7427. East of U.S. 101, in town. Dinner daily. Chicken, beef ribs, and baby back ribs served with baked potatoes, baked beans, coleslaw, and freshly baked cornbread with honey butter. Tri-tip dinner includes salad, garlic bread, baked potato, and baked beans. Free delivery to motels. Inexpensive to moderate.

SLO Brewing Company, 1119 Garden Street, 93401; (805)

Historic Andrews Bank Building, San Luis Obispo

543–1843. Downtown, between Higuera and Marsh Streets, upstairs. Monday through Saturday, 11:30 A.M. to 10:30 P.M.; Thursday through Saturday, 11:30 A.M. to 1:30 A.M. Summer and fall, also open Sunday, 11:00 A.M. to 10:30 P.M. Historic brewpub offering an assortment of appetizers, great burgers, lunch and dinner specials, and beers and ales brewed on the premises—pale ale, porter, and seasonal brewmaster's specials on tap. Moderate.

Tortilla Flats, 1051 Nipomo Street, 93401; (805) 544–7575. Nipomo at Higuera Street, east of U.S. 101, in town. Daily lunch and dinner, Sunday brunch. Superb Mexican food and plenty of it. Homemade tortilla chips and salsa at each table. Appetizers include nachos, guacamole, chile con queso, and the Tortilla Flats sampler—big enough for two. Soups, salads, and taco-and-tostada bar. Beef, chicken, or shrimp fajitas. Tacos, burritos, enchiladas, chicken entrees, steaks, and more. Full bar. Inexpensive to moderate.

SHOPPING AND BROWSING

San Luis Obispo has several shopping centers and one covered mall, but the best place to shop and browse is the lovely downtown area. Here, fine old buildings along the tree-shaded streets of this clean city hub contain hundreds of galleries, boutiques, and specialty shops.

In an era of suburban sprawl, it's a pleasure to stroll these downtown streets where couples young and old walk hand in hand from shop window to sidewalk display. Appetite-whetting aromas of freshly baked breads and pastries, homemade soups, and sizzling burgers and steaks waft from doorways and walkways. It can get crowded, but it's never rushed.

This is life in the SLO lane. Don't miss it.

RENTALS

Art's SLO Cyclery, 2140 Santa Barbara Street, 93401; (805) 543–4416. Rents fully equipped bicycles with water bottles, racks, spare tubes, pumps, and locks. Helmets available. Bike sales, supplies, and service.

GOLF

Laguna Lake Municipal Golf Course, 11175 Los Osos Valley Road, 93402; (805) 781–7309. West of U.S. 101, south of town, via Los Osos Valley Road exit. A nine-hole executive course with pro shop, resident pro, club and cart rentals and repairs, driving-range cage, and snack bar.

WINERIES AND VINEYARDS

More than a dozen wineries and vineyards dot the rolling hills just outside San Luis Obispo. Most have tasting rooms and offer tours. Following are several of the nearest ones. You'll find others north of San Luis Obispo, near Paso Robles, and a couple more farther south.

Claiborne & Churchill Vintners, 264 Carpenter Canyon Road, 93401; (805) 544–4066. Just off the south end of Broad Street (Route 227), south end of town. Tours and tasting Thursday through Sunday, 11:00 A.M. to 4:00 P.M. A small winery featuring premium gewürztraminer, chardonnay, and Pinot noir.

Corbett Canyon Vineyards, 2195 Corbett Canyon Road, 93403; (805) 544–5800. South of San Luis Obispo, southeast of U.S. 101 via Route 227, about 6½ miles to Corbett Canyon Road, then east just over a mile. Tasting by appointment. Specialties include chardonnay, chenin blanc, gewürztraminer, Pinot noir, sauvignon blanc, and both red and white zinfandels, among others.

The Crushed Grape, 319 Madonna Road, 93401; (805)

544-4449. In the Central Coast Plaza, south end of town, west of U.S. 101 via Madonna Road exit. Monday through Friday, 10:00 A.M. to 9:00 P.M.; Saturday, 10:00 A.M. to 6:00 P.M.; Sunday, 11:00 A.M. to 5:00 P.M. Sample any of a variety of California wines and buy wines by the bottle. Gift baskets available include locally produced gourmet foods.

Edna Valley Vineyard, 2585 Biddle Ranch Road, 93403; (805) 544-5855. About 5 miles south of San Luis Obispo, southeast of U.S. 101 via Route 227 to Biddle Ranch Road. Tours and tasting daily, 10:00 A.M. to 4:00 P.M. Specializes in chardonnay and Pinot noir.

Meridian Vineyards, 7000 Highway 46 East, Paso Robles, 93446; (805) 237-6000. Tasting room open daily 10:00 A.M. to 5:00 P.M. Specializing in chardonnay, Pinot noir, syrah, and cabernet.

OTHER ATTRACTIONS

Mission San Luis Obispo, San Luis Obispo 93401; (805) 543-6850. East of U.S. 101 in downtown San Luis Obispo, on Monterey Street at Chorro Street. Monday through Friday, 7:00 A.M. to 6:00 P.M.; Saturday, 7:00 A.M. to 6:30 P.M.; Sunday, 7:00 A.M. to 7:00 P.M. A beautiful old mission, right in the heart of downtown, founded in 1772 by Father Junípero Serra; the fifth of California's missions. Built of adobe bricks made by local Chumash Indians.

TRAVEL INFORMATION

San Luis Obispo Chamber of Commerce, 1039 Chorro Street, 93401; (805) 543-1323; www.slochamber.org

San Luis Obispo County Visitors & Conference Bureau, 1041 Chorro Street, Suite E, 93401; (805) 541-8000

EVENTS

March	Farmer's Market Rib Cookoff, (805) 543–1323
April	Mandonnari Italian Street Painting Festival, (805) 543–1323
May	California Festival of Beers, (805) 543–1323
June	Farmer's Market Father's Day Jazz Festival, (805) 543–1323
July	Fourth of July Fireworks, (805) 543–1323
	KCBX Central Coast Wine Classic, (805) 543–1323
	San Luis Obispo Mozart Festival, (805) 543–1323
	SLO Triathlon, (805) 543–1323
	Shakespeare Festival, (805) 543–1323
	Renaissance Festival, (805) 543–1323
August	International Orchid Show, (805) 543–1323
	Central Coast Wine Festival, (805) 543–1323
	Obon Festival, (805) 543–1323
September	Taste of San Luis, (805) 543–1323
October	International Film Festival, (805) 546–3456
	Harbor Festival, (805) 772–1155
	Pismo Beach Clam Festival, (805) 773–4382
November	Arroyo Grande Edna Valley Harvest Festival, (805) 541–5856
	Holiday Craft Fair, (805) 543–1323
December	Holiday Parade, (805) 543–0286

MORRO BAY

Population: 9,700

Location: *Morro Bay is on California Highway 1, 18 miles south of Cambria, 16 miles northwest of San Luis Obispo; neighboring Los Osos (population 8,000) is 5 miles to the south, and Cayucos (population 3,000) is 4 miles to the north.*

Resting on the east shore of a small estuary of the same name, Morro Bay is a compact and charming resort community with a busy and interesting port minutes from the open ocean. The city, bay, sand spit, and state park are all named after the area's most prominent landmark—the huge rock early Spanish explorers dubbed El Morro, meaning "The Knob" or "The Knoll."

Morro Rock stands 576 feet high and is the core of an ancient volcanic plug, one of several in a chain stretching from here to San Luis Obispo. When early settlers first came to these shores, Morro Rock was an islet standing 1,000 feet offshore and was larger than it is today. In the 1930s, construction of a revetment and causeway connected the rock to the mainland. From the late 1800s until 1969, when the state designated Morro Rock an ecological reserve, more than a million tons of rock were quarried from the face of the dome to build breakwaters and the causeway.

The reserve was established to protect the endangered peregrine falcons that nest on the rock and feed on the abundant local and migratory birds and waterfowl. Although climbing the rock is prohibited, it's possible to drive or hike to the base and to view it from anywhere on the Morro Bay waterfront or the hills above town. Alert and lucky observers spot the raptors on hunting forays, diving on their prey at speeds in excess of 200 miles per hour, making them the fastest birds in the world.

Visitors flock to Morro Bay to dine on fresh local seafood and to enjoy outdoor activities on the bay, on the beaches, and at nearby state parks. There are a beautiful golf course and superb museum here, as well as numerous natural areas to explore. The many shops and galleries of Cambria are a short drive north; downtown San Luis Obispo is an equal distance to the southeast.

LODGING

Bay View Lodge, 225 Harbor Street, 93442; (805) 772–2771 or (800) 742–8439. Southwest of Highway 1, 1 block from the waterfront. Queen and king beds in 22 rooms with cable TV, cable movies, and coffeemakers. Some rooms with fireplaces, refrigerators, and views of the waterfront and ocean. Whirlpool. Laundry facilities. Walk to shops and restaurants. Moderate.

Best Western San Marcos Motor Inn, 250 Pacific Street, 93442; (805) 772–2248 or (800) 772–7969. Southwest of Highway 1 via Morro Bay exit to Morro Avenue at Pacific Street. King beds in 32 rooms with cable TV, cable movies, and refrigerators. Whirlpool, balconies, and ocean view. One block to the waterfront. Moderate to expensive.

Blue Sail Inn, 851 Market Avenue, 93442; (805) 772–7132 or (888) 337–0707. Southwest of Highway 1, 1 block from the waterfront. Cable TV and cable movies in 47 rooms with refrigerators, wet bars, coffeemakers, and private balconies; some fireplaces. Whirlpool. Bay view. Moderate to expensive.

The Breakers Motel, P.O. Box 110, 93442; (805) 772–7317 or (800) 932–8899. Southwest of Highway 1, Morro Bay Boulevard at Market Avenue. Double, queen, and king beds in 25 rooms with remote-control cable TV, cable movies, and refrigerators. In-room coffee and tea. Heated pool, ocean view, some fireplaces. Walk to shops, restaurants, and waterfront. Moderate.

El Morro Masterpiece Motel, 1206 Main Street, 93442; (805) 772–5633 or (800) 527–6782. Southwest of Highway 1. Queen and king beds in 27 rooms and suites with cable TV, cable movies, coffeemakers, and hair dryers. Some rooms with refrigerators, ceiling fans, and fireplaces. Penthouse suite with Roman spa, fireplace, wet bar, VCR, Sundeck, and great panoramic view. Whirlpool and ocean view. Moderate to expensive.

Embarcadero Inn, 456 Embarcadero, 93442; (805) 772–2700

Morro Rock, Morro Bay

or (800) 292-7625. Southwest of highway 1, on the waterfront. Queen and king beds in 32 bay-view rooms and suites with refrigerators, remote-control TV, and VCRs; 30 of the rooms with balconies. Suites also have fireplaces and wet bars. Walk to shops and restaurants. Moderate to expensive.

CAMPGROUNDS AND RV PARKS

Bay Pines Travel Trailer Park, 1501 Quintana Road, 93442; (805) 772-3223. South of Morro Bay on Highway 1 at Los Osos exit. Has 112 full-hookup sites with satellite TV. Heated pool, showers, and laundry. Moderate.

Montana de Oro State Park, Pecho Road, Los Osos 93402; (805) 528-0513 or (800) 444-7275. Near park headquarters along Islay Creek. Has 50 sites with tables and stoves for tents, trailers, and motor homes to 24 feet. Also a horse camp east off Pecho Valley Road, at northern park boundary: 3 individual horse camps and 2 group camps with tables, wood stoves, pit toilets, and corrals. Inexpensive to moderate.

Morro Bay State Park, State Park Road, (805) 772-2560 or (800) 444-7275. Has 135 campsites, 20 with electricity and water hookups. Table, stove, and food locker at each site. Showers, laundry tubs, and tank dump. Campground set amid a pine and eucalyptus forest. Exercise trail and Frisbee golf course. Moderate.

Morro Dunes Travel Trailer Park and Resort Campground, 1790 Embarcadero, 93442; (805) 772–2722. Has 178 campsites, 68 with full hookups. Table and stove at each site. Showers, laundry, tank dump, ocean view, and beach access. Store, RV supplies, firewood, and ice. Moderate.

Morro Strand State Beach, (805) 772–2560 or (800) 444–7275; in winter, (805) 772–7434. West of Highway 1, between Ascadero Road and Yerba Buena Avenue. Has 104 sites with tables and stoves for tents, trailers, and RVs to 24 feet. Showers. Campground is protected from wind by small dunes. Moderate.

Tratel Morro Bay, 1680 Main Street, 93442; (805) 772–8581. East of Highway 1, south of Route 41. Has 53 full-hookup sites with cable TV and concrete patios. Showers and laundry. Minimarket 1 block away. Moderate.

FOOD

The Coffee Pot Restaurant, 1001 Front Street, 93442; (805) 772–3176. On the waterfront, downtown. Breakfast and lunch daily. More than a dozen omelets, quiche, and egg dishes, served with O'Brien hash browns and choice of biscuit, muffin, or toast. Pancakes and French toast. Soups, salads, sandwiches, and fish-and-chips. House specialties include huge homemade cinnamon rolls, blueberry muffins, and French toast stuffed with cream cheese, walnuts, and marmalade. Inexpensive to moderate.

Dorn's Original Breakers Cafe, 801 Market Street, 93442; (805) 772–4415. Southwest of Highway 1, 1 block east of Embarcadero. Breakfast, lunch, and dinner daily; breakfast served till 2:00 P.M. daily. Almost a dozen omelets to choose from, including Dorn's special seafood omelet. Choice of seven kinds of pancakes. Waffles, French toast, and eggs. Large assortment of lunch appetizers, salads, soups, chowder, sandwiches, and seafood entrees. Large dinner menu includes steaks, fish, and shellfish, and such house specialties as abalone, seafood brochette, linguine and clam sauce, sole Florentine, and "sea shells"—assorted shellfish sautéed in wine sauce with garlic, tomatoes, mushrooms, and pasta shells. Full bar. Moderate.

The Great American Fish Company, 1185 Embarcadero, 93442; (805) 772–4407. Southwest of Highway 1, on the waterfront. Lunch and dinner daily. A variety of seafood and meat sandwiches, seafood crepes, and fish-and-chips. More than a dozen appetizers, including smoked albacore, squid strips, artichokes, oysters, and stuffed potato skins. In addition to steaks, chicken, and ribs, mesquite-broiled shark, salmon, shrimp, halibut, swordfish, albacore, giant squid, and mahimahi. Full bar. Moderate.

Harbor Hut, 1205 Embarcadero, 93442; (805) 772-2255. On the waterfront, in town. Daily lunch and dinner, Sunday brunch. Lunch menu features award-winning clam chowder, salads, omelets, crepes, stuffed potato skins, deli-style sandwiches, and such seafood entrees as calamari, clam strips, oysters, prawns, and fresh fish. Half-dozen seafood appetizers. Dinners include five different steaks, teriyaki chicken, and such seafood favorites as king-crab legs, bouillabaisse, lobster, and seafood platter, as well as fresh salmon, halibut, and abalone when available. Full bar. Moderate.

Margie's Diner, 1698 Main Street, 93442; (805) 772-2510. North of downtown, east of Highway 1, just south of Route 41 intersection. Breakfast, lunch, and dinner daily. Good selection of omelets and other egg dishes, pancakes, French toast, and biscuits and gravy. Lunch includes soup, chili, salads, juicy burgers, deli-style sandwiches, and open-face turkey and roast-beef sandwiches with mashed potatoes and gravy. All lunch items available through dinner, plus such entrees as barbecued chicken, fried chicken, ham steak, and roast beef. Milk shakes, malts, and root-beer floats. Homemade pies. Inexpensive to moderate.

MUSEUM

Museum of Natural History, Morro Bay State Park, 93442; (805) 772-2694. At White Point, in the park, southeast of town. Daily, 10:00 A.M. to 5:00 P.M.; closed Thanksgiving, Christmas, and New Year's Day. Interpretive displays of the wildlife and history of the Morro Bay area. Slide shows, movies, lectures, and field trips. Superb view of bay and ocean. Good place for watching whales in season.

BEACHES, PARKS, TRAILS, AND WAYSIDES

Montana de Oro State Park in Los Osos is a large, relatively undeveloped natural area lying south of Morro Bay. Within its 8,000 acres are creeks, woodlands, grassy coastal plains rising to 1,500-foot hills, and 7 miles of ocean shoreline varying from sandy beaches to rocky bluffs and cliffs.

Trails wind among the pine, eucalyptus, and live oak trees on the hillsides and along creek bottoms where willow, myrtle, maple, box elder, and cottonwood trees grow. A variety of small mammals reside here, as do fox, bobcat, deer, and even cougar.

From Morro Bay, take South Bay Boulevard to Los Osos Valley Road, and turn west. From U.S. 101, Los Osos Valley Road leads west to Pecho Road.

Morro Bay State Park borders the southeast end of the city and lies adjacent to the bay. It contains the Natural History Museum and an eighteen-hole golf course, as well as hiking trails and picnic areas.

The Morro Bay State Park Sand Spit is a long finger of land separating the ocean from the bay. This undeveloped stretch of beach and dunes, popular with bird-watchers and clam diggers, is reached on foot by trail off Pecho Road or by boat, which is the easier and more popular way to go. Those who don't have boats can rent them or take the water taxi from the Embarcadero.

Morro Strand State Beach and Cayucos State Beach lie north of town, west of Highway 1, with access at the end of Twenty-fourth Street and in the town of Cayucos near the pier.

The Morro Bay area is a popular spot for watching and photographing a wide variety of birds. The large salt marsh attracts puddle ducks, diver ducks, seabirds, shorebirds, and songbirds by the thousands. Eucalyptus trees near the bay also serve as roosts and rookeries for great blue herons and egrets.

The eucalyptus trees also attract beautiful monarch butterflies, which arrive by the tens of thousands in October and remain through the winter months. Each evening, the butterflies gather in the trees in great clusters to keep warm.

WATER SPORTS AND ACTIVITIES

Surfers like the beaches near Morro Rock and north of town. The bay is popular with sailboarders, canoeists, and kayakers. And on minus tides, mudflats are exposed, providing access to clam beds. Both Dungeness and rock crabs are found in the bay, and local bait shops rent crabbing gear.

Anglers take surfperch, mackerel, rockfish, and various bottom fish from several small piers on the bay. The Cayucos Pier is on the ocean and serves as a popular fishing spot north of town. It's lighted for fishing at night, and there's no need for a fishing license.

Offshore anglers take chinook salmon from spring well into fall. Fall months are good for albacore, and the halibut fishery runs from midsummer through autumn. Lingcod, rockfish, cabezon, and a host of reef and bottom species are available all year, weather permitting.

RENTALS AND SUPPLIES

Liquid Soul, 701 Embarcadero, 93442; (805) 772–3244. On the waterfront, downtown. Monday through Friday, 10:00 A.M. to 8:00 P.M., Saturday and Sunday, 10:00 A.M. to 9:00 P.M. Sells surfboards, boogieboards, and other water gear.

Morro Bay Marina, 699 Embarcadero #11, 93442; (805) 772–8085. On the waterfront, downtown Pacific at Embarcadero. Rents boats by the hour.

Morro Bay State Park Marina, 10 State Park Road, 93442; (805) 772–8796. South of town. Daily, 9:00 A.M. to 5:00 P.M. Rents canoes and rowboats by the hour.

Wavelengths Surf Shop, 998 Embarcadero, 93442; (805) 772–3904. West of Highway 1, downtown. Monday through Saturday, 9:30 A.M. to 8:00 P.M.; Sunday, 9:30 A.M. to 6:00 P.M. Rents surfboards, boogieboards, and wet suits by the day.

TOURS AND TRIPS

Bay Taxi, Virg's Landing, 1215 Embarcadero, 93442; (805) 772–1222. Transportation to the sand spit for hikers, bird-watchers, clam diggers, and picnickers. Also, thirty-minute bay tours.

Tiger's Folly II, 1205 Embarcadero, 93442; weekdays, (805) 772–2257; weekends, (805) 772–2255. Docked at the Harbor Hut Restaurant. One-hour harbor cruises, weekends only. Full bar on board. Reservations not required. Also Sunday champagne brunch cruises, for which reservations are required.

GOLF

Sea Pines Golf Club, 1945 Solaro Street, Los Osos 93402; (805) 528–1788. A mile west of Los Osos via Los Osos Valley and Pecho roads. A nine-hole, par-twenty-eight, 1,465-yard public course. Clubhouse, pro shop, resident pro, club and cart rentals, driving range, and restaurant.

TRAVEL INFORMATION

Cayucos Chamber of Commerce, 241 South Ocean Avenue, P.O. Box 141, Cayucos 93430; (805) 995–1200 or (800) 563–1878; www.cayucosbythesea.com

Los Osos Chamber of Commerce, 781 Los Osos Valley Road, P.O. Box 6282, Los Osos 93402; (805) 528–4884; www.losososbay woodpark.org

Morro Bay Chamber of Commerce, 880 Main Street, P.O. Box 876, 93442; (805) 772–4467; in California, (800) 231–0592; www. morrobay.org; e-mail: baywatch@thegrid.net

EVENTS

January	Polar Bear Dip, Cayucos, (805) 995–1200
July	Fireworks and Fourth of July Celebration, Cayucos, (805) 995–1200
	Fourth of July Parade, Cayucos, (805) 995–1200
	Fourth of July Fireworks, Morro Bay, (805) 772–4467
	Portuguese Festival, Cayucos, (805) 995–1200
September	Peddler's Faire, Cayucos, (805) 995–1200
October	Harbor Festival, Morro Bay, (805) 772–1155
	Oktoberfest, Los Osos, (805) 528–4884
	Cayucos Music Festival, (805) 995–1200
December	Christmas Street Faire, Morro Bay, (805) 772–2489
	Lighted Boat Parade, Morro Bay, (805) 772–4467

CAMBRIA

Population: 5,000

SAN SIMEON

Population: 600

Location: *Cambria is on California Highway 1, 16 miles north of Morro Bay and 34 miles northwest of San Luis Obispo; San Simeon, on California Highway 1, is 6 miles north of Cambria and 67 miles south of Big Sur.*

C ambria is on the coast in the pine-forested foothills. San Simeon, also on the coast, is situated on the coastal benchlands that rise into rolling ranch country on the west slope of the Santa Lucia Mountains. Although the two communities evolved in the mid-nineteenth century nearly simultaneously, to some extent for similar reasons, they could scarcely be more different from each other today.

When copper and cinnabar, from which mercury is extracted, were discovered in the nearby mountains in the early 1860s, the Cambria area expanded rapidly. Dairy farming and cattle ranching grew with it, and soon dairy products, tallow, and hides were being shipped from here.

The cove just south of San Simeon Point developed as a whaling station in the early 1850s. During the annual migration of gray whales past the point, whale spotters watched for the spouting mammals and signaled the whalers, who set out after them in small boats. The blubber was rendered and oil shipped from here until the industry declined in the 1870s.

George Hearst, father of William Randolph Hearst, was an illiterate Missourian who made millions mining California silver and gold and later became a U.S. senator. He bought Rancho San Simeon in 1865 and in 1878 built a new wharf at the cove near San Simeon

93

Point, where schooners could load cattle hides, quicksilver, and other locally produced goods.

The coastal shipping trade flourished until 1894, when the railroad came to Cambria. Completion of the Coast Highway between Carmel and Cambria began a new era. But even before then, changes were taking place that would have far-reaching effects on the local landscape and economy.

In 1919, construction began on what would eventually become the greatest tourist attraction on this stretch of coast: William Randolph Hearst's extravagant monument to himself at San Simeon, known as the Hearst Castle. More than a million people visit this complex every year to see the hundred-room Casa Grande, three guest houses, works of art collected from around the globe, and grounds landscaped with shrubs, flowers, and more than 100,000 trees.

Construction, modification, and alteration continued for more than thirty years, leaving the complex still unfinished at Hearst's death in 1951. His heirs deeded the property to the state in 1958, and it's now operated as the Hearst San Simeon Historical Monument.

Cambria burgeoned in the 1950s and ultimately flowered into a busy artists' hamlet where dozens of galleries and shops, restaurants, and pubs stand amid the mixed architecture of California contemporary and English Tudor styles.

Between trips to the beach, visitors to the area can combine tours of Hearst Castle with shopping, browsing, and dining.

LODGING

Beach House Bed & Breakfast, 6360 Moonstone Beach Drive, Cambria 93428; (805) 927–3136. West side of Highway 1, on the beach. Has 7 rooms, some with fireplaces and oceanviews, all with private baths and cable TV. Decks, patios, and living room with fireplace. Bicycles available. Continental breakfast. Expensive.

Best Western Cavalier Beachfront Resort, 9415 Hearst Drive, San Simeon 93452; (805) 927–4688 or (800) 826–8168. West side of Highway 1, on the ocean, 3 miles south of Hearst Castle. Remote-control cable TV, cable movies, and VCRs in 90 rooms, some with fireplaces, wet bars, and refrigerators. Two heated pools, whirlpool, ocean view. Two restaurants, cocktail lounge, room service, and adjacent shopping plaza. Moderate to expensive.

Castle Inn by the Sea, 6620 Moonstone Beach Drive, Cambria 93428; (805) 927–8605. West of Highway 1, on the beach. Queen and king beds in 31 rooms with cable TV, VCRs, and refrigerators.

Moonstone Beach Boardwalk, Cambria

Large picnic area, heated pool, and whirlpool. Continental breakfast. Moderate.

El Rey Garden Inn, 9260 Castillo Drive, P.O. Box 200, San Simeon 93452; (805) 927–3998 or (800) 821–7914. East side of Highway 1. Queen and king beds in 56 rooms and suites with cable TV, some with fireplaces, in-room whirlpool, wet bars, and refrigerators. Garden courtyard with waterfalls. Heated pool and whirlpools. Restaurant on premises. Moderate to expensive.

Olallieberry Inn, 2476 Main Street, Cambria 93428; (805) 927–3222 or (888) 927–3222. One mile east of Highway 1. Has 9 individually decorated rooms with private baths, 6 with fireplaces. On weekends, wine and appetizers served in the parlor. Continental breakfast. Moderate to expensive.

CAMPGROUNDS AND RV PARKS

San Simeon State Park, P.O. Box 8, San Simeon 93452; (805) 927–2020 or (800) 444–7275. Beach is west of Highway 1, campground east of the highway. Has 132 developed campsites and 70 primitive sites with tables and fire pits. Showers, tank dump, ocean view, fishing, hiking, and nature trails, and a ⅛-mile walk to the beach. Moderate.

FOOD

The Brambles Dinner House, 4005 Burton Drive, P.O. Box 746, Cambria 93428; (805) 927–4716. East of Highway 1, 2 blocks southwest of Main Street. Dinner daily. Clam chowder, oyster soup, and pea soup. Top sirloin, rib eye, filet mignon, and New York steaks, as well as tenderloin teriyaki brochette and lamb chops broiled over oak. Barbecued chicken, baby pork ribs, and beef ribs. Prawns, scallops, scallone, fish, and bouillabaisse. One house speciality is salmon grilled over oak; another is prime rib with Yorkshire pudding. Full bar. Moderate.

The Hamlet Restaurant, Highway 1, Cambria 93428; (805) 927–3535. At Moonstone Gardens, Highway 1 at Moonstone Beach Drive. Daily lunch and dinner, Sunday brunch. Such lunch offerings as quiche Lorraine, brisket of beef sandwich, fish-and-chips, calamari and chips, clam chowder and salad, and mariner's salad. Dinners include seafood platter, breast of chicken, filet mignon, king-crab legs, poached salmon, brisket of beef, and rack of lamb. Full bar; great ocean view from inside restaurant; lunch outdoors on garden patio. Moderate.

Linn's Main Bin, 2277 Main Street, Cambria 93428; (805) 927–0371. East of Highway 1. Breakfast, lunch, and dinner daily. Extraordinary three-egg omelets, such as the Moonstone Beach, stuffed with seafood, Jack cheese, and sour cream; the Mexi-cali, stuffed with Jack cheese, chili peppers, onions, and bell peppers and topped with salsa and guacamole; and the Granatino Special, filled with Italian sausage, mozzarella cheese, onions, and bell peppers, then topped with marinara sauce. Other breakfast offerings are Belgian waffles, fresh fruit plate, and freshly baked muffins and granola. Quiches and hearty soups are lunch favorites, as are specialty sandwiches. For lunch and dinner, chicken and beef pot pies in two sizes are local favorites. Wonderful homemade cakes, pies, and cheesecakes. Inexpensive to moderate.

Mustache Pete's Italian Eatery, 4090 Burton Drive #1, Cambria 93428; (805) 927–8589. East of Highway 1, 1 block southwest of Main Street, Burton at Center Street. Lunch and dinner daily. Among the appetizers are shrimp cocktail, steamer clams, and escargot. Soups, salads, shrimp Louis, and such sandwiches as veal parmigiana hero, turkey and Swiss, and Italian submarine. Fettuccine, linguine, tortellini, rigatoni, ravioli, lasagna, manicotti, cannelloni, and spaghetti served for lunch and dinner. Also a large selection of veal, beef, poultry, and seafood entrees served with soup or salad and pasta.

Carryout service available. Full bar. Moderate.

The Sow's Ear Cafe, 2248 Main Street, Cambria 93428; (805) 927–4865. East of Highway 1. Dinner daily. Appetizers include fried Brie, stuffed mushrooms, and calamari strips. Among dinner entrees are salmon in parchment, beer-spiced shrimp, chicken and dumplings, baby pork ribs, sautéed calamari, and chicken-fried steak with country gravy. Fresh seafood specials nightly. Freshly baked breads and homemade desserts. Local wines. Moderate.

SHOPPING AND BROWSING

California Carvers Guild Gallery & Museum, Plaza del Cavalier, Suite 9, 250 San Simeon Avenue, San Simeon 93452; (805) 927–3624. West of Highway 1. Sunday through Thursday, 10:00 A.M. to 6:00 P.M.; Friday and Saturday, 10:00 A.M. to 9:00 P.M. Home base for the 2,200-member guild, also a showplace for the work of more than 150 members. Carvings, from primitive to exquisitely detailed, in domestic and exotic hardwoods and softwoods. Good selection of wildlife carvings, some whimsical pieces.

Cambria Antique Center Mall, 2110 Main Street, Cambria 93428; (805) 927–2353. Five thousand square feet of art and antiques; multiple dealers. Open daily, 9:00 A.M. to 5:00 P.M.

Linn's Fruit Bin Farmstore, Rural Route #1, Box 600, Cambria 93428; (805) 927–1499. On Santa Rosa Creek Road, 5 miles east of Cambria. Daily, 8:00 A.M. to 5:00 P.M. Fruit and berry preserves, fruit and nut pies, chicken and beef frozen pot pies, and country craft items.

Moonstones American Craft Gallery, 4070 Burton Drive, Cambria 93428; (805) 927–3447 or (800) 424–3827. Daily, 10:00 A.M. to 10:00 P.M. Boxes and carvings of exotic woods, kaleidoscopes, sculptured glass, crystals, ceramics, kinetic sculpture, jewelry, and candles.

Seekers Glass Gallery, 4090 Burton Drive, P.O. Box 521, Cambria 93428; (805) 927–4352. Southwest of Main Street, Burton Drive at Center Street, East Village. Daily, 10:00 A.M. to 10:00 P.M. An exquisite collection of contemporary American glass artwork, beautifully displayed. More than 250 artists represented.

MUSEUM

Hearst San Simeon State Historical Monument, P.O. Box 8, San Simeon 94352; (805) 927–2020 or (800) 444–4445; reservations from outside California, (619) 452–1950. Daily, except Thanksgiving, Christmas, and New Year's Day, 8:00 A.M. to 4:00 P.M. in winter; extended summer hours. Evening tours, spring and autumn, with costumed actors representing the guests who frequented the castle. Commonly known as Hearst Castle, this was once the opulent home of newspaper publisher William Randolph Hearst. Since the Hearst family donated it to the state, it has become one of the most popular attractions on the West Coast. Architect Julia Morgan designed and implemented all the plans, seeing to every detail of the vast undertaking. Four different guided tours take place concurrently—each lasting about an hour and three-quarters and each with limited capacity. Tour 1 (fifty-three persons): guest house, esplanade and gardens, the castle, assembly room, refectory, morning room, billiard room, and theater. Tour 2 (twelve persons): Doge's Suite, The Cloisters, the library, Gothic Suite, Celestial Suite, Della Robbia Room, and the pantry and kitchen. Tour 3 (fourteen persons): "B" House (or Casa del Monte), new wing, the old versus the new, and special feature—a film of celebrity guests of the 1920s and 1930s. Tour 4 (fourteen persons): "A" House (or Casa del Mar), wine cellar, hidden terrace, and Neptune Pool dressing rooms. Tickets cost $14 to $25 and you can order by calling (800) 444-4445. In summer, reservations are essential.

BEACHES, PARKS, TRAILS, AND WAYSIDES

Leffingwell Landing, west of Highway 1, off Moonstone Beach Drive, provides vantages for watching whales and sea otters. Trails along the bluffs overlook a rocky beach and tidepools.

Moonstone Beach, west of Moonstone Beach Drive, is a good spot for hiking and exploring tidepools. It's also a popular beachcombing area for driftwood and gemstones. In fact, it's named after the moonstone agates—along with jasper and jade—found here.

The William R. Hearst Memorial State Beach, west of Highway 1 on San Simeon Road, is a favorite swimming area, because San Simeon Point protects it from wind and moderates the surf. A grassy picnic area can be found in a nearby eucalyptus grove.

Most of the year, sea otters and sea lions are visible off the beaches. Binoculars help in finding these sea mammals. In the vicinity of the San Simeon Ranch near Hearst Castle, turn your binoculars on the hillsides east of the highway, and you might spot zebra grazing. They're remnants of the herds of exotic animals the Hearsts imported years ago.

WATER SPORTS AND ACTIVITIES

Rock and surf fishing are productive along Moonstone Beach. The 1,000-foot pier at William R. Hearst Memorial State Beach is another favorite angling spot, with tackle and bait available nearby.

OTHER ATTRACTIONS

Pewter Plough Playhouse, Main Street at Sheffield, West Village, Cambria 93428; (805) 927–3877. Live local theater; call for dates, times, and a list of shows.

TRAVEL INFORMATION

Cambria Chamber of Commerce & Visitor Information, 767 Main Street, Cambria 93428; (805) 927–3624; www.cambria chamber.org; e-mail: cambriachamber@thegrid-net

San Simeon Chamber of Commerce, 9511 Hearst Drive, P.O. Box 1, San Simeon 93452; (805) 927–3500; www.sansimeonsbest. com

EVENTS

January	Castle to Coast Run, San Simeon, (805) 528–6576
March	The Famous Jazz Series, Cambria, (805) 927–0567
	Chili Cookoff and Classic Car Show, Cambria, (805) 927–3624
May	A Day in Old San Simeon Barbecue, (805) 927–2014
June	Cambria Heritage Celebration, (805) 927–1017
	Arts & Craft Faire, Cambria, (559) 887–3474
July	Picnic in the Park and Fireworks, Cambria, (805) 927–8020
August	Cambria Farmers Market, (805) 927–4715
	Greenspace Art Auction, Cambria, (805) 927–2866
September	Central Coast Woodcarvers Show, Cambria, (805) 534–1292
	Allied Arts Art Show, Cambria, (805) 927–0528
	Almost 10K Run, Cambria, (805) 927–4805
	Arts & Craft Faire, Cambria, (559) 877–3474
November	Cambria Crafters Guild Christmas Boutique, (805) 929–3391
	Rosemary Festival, Cambria, (805) 927–5224 or (800) 266–4372
December	Cambria Farmers Market Christmas at the Market, (805) 927–4715

BIG SUR

Population: 520

Location: *On California Highway 1, about 65 miles north of San Simeon and about 25 miles south of Carmel.*

Draped along the western slope of the Santa Lucia Mountain Range between San Simeon and Carmel, California Highway 1 achieves its reputation for being one of the nation's scenic wonders. For 90 miles this narrow, winding, two-lane road climbs the chaparral-covered shoulders of the mountains, descends into the wooded canyons, clings to oceanside bluffs, and courses through switchback after switchback, sending travelers east and west to get north or south.

Construction began on this highway in 1919 and took until 1937 to complete, at a cost of $10 million. But those were Depression-era dollars. To put that figure in better perspective, in 1983 a major slide closed the highway and took one year to repair. That cost $7.4 million.

Certainly, the cost of labor was cheaper when the highway was built. Most of the work was done by convicts who lived at several labor camps along the course of the highway. The prisoners, from San Quentin, earned from 35 to 75 cents a day in cash and were credited with three days' shortening of their sentences for every two days they worked.

This is no hurry-up highway; nor should it be. It's a scenic route through spectacular mountain and ocean vistas that must be savored. Those in a rush to reach destinations north or south should use U.S. 101 instead.

Although there is a spot on the map named Big Sur, don't expect to find a city, or a village for that matter. Even *community* is an inappropriate term to describe the loose gathering of people and property called Big Sur. It's better to think of Big Sur as a region, an overwhelming presence, even an attitude or notion or experience. Many of us think of this whole 90-mile expanse of rugged coastline and highway with its unmarked trails to hard-to-find beaches as Big Sur, and we're probably as close to the right idea as anyone.

The river after which the area and several specific locations are named the Spaniards called *El Rio Grande del Sur*, meaning, quite unromantically, "The Big River of the South." They dubbed another smaller stream *El Rio Chiquito del Sur*, which means "The Little River of the South." We have shortened and Americanized them to Big Sur River and Little Sur River.

Big Sur has few amenities to distract the traveler or detract from the area's scenic splendor—no nightclubs, golf courses, theaters, trendy boutiques, or fast-food joints. Mostly, what you see is what you get. Big Sur is an outdoor experience. It's having a scenic drive, hiking up a canyon or along a coastal bluff, fishing the surf or one of several mountain streams, hunting jade in a rocky cove, photographing seascapes, watching birds on a coastal lagoon, or camping among the redwoods.

Campgrounds are fairly plentiful, but they fill up fast. Those that take reservations are often booked weeks or months ahead for the summers and weekends, especially weekends. Those available on a first-come, first-served basis fill up early in the day. So plan ahead, and make reservations for the busy times.

Although lodging is relatively scarce, a few resorts and cabins provide overnight accommodations. They can be booked solid much of the year, so make reservations, no matter when you plan to travel.

Big Sur climate is considered moderate, with January temperatures usually from the low forties to the low sixties and July temperatures from the low fifties to the high sixties. Summer days can get hot, though, especially inland. Rain, which averages about 40 inches a year, falls mainly from October to April. May through September is dry.

Rock hounds enjoy searching creek beds and rocky beaches along the surf line. In addition to agates and jasper, jade and garnets are among the treasures found.

Big Sur wildlife is abundant and varied. The entire shoreline is a sea-otter refuge that is also frequented by California and Steller sea lions. Gray whales migrate up and down the coast from summer feeding grounds in Alaska to winter calving grounds in Mexico, and strag-

Coastline, Big Sur

glers linger and feed near shore much of the year.

Cormorants and tufted puffins use the cliffs and rocks as rookeries. Shorebirds, such as sanderlings and willets, feed along the shoreline, while red-tailed hawks and golden eagles soar on the updrafts, hunting rodents and reptiles.

Among the numerous small mammals are ground squirrels, gray squirrels, possums, rabbits, raccoons, and ring-tailed cats. Gray fox and bobcat compete with the raptors for food. Large mammals include deer, wild pig, and the occasional black bear and cougar.

For years Big Sur has also attracted an odd admixture of humankind from ranchers to mystics, but has been particularly attractive to writers, artists, photographers, and self-styled intellectuals and eccentrics. Artist and novelist Henry Miller lived here, part of the time in an abandoned labor camp. Poet Lawrence Ferlinghetti called Big Sur home, and author Jack Kerouac based his novel *Big Sur* on his many visits with the beat-generation poet. Photographer Ansel Adams lived here and photographed Big Sur extensively.

In its December 1988 issue, the slick monthly *M* magazine (for "The Civilized Man") listed offshore sailing, Swiss railroads, the Tibetan side of the Himalayas, *The Oxford English Dictionary*, "The William Tell Overture" (with fireworks), gold, real Bermuda onions, and Big Sur among the one hundred things on earth that haven't been ruined yet.

103

LODGING

Big Sur Campground and Cabins, Highway 1, 93920; (831) 667–2322. Just over 67 miles north of San Simeon, just under 24 miles south of Carmel. Three A-frames and 9 cabins with fireplaces, fully equipped kitchens, queen beds, and sleeping lofts. River units with redwood decks. Moderate.

Big Sur Lodge, P.O. Box 190, 93920; (831) 667–3100 or (800) 424–4787. At Pfeiffer Big Sur State Park, 64 miles north of San Simeon, 26 miles south of Carmel. Has 61 lodge rooms and cabins, some with kitchens, some with fireplaces. Heated pool, restaurant, gift shop, 2 grocery stores, and coin-operated laundry on premises. Moderate.

Big Sur River Inn, 47225 Highway 1, Pheneger Creek, 93920; (831) 667–2700 or (800) 548–3610. About 65 miles north of San Simeon, 25 miles south of Carmel. Queen beds in 20 rooms and family suites—all with private baths. Suites have balconies overlooking the river. Heated pool, restaurant, bar, general store, and gift shop on premises. Live entertainment in the bar on weekends. Moderate.

Ventana Inn; (831) 667–2331 or 624–4812, (800) 628–6500. About 63 miles north of San Simeon, 27 miles south of Carmel. Queen and king beds in 62 rooms, suites, town-house suites, and cottages, most with fireplaces, some with hot tubs as well. Suites with dining alcoves and wet bars available. TVs and VCRs. Refrigerators in some suites, including the town houses. Private terraces with mountain or ocean views. One-day reservations Sunday through Thursday only; nonholiday weekends, 2-day reservations only; holiday weekends, 3-day reservations only. Continental breakfast served in lobby, library, or guests' rooms. Complimentary wine and cheese buffet every afternoon. Expensive to extremely expensive.

CAMPGROUNDS AND RV PARKS

Camping outside designated areas in the Los Padres National Forest requires permits, available at two ranger stations on Highway 1. The Big Sur Station is less than 1 mile south of Pfeiffer Big Sur State Park; Pacific Valley Station is 32 miles north of San Simeon. Information, permits, and maps are also available from the U.S. Forest Service, District Headquarters, 406 South Mildred Street, King City 93930; (408) 385–5434.

Andrew Molera State Park, P.O. Box A, 93920; (831) 667–2315. About 21 miles south of Carmel, 3 miles south of Point

Sur. Has 50 campsites with fire pits at a walk-in campground about ¼-mile from the parking area. Trail to beach. Guided hikes July and August. Miles of hiking trails. Inexpensive.

Big Sur Campground & Cabins, Highway 1, 93920; (831) 667–2322. Just over 67 miles north of San Simeon, just under 24 miles south of Carmel. Has 81 full-hookup campsites in the redwoods and along the river, 36 pull-through sites, plus 4 tent cabins. Tables, fire pits, showers, laundry, and tank dump. Store. Tent rentals. Swimming, fishing, playground, volleyball, basketball. Tent cabins available May 1 to October 1 only. Also 8 A-frame cabins available. Moderate to expensive.

Fernwood Resort Campground; (831) 667–2422. About 65 miles north of San Simeon, about 25 miles south of Carmel. Has 60 campsites with electricity hookups and fire pits. Showers, restaurant, bar, and grocery store on premises. Firewood available. Moderate.

Kirk Creek Campground, Los Padres National Forest; (800) 444–7275 or (877) 444–6777. West of Highway 1, 35 miles north of San Simeon, 55 miles south of Carmel. Has 34 campsites with fire pits and a bike-camp area. Trails to the beach. Inexpensive to moderate.

Limekiln Creek Redwoods Campground State Park, Highway 1, 93920; (831) 667–2403 or (800) 444–7275. About 26 miles south of Big Sur, 2 miles south of Lucia. Has 43 campsites with water hookups and fire pits for tents, trailers, and RVs to 30 feet. Showers, tank dump, trail to beach, hiking trails, trout stream, and nearby surf fishing. General store with groceries, beer, wine, bait, tackle, firewood, and ice. Moderate.

Pfeiffer Big Sur State Park Campground, Highway 1, 93920; (831) 667–2315 or (800) 444–7275. East of Highway 1, 26 miles south of Carmel, 64 miles north of San Simeon. Has 218 campsites with tables, stoves, and food lockers along the river, in redwood groves, in oak forests, and in meadows. Accommodates RVs to 32 feet, but no hookups. Showers, laundry, tank dump, and store. Hiking trails with swimming spots, summer guided nature walks, campfire programs, and Junior Ranger programs. Moderate.

Plaskett Creek Campground, Los Padres National Forest; (877) 444–6777. East of Highway 1, 35 miles north of San Simeon, about 40 miles south of Big Sur. Has 44 campsites with tables, fire pits, and grills. Water available, but no hookups. Also has hike and bike sites. Moderate.

Riverside Campground and Cabins, P.O. Box 3, 93920; (831) 667–2414. About 66 miles north of San Simeon, 24 miles south of Carmel. Has cabins and 46 campsites with electricity hookups, tables, and fire pits. Tent rentals, firewood, showers, laundry, playground, and hiking trails. Inexpensive to moderate.

BEACHES, PARKS, TRAILS, AND WAYSIDES

The Big Sur area is a vast system of canyons and streams, beaches and coves, cliffs and bluffs, and many miles of trails. Although there are plenty of sandy beaches, swimming is not a major pastime at most, because of cold ocean water and dangerous currents.

The steep, unstable terrain can be hazardous, so stay on established trails when possible, especially when descending hills and bluffs to beach areas. Poison oak grows throughout the Big Sur region and is abundant in some places. Learn to recognize it so that you can avoid it. Be aware, too, that this is rattlesnake country. Don't let unnecessary fear of these interesting reptiles prevent your enjoying Big Sur; just exercise caution, and watch where you walk.

More of a nuisance than a hazard is the fact that so many trails, gravel roads, and beach areas are unmarked; it's sometimes difficult to tell where trails and roads lead and whether you're on public land or private property. Seems some of the locals have an aversion for signs of any sort and take them down about as fast as they're put up. Rely on maps to guide you.

At the south end of the Big Sur area, about 25 miles north of San Simeon, just north of Gorda, lies Willow Creek Picnic Area, on the west side of Highway 1. On the east side of the highway, at the south end of the bridge, a road leads to the rocky beach where rock hounds sometimes find jade. Upstream, gold and silver mines operated in the late 1800s and early 1900s but have been closed since 1915.

North of Willow Creek, about 12½ miles south of Lucia, is Jade Cove, so named for the deposits of nephrite jade here. Rock hounds are allowed to take this jade only below the mean high-tide line. This cove is where divers worked in 1971 to remove a chunk of jade weighing 9,000 pounds.

Limekiln Beach, 26 miles south of Big Sur, is privately operated, and a nominal day-use fee is charged. The beach at the creek mouth was once the site of Rockland Landing. A trail leads about ½-mile to four old lime kilns once used to smelt lime that was shipped in kegs from Rockland Landing in the 1870s.

About 11 miles south of Pfeiffer Big Sur State Park and 37 miles south of Carmel is Julia Pfeiffer Burns State Park, encompassing 2,405 acres of mountainous and forested terrain. A paved trail leads to a viewpoint overlooking McWay Waterfall. Another trail leads to a picnic area.

Pfeiffer Beach is south of Pfeiffer Big Sur State Park, west of Highway 1, 1 mile south of the park entrance via Sycamore Canyon Road. This picturesque beach, popular with hikers and photographers, provides views of spectacular surf crashing amid sea stacks and rocky rubble. Parts of the Richard Burton–Elizabeth Taylor movie *The Sandpiper* were filmed here. This beach is also a good place for watching and photographing shorebirds.

Pfeiffer Big Sur State Park offers a wide variety of activities, including picnicking, hiking, photography, and wildlife watching. The park is east of Highway 1, 26 miles south of Carmel. During summer months, docent-led nature walks are among the activities.

The Big Sur River flows through Andrew Molera State Park, then empties into the ocean. A lagoon near the river mouth is a sanctuary that attracts a variety of shorebirds. There are 10 miles of hiking trails and 2½ miles of sandy beach in this 4,749-acre park. Coast redwoods and big-leaf maples grow in the park. The eucalyptus grove along the river attracts monarch butterflies, which overwinter here. The park lies 21 miles south of Carmel.

Two miles south of Malpaso Creek is Garrapata State Park. Here a 1³⁄₁₀-mile trail leads along coastal bluffs to Soberanes Point, a good spot for watching whales and sea otters.

WATER SPORTS AND ACTIVITIES

Many pocket beaches and coves along this great stretch of Pacific coastline are popular with divers. A major attraction is 35 miles south of Carmel at Julia Pfeiffer Burns State Park, where a trail leads through Partington Canyon to Partington Cove. Offshore is the 1,680-acre Julia Pfeiffer Burns Underwater Area.

Surf and rock anglers catch fish from about any stretch of beach or rocky shore where there's access. Among the most plentiful species are surfperch, flounder, sanddabs, croaker, rockfish, cabezon, and lingcod.

Freshwater fishing is restricted to those coastal streams with sufficient year-round flow to support a native population of trout and to attract the anadromous steelhead. Both the Big Sur and Little Sur rivers are such streams, as are Big Creek, Garrapata Creek, Limekiln Creek, and Salmon Creek.

OTHER ATTRACTIONS

Point Sur State Historic Park and Lighthouse; recorded message, (831) 625–4419; additional information available from Andrew Molera State Park Headquarters. West of Highway 1, 3 miles north of Andrew Molera State Park. Docent-guided tours of the park and lighthouse start at 10:00 A.M. and 2:00 P.M. on Saturday, 10:00 A.M. on Sunday; visitors advised to arrive half an hour before the tour starts. Moonlight tours are given in the evening. Drive past the gate to the small parking area (no motor homes or trailers). Tours, which last two hours or so, require hiking along a trail that rises 300 feet and is ½-mile each way. Not a good tour for young children.

TRAVEL INFORMATION

Big Sur Chamber of Commerce, P.O. Box 87, 93920; (831) 667–2100; www.bigsurcalifornia.org; e-mail: info@bigsurcalifornia.org

Big Sur Natural History Association, P.O. Box 189, Big Sur 93920

	EVENTS
April	Big Sur International Marathon, Pfeiffer Big Sur State Park, (831) 625–6226
May	Big Sur JazzFest, (831) 667–1530
June	Big Sur Garden Tour, (831) 667–1530
October	Big Sur 10K River Run, Big Sur State Park, (831) 624–4112
	Big Sur Jade Festival, (805) 927–5574
	Big Sur Blues Festival, (831) 667–2422
November	Big Sur Harvest & Craft Fair, (831) 667–2557

CARMEL
Population: 4,400

☆
PEBBLE BEACH
Population: 4,700

Location: *Carmel is on California Highway 1, 26 miles north of Big Sur, 90 miles north of San Simeon, 350 miles north of Los Angeles, and 130 miles south of San Francisco; Pebble Beach lies west of Carmel, via 17-Mile Drive.*

Imagine a village so quaint it has no parking meters along its narrow, shaded streets and no neon signs advertising its many chic shops and charming cafes. Imagine a coastal hamlet with more than a hundred galleries but no streetlights, where houses have names instead of addresses, and where all the trees are registered.

If you're planning to visit the village of Carmel at the north end of the Monterey Peninsula, you can stop imagining—you've found the place described. For years, Carmel has been just such a village, as well as a home to artists, poets, novelists, musicians, and freethinkers. It also attracts the affluent and the famous, as does the neighboring Pebble Beach.

There are four ways to get into the exclusive community of Pebble Beach, all of them guarded gateways where starched-and-pressed security personnel will charge you five bucks a car for the privilege— money well spent if you're interested in the scenic drive. In the vicinity of Carmel, the Highway 1 Gate is just north of town and west of the highway. To reach the Carmel Gate, take Ocean Avenue west from Highway 1; then go right on San Antonio. In Pacific Grove, the Pacific Grove Gate and the Country Club Gate are off Sunset Drive.

If you're a guest at The Inn at Spanish Bay, or if you plan to dine, the gate fee is refunded. If you're planning to visit a Pebble Beach

109

resident, have that person leave word at the gate so that you can enter free of charge.

Without the toll, no doubt the narrow and winding roadways of Pebble Beach would be congested, noisy, and littered, instead of as wonderfully enjoyable, quiet, and scenic as they are.

LODGING

Carmel River Inn, P.O. Box 221609, Carmel 93922; (831) 624–1575 or (800) 882–8142. At the south end of Carmel on Highway 1 at the bridge. Twin, double, and king beds in 43 rooms, suites, and cottages with cable TV, some with fireplaces, some with kitchens. Perhaps the best lodging bargain in the Carmel area. Moderate to expensive.

The Cobblestone Inn, P.O. Box 3185, Carmel 93921; (831) 625–5222 or (800) 833–8836. At Eighth and Junipero Avenues, west of Highway 1 on Ocean Avenue, then north on Junipero. Cable TV in 24 rooms with private baths. Quilts, pillows, fireplaces, and antiques enhance the country comfort of the inn. Complimentary tea, sherry, wine, and hors d'oeuvres in the afternoon. Buffet breakfast served in the dining room each morning. Picnic lunches provided on request. Easy walk to village shops and restaurants. Moderate to expensive.

Highlands Inn, P.O. Box 1700, 120 Highlands Drive, Carmel 93923; (831) 624–3801 or (800) 682–4811. Just south of Carmel on Highway 1. "Understated elegance" perhaps best describes this California-style inn, with its ocean-view rooms, 1-bedroom suites, townhouse suites, and 2-bedroom town-house suites. Fireplaces, decks, kitchens, and spa baths available. Heated pool and hot tubs. Wine tasting and afternoon tea. Cocktail lounge, superb restaurant, gift shop, and deli-cafe on premises. Valet parking, concierge service, and room service. Very expensive to extremely expensive.

Hofsas House, P.O. Box 1195, Carmel 93921; (831) 624–2745 or (800) 221–2548. On San Carlos Street, near Fourth, west of Highway 1, via Ocean Avenue, only 2 blocks from village center. Queen and king beds in 38 individually decorated rooms and suites with cable TV, some with fireplaces, some with kitchens, some with balconies. Also available are 2-bedroom, 2-bath suites with wet bars. Walk to shops, galleries, and restaurants, and avoid Carmel's parking hassles. Heated pool and sauna. Moderate to expensive.

Inn at Spanish Bay, 2700 17-Mile Drive, Pebble Beach 93953; (831) 624–3811 or (800) 654–9300. West of Highway 1, between

Carmel and Pacific Grove. A beautiful, full-service resort with 271 rooms and suites, offering fireplaces, sofas, chairs, four-posters, and marble baths. Most rooms with balconies or patios. Ocean-view rooms and suites. Two restaurants, 24-hour room service, 2 cocktail lounges, 8 tennis courts, eighteen-hole golf course and privileges at 3 others. Pool, spa, and beach access. Extremely expensive.

Lamplighters Inn, P.O. Box 604, Carmel 93921; (831) 624–7372. West of Highway 1 on Ocean Avenue to Camino Real. Twin, queen, and king beds in 5 rooms, 2 cottages to accommodate 2 to 6 guests. Cable TV and fireplaces. Three blocks to the beach, easy walk to village shops. This is the most photographed inn in California. Moderate to expensive.

Pine Inn, P.O. Box 250, Carmel 93921; (831) 624–3851 or (800) 228–3851. West of Highway 1 on Ocean Avenue at Lincoln Street. Twin, double, queen, and king beds in 49 rooms in this beautiful, full-service, 1889 hotel decorated with period furnishings, artwork, and fabrics. Shops, boutiques, cocktail lounges, and restaurant on premises, fireplace in the library. Walk to other village attractions. Moderate to expensive.

CAMPGROUNDS AND RV PARKS

Carmel by the River RV Park, 27680 Schulte Road, Carmel 93923; (831) 624–9329. East of Highway 1, 4½ miles on Carmel Valley Road, then south 1 mile on Schulte Road. Has 35 sites on the Carmel River with full hookups and cable TV. Showers, barbecue area, and horseshoe pits. Pets allowed. Expensive.

FOOD

Anton & Michel Restaurant, P.O. Box 4425, Carmel 93921; (831) 624–2406. West of Highway 1, on Mission Street between Ocean and Seventh Avenues. Daily lunch and dinner, Sunday brunch. Cold appetizers include prawn cocktail, smoked salmon, and pâté maison. Among the hot appetizers are escargots, scampi marinara, and fettuccine Alfredo. Such dinner specialties as scallops in saffron sauce, abalone steak, lamb medallions with fresh mint pesto, pepper-steak flambé, filet mignon bordelaise, and rack of lamb or tenderloin of beef for two. Extensive wine list and full bar. Expensive.

Flaherty's Seafood Grill and Oyster Bar, P.O. Box 2265, Carmel 93921; (831) 625–1500 or 624–0311. West of Highway 1, on Sixth Avenue between San Carlos and Delores Streets. Lunch and dinner daily. Fresh seafood is the specialty here: oysters, scallops, clams, Maine lobster, Dungeness crab, and abalone. Superb soups and chowders. Shellfish kept alive in large saltwater tanks. Cocktails and imported and domestic beers and wines. Moderate.

Rio Grill, 101 Crossroads Boulevard, Carmel 93923; (831) 625–5436. Just east of Highway 1, via Crossroads Boulevard. Lunch and dinner daily. A local favorite with a creative menu. Start with a marinated and fire-roasted artichoke with sun-dried tomatoes, crisp-fried calamari with orange-sesame dipping sauce, smoked-salmon tostada, crisp rock-shrimp taco, or any of several other tempting appetizers. House-made soups and big, meal-size salads. Oak-grilled burgers and inventive deli-style sandwiches. Entrees include barbecued baby back ribs, herb-crusted chicken breast, smoked duck, grilled prawns on penne pasta, pumpkin seed–crusted salmon, and lamb shank with wild mushrooms braised in ale. Among the great desserts are caramel apple bread pudding, pecan brownies with chocolate sauce and vanilla cream, and the house-famous ice cream sandwich. Full bar. Moderate to expensive.

SHOPPING AND BROWSING

The Barnyard, 3618 The Barnyard, Carmel 93923; (831) 624–8886. About ½-mile east of Highway 1, via Carmel Valley Road or Rio Road to Carmel Rancho Boulevard. Nothing here even faintly resembles the typically homogenized suburban mall. Instead, fifty-five shops and boutiques and eleven restaurants are housed in pleasing buildings in the California-country style of architecture. Cobblestone walks meander amid colorful gardens. Among the shops are those specializing in men's and women's apparel, gifts, toys, jewelry, antiques, collectibles, and kitchenware.

Carmel Plaza, P.O. Box 4814, Carmel 93921; (831) 624–0137. West of Highway 1, on Ocean Avenue between Junipero and Mission Streets. Monday through Sunday, 10:00 A.M. to 6:00 P.M. Restaurants and some stores open later. In the village of Carmel with courtyard, fountain, flowers, and more than fifty stores, shops, galleries, and restaurants. Shops include Banana Republic, Carmel Shirtworks, Leather Bound, New Zealand Sheepskin, Saks Fifth Avenue, Sharper Image, Shells of Carmel, Thinker Toys, and Poster Graphics.

Cottage Gallery, P.O. Box 335, Carmel 93921; (530) 672–9702. West of Highway 1, Mission Street at Sixth Avenue, across from the firehouse. Daily, 10:00 A.M. to 5:30 P.M. Original oil paintings, watercolors, and sculpture. Contemporary art by a number of noted artists. Landscapes, seascapes, and pastoral scenes.

The Crossroads, 159 Crossroads Boulevard, Carmel 93921; (831) 625–4106. East side of Highway 1 at Rio Road. Monday through Saturday, 10:00 A.M. to 6:00 P.M.; Sunday, noon to 5:00 P.M. Among the more than 100 establishments in this English-style shopping village are 18 restaurants and cafes and more than 80 boutiques and shops.

Masterpiece Gallery, P.O. Box 6477, Carmel 93921; (831) 624–2163. West of Highway 1, on Delores Street at Sixth Avenue. Daily, 11:00 A.M. to 5:00 P.M. Closed on Saturday. A gallery featuring the works of a number of contemporary masters, as well as Californian and French Impressionists of the late nineteenth and early twentieth centuries. Paris street scenes, California and East Coast landscapes, and waterscapes.

BEACHES, PARKS, TRAILS, AND WAYSIDES

The Point Lobos State Reserve is a 1,300-acre natural area west of Highway 1, 3 miles south of Carmel at Riley Ranch Road. *Lobo* is Spanish for "wolf"; however, it's not the wild canine that the point was named for but, rather, the abundant "sea wolves" or sea lions that haul out on nearby rocks. The name has been shortened from the original Spanish *Punta de los Lobos Marinos,* or "Point of the Sea Wolves."

Many consider the reserve to be the best of California's state parks. The rocky shoreline is intriguing and beautiful, and stands of Monterey pine and Monterey cypress add to its natural splendor. Hikers enjoy more than a dozen trails, and park rangers carefully limit the number of visitors to prevent crowding.

Off Point Lobos, 750 submerged acres have been designated the Point Lobos Ecological Reserve, where all marine life is protected. In fact, everything natural in the park is protected. So don't remove anything but litter. If something occurs naturally, leave it.

Along the 6 miles of coastline in the reserve are many tidepools, rock formations, coves, and headlands to explore. There are picnic areas and places to observe the plentiful wildlife, which includes seabirds, harbor seals, sea lions, sea otters, and even occasional blue and minke whales.

Diving is permitted in the reserve, but only at Whalers and Bluefish coves. No more than ten pairs of divers per day are allowed in the reserve, and permits—available at the gate—are required.

Carmel Mission

The reserve is usually open from 9:00 A.M. to 5:00 P.M., but it often remains open later in the summer. Guides and maps are available as are docent-led tours.

Carmel River State Beach, west of Highway 1, off Scenic Road, is a favorite place for hiking and picnicking and a good area for watching and photographing birds. The Carmel Submarine Canyon, just offshore, creates some dangerous currents, however, so this is not a good swimming area.

Swimming and surfing conditions are better at Carmel City Beach, west of Highway 1 at the foot of Ocean Street. This is also a popular picnic spot.

Opportunities for hiking, picnicking, exploring tidepools, and photographing exciting coastal scenery and marine wildlife are around every bend of 17-Mile Drive at Pebble Beach. The gate guard who takes your toll will provide you with a map and guide to more than two dozen attractions and points of interest.

Binoculars and telephoto lenses come in handy along this route. Sea otters frequent the area and are easy to spot in the kelp beds. Seals and sea lions haul out on offshore rocks. Seabirds are plentiful on shore and off. And on cool mornings you are sure to see plenty of black-tailed deer.

GOLF

The Links at Spanish Bay, 2700 17-Mile Drive, P.O. Box 1418, Pebble Beach 93953; (831) 647–7495. An eighteen-hole, par-seventy-two, 6,820-yard Scottish-style course with spectacular ocean views. Driving range, practice greens, pro shop, resident pro, clubhouse, club and cart rental, restaurants, and bar.

Pebble Beach Golf Links, P.O. Box 658, Pebble Beach 93953; (831) 624–3811, extension 250 or (800) 654–9300. At The Lodge on 17-Mile Drive, overlooking Carmel Bay and Pebble Beach. An eighteen-hole, par-seventy-two, 6,799-yard course open to the public. Driving range, practice greens, club and cart rental. Pro shop, resident pro, restaurants, and cocktail lounges.

Peter Hay Par 3 Golf Course, P.O. Box 658, Pebble Beach 93953; (831) 625–8518. At The Lodge, on 17-Mile Drive, overlooking Carmel Bay and Pebble Beach. Public nine-hole, par-twenty-seven course. Driving range, practice greens, club and cart rental. Restaurants and cocktail lounges nearby.

Rancho Canada Golf Club, P.O. Box 22590, Carmel 93922; (831) 624–0111. One mile east of Highway 1 on Carmel Valley Road. Two lovely public courses in the Carmel River Valley. East course, eighteen holes, par seventy-one, 6,109 yards; west course, eighteen holes, par seventy-two, 6,324 yards. Driving range, practice greens, club and cart rental. Huge pro shop, resident pro, restaurant, bar, and cocktail lounge.

Spyglass Hill Golf Course, P.O. Box 658, Pebble Beach 93953; (831) 625–8563. On Spyglass Hill Road. A tough eighteen-hole, par-seventy-two, 6,855-yard course with driving range, practice greens, pro shop, resident pro, clubhouse, and equipment rental. Restaurant and bars nearby.

WINERY

Chateau Julien Winery, 8940 Carmel Valley Road, Carmel 93923; (831) 624–2600. In Carmel Valley, 5 miles east of Highway 1. Wine tasting, 8:30 A.M. to 5:00 P.M. Monday through Friday and 11:00 A.M. to 5:00 P.M. Saturday and Sunday; winery tours, 8:00 A.M. and 2:30 P.M. Monday through Friday; weekends 12:30 and 2:00 P.M. Tour the winery and sample the award-winning wines. T.G.I.F. tour limited to eight persons and includes wine tasting and evaluation.

OTHER ATTRACTIONS

Carmel Mission, 3080 Bio Road, P.O. Box 2235, Carmel 93921; (831) 624–1271; museum, (831) 624–3600. West of Highway 1 via Rio Road, south end of Carmel. Monday through Saturday, 9:30 A.M. to 5:00 P.M.; Sunday, 10:30 A.M. to 5:00 P.M. Founded in 1770 by Father Junípero Serra as the second California mission. After secularization in 1833, the mission fell into disrepair and languished for a century before being fully restored. Father Serra and Father Crespi are interred at the basilica.

Tor House, P.O. Box 1887, Carmel 93921; (831) 624–1813. West of Highway 1, on Carmel Point, Ocean View Avenue at Stewart Way. Friday and Saturday, 10:00 A.M. to 4:00 P.M. Home of poet Robinson Jeffers and his family. Docent-led tours of the Tor House, Hawk Tower, and Old World gardens limited to six persons per hour.

TRAVEL INFORMATION

Carmel Business Association, San Carlos between Fifth and Sixth, P.O. Box 4444, Carmel 93921; (831) 624–2522; www.carmel california.org

Point Lobos Natural History Association, Route 1, Box 62, Carmel 93923; www.carmelcalifornia.org

Point Lobos State Reserve, Route 1, Box 62, Carmel 93923; (831) 624–4909; www.point-lobos.parks.state.ca.us; e-mail: ptlobos@ mbay.net

March	Carmel Kite Festival, (831) 626–1255
April	Chateau Julien Wine & Art Festival, (831) 624–2600
	Carmel Garden & Design Show, (831) 625–6026
May	Robinson Jeffers Tor House Garden Party, Carmel, (831) 624–1813
	Pebble Beach Spring Horse Show, (831) 624–2756
	Carmel Art Festival, (831) 625–2288
	Memorial Day Regatta, Pebble Beach, (831) 625–8507
June	Art & Wine Festival at The Barnyard, Carmel, (831) 624–8886
	Friday Concerts in the Park, Carmel, (831) 626–1255
July	Carmel Bach Festival, (831) 624–1521
August	Carmel Valley Fiesta, (831) 659–2038
	Carmel Shakespeare Festival, (831) 622–0700
	Pebble Beach Concours D' Elegance, (831) 372–8026
September	Labor Day Regatta, Pebble Beach, (831) 625–8507
	Carmel Outdoor Art Festival, (831) 624–3996
	Strides & Tides Horse Show, Pebble Beach, (831) 624–2756
	Fiesta De San Carlos Borromeo, Carmel, (831) 624–1271
October	Carmel Sand Castle Contest, (831) 624–2522
	Taste of Carmel, (831) 624–2522
	Carmel Performing Arts Festival, (831) 624–7675
	Robinson Jeffers Tor House Festival & Poetry Walk, Carmel, (831) 624–1813
November	Pebble Beach Equestrian Championships, (831) 624–2756
	Homecrafter's Marketplace, Carmel, (831) 659–5208
	Carmel-by-the-Sea's Annual Tree Lighting, (831) 624–2522

CARMEL/PEBBLE BEACH

117

MONTEREY
Population: 35,000

☆

PACIFIC GROVE
Population: 17,000

Location: *Monterey is on California Highway 1, about 32 miles north of Big Sur, 99 miles north of San Simeon, and 95 miles south of Half Moon Bay; adjacent Pacific Grove is at the northwest tip of the Monterey Peninsula.*

When the Spanish named the Big Sur River El Rio Grande del Sur, or "The Big River of the South," they meant south of Monterey, which was California's capital during its Spanish and Mexican periods. When the Mexicans gave up the Monterey Peninsula to the Americans in 1846, Monterey retained its importance as a political and cultural center. In fact, the California Constitutional Convention was held in 1849 at Colton Hall, which is now a Monterey museum. The following year, California became the thirty-first state.

Industries here have flourished and vanished, beginning with the brisk hide and tallow trade with English and Americans in the early 1800s. The first pier was built on the bay in 1846 to service trading vessels. In the 1850s it became part of a Portuguese whaling station. At the begining of the twentieth-century, a commercial fishery for Pacific sardines burgeoned and soon mushroomed as seining and canning technology improved. Annual landings of the tiny fish grew from a few thousand tons in the early 1900s to a quarter-million tons in the mid-1940s. Such harvests continued until the sardines "mysteriously disappeared" in 1951.

During the heyday of the sardine fishery, twenty-three canneries and nineteen reduction plants were strung along the shore of Monterey Bay. Known as Cannery Row and immortalized in the John

Steinbeck novel of that title, the area deteriorated after the sardine fishery collapsed, but it was revived and refurbished in the 1970s. It's now a major tourist attraction, with seven hotels and inns; ten candy and pastry shops; four wine-tasting rooms; nine clubs, pubs, and watering holes; twenty-eight restaurants, delis, and pizzerias; more than sixty-five stores, shops, and galleries; and such attractions as the Steinbeck Museum and the Monterey Bay Aquarium.

Near downtown and just a few blocks southeast of Cannery Row is the famed Fisherman's Wharf, crowded with browsers, shoppers, diners, sight-seers, and anglers. Among the gift shops and galleries are fish markets, delis, and restaurants selling all sorts of seafood. This is also where the sportfishing fleet is moored. Those who aren't interested in angling but who would like to explore the bay can board one of the vessels offering sight-seeing and whale-watching excursions.

The natural beauty of the bay and peninsula led to the development of tourism in the late nineteenth century. Tourism is now Monterey's leading industry, and the city has an abundance of superior accommodations and superb restaurants to serve its many visitors—something for everyone's budget and appetite.

Next door is Monterey's sister city, Pacific Grove—a late bloomer, but charming nonetheless. Founded in 1875 as a Methodist retreat, it stayed straitlaced for nearly a century, prohibiting the sale of alcohol within city limits, except for medicinal purposes, until 1969.

Reminders of Pacific Grove's Victorian past are everywhere, including more than 250 houses built before 1910. A number of these handsome structures are now bed-and-breakfast inns.

Tourists aren't the only ones drawn regularly to the pleasant climate and tranquility of Pacific Grove. Monarch butterflies begin arriving in October and overwinter in the groves of Monterey cypress, Monterey pine, and eucalyptus trees.

Pacific Grove is easy to reach from Highway 1 by taking the Route 68 exit west, or by driving through Monterey past Cannery Row. From Carmel and Pebble Beach, 17-Mile Drive also leads to Pacific Grove.

LODGING

The Gosby House Inn, 643 Lighthouse Avenue, Pacific Grove 93950; (831) 375–1287. West of Highway 1 via Route 68 and Forest Avenue to Lighthouse Avenue, then left 3 blocks. Built as a private dwelling in 1887 but began accommodating guests in 1894. The beautiful Queen Anne has 22 rooms, some with fireplaces, most with private baths. Hors d'oeuvres and fresh fruits served with sherry or tea each afternoon. Breakfast served in the parlor. Near golf courses, bay, and other peninsula attractions. Moderate to expensive.

Lighthouse Lodge and Suites, 11150 Lighthouse Avenue, Pacific Grove 93950; (831) 655–2111 or (800) 858–1249. Three miles west of Monterey. Queen and king beds in 64-room lodge and 1- and 2-bedroom suites, all with cable TV and some with fireplaces, ocean views, kitchenettes, wet bars, and microwaves. Heated pool, hot tub in suites, complimentary afternoon wine and cheese in lodge, free barbecue buffet dinner, and complimentary continental breakfast. Three blocks to the ocean. Moderate to extremely expensive.

Monterey Bay Inn, 242 Cannery Row, Monterey 93940; (831) 373–6242; in California, (800) 424–6242; elsewhere, (800) 225–2902. West of Highway 1, between downtown Monterey and Pacific Grove, on Cannery Row. King beds in 47 rooms and 3 suites, all with sleeper sofas, private balconies, snack bars, refrigerators, and remote-control cable TV. Suites also have desks and easy chairs. Whirlpool, sauna, and health club. Special facilities for divers include outside showers and gear lockers. Walk to shops, restaurants, and aquarium. Expensive to very expensive.

Monterey Plaza Hotel, 400 Cannery Row, Monterey 93940; (831) 646–1700 or (800) 368–2468. West of Highway 1 and downtown, on the bay. Twin, sofa-queen, and king beds in 290 rooms and 20 suites, many with bay views, most with patios or balconies. Ristorante Delfino, on premises, serves breakfast, lunch, and dinner. Delfino Lounge overlooks the bay. Walk to shops and aquarium. Moderate to very expensive.

Sand Dollar Inn, 755 Abrego Street, Monterey 93940; (831) 372–7551 or (800) 982–1986. West of Highway 1 via Munras Avenue, which becomes Abrego Street. Queen and king beds in 63 rooms and suites with remote-control cable TV, some with fireplaces, some with wet bars, and some with private balconies. Two-bedroom suites also have minirefrigerators. Heated pool, exercise room, and whirlpool. Inexpensive to moderate.

Seven Gables Inn, 555 Ocean View Boulevard, Pacific Grove 93950; (831) 372–4341. West of Highway 1 via Route 68 and Forest Avenue to Ocean View, then right 2 blocks. Queen beds in 14 rooms in a beautiful Victorian bed-and-breakfast inn on the edge of Monterey Bay. Each room has a private bath and ocean view. Furnished with fine antiques. English-style high tea every afternoon, full breakfast each morning. Expensive to very expensive.

Victorian Inn, 487 Foam Street, Monterey 93940; (831)

Cannery Row, Monterey

373–8000 or (800) 232–4141. West of Highway 1, 2 blocks from Cannery Row, between Hoffman and McClellan. Remote-control cable TV, cable movies, and fireplaces in 68 rooms with private patios or balconies, some with ocean view. Each bathroom with second phone and shower massage. Hot tub. Afternoon wine and cheese, continental breakfast. Moderate to expensive.

CAMPGROUNDS AND RV PARKS

Laguna Seca Recreation Area, Monterey County Parks, 1025 Monterey Road, P.O. Box 5279, Salinas 93915; (831) 422–6138. (But there isn't always someone there to answer the phone.) Eight miles east of Highway 1 via Route 68 (Salinas exit). Has 180 developed campsites. Water and electrical hookups available. Tent sites available; sites are in the hills among the oaks. Showers and tank dump. Moderate.

FOOD

Bubba Gump Shrimp Company Restaurant & Market, 720 Cannery Row, Monterey 93940; (831) 373–1884. West of downtown Monterey. Lunch and dinner daily. From the appetizer menu, choose from peel-and-eat shrimp, garlic-bread basket, cheesy fries,

121

calamari fritti, among others. New England clam chowder, Caesar salad, or shrimp salad. Among the sandwiches are burgers, fish, barbecued pork, and grilled chicken. Shrimp specialties include fried, barbecued, with coconut, steamed in beer, in bourbon sauce, scampi, or in dipping sauce with French bread. Try such entrees as fish-and-chips, mahimahi, baby back ribs, salmon, ribeye steak, crab legs, veggie plate, or steak-and-crab combo. Specialty desserts include Alabama mud pie, Key lime pie, and cobbler. Full bar. Moderate.

Bullwacker's Restaurant and Pub, 653 Cannery Row, Monterey 93940; (831) 373-1353. Breakfast, lunch, and dinner daily. A casual English-style eatery and watering hole that serves omelets, burgers, steaks, seafood, fish-and-chips, pasta dishes, sandwiches, and vegetarian dishes. Full bar. Moderate.

Chart House, 444 Cannery Row, Monterey 93940; (831) 372-3362. West of downtown Monterey. Dinner daily. For starters, choose from more than a half-dozen appetizers, such as crunchy calamari medallions, coconut shrimp, shrimp martini, or seared peppered ahi tuna. Try the New England clam chowder or house-signature Caesar salad. House seafood specialties include sesame-crusted salmon, mahimahi, shrimp scampi, Alaskan king crab legs, and fresh fish of the day. From the grill come such entrees as Teriyaki-glazed double-cut pork loin chop, Teriyaki beef medallions, filet mignon with cracked black-peppercorn crust, glazed rack of lamb, and glazed lemon chicken. For dessert, try the chocolate lava cake. Full bar. Moderate.

Old Bath House Restaurant, 620 Ocean View Boulevard, Pacific Grove 93950; (831) 375-5195. Near Lover's Point Park, west of Highway 1 via Route 68 and Forest Avenue. Dinner daily. Start with an appetizer, such as baked oysters, mesquite-grilled prawns and duck sausage, or truffle mousse pâté. Salad might be avocado and grilled artichoke heart or sautéed quail and spinach. Soups are Monterey mushroom and cream of lobster. Dinner offerings include mesquite-grilled pork medallions, rack of lamb, Australian lobster in pastry, prawns chardonnay, and duck merlot. Finish with chocolate truffle torte with raspberry sauce, hot pecan-ice-cream fritters, or Grand Marnier crepe. Full bar. Moderate to expensive.

Sardine Factory, 701 Wave Street, Monterey 93940; (831) 373-3775. Dinner daily in the elegant surroundings of four dining areas and the cocktail lounge. Generous and tasty appetizers include whole Dungeness crab with vinaigrette dressing or mustard sauce, baked abalone and oysters Rockefeller, seared sea scallops, smoked king salmon and sardines, Gulf prawns with chili salsa, steamed clams or mussels, and escargot. Sensational soups include the house-famous abalone bisque or such offerings as lobster bisque, forest mushroom soup, or artichoke bisque. Try the house Caesar salad or Carmel Valley tomato salad. In addition to vegetarian, chicken, veal, beef, and pork entrees are such seafood specialties as abalone steak, grilled Monterey sanddabs, bay prawns, king salmon, and Cannery Row cioppino. Catch of the day might include sea bass, halibut, or tuna. Wine list features more than 1,000 domestic and imported selections. Full bar. Moderate to expensive.

SHOPPING AND BROWSING

Both Monterey and Pacific Grove have stores, shops, and galleries scattered throughout downtown areas and concentrated in plazas, malls, and shopping centers, as well as in such places as Cannery Row and Fisherman's Wharf. And if that's not enough, a short drive will put you in Carmel, where shopping and browsing were invented.

American Tin Cannery Premium Outlets, 125 Ocean View Boulevard #110, Pacific Grove 93950; (831) 372–1442. West of Highway 1 via Route 68 and Forest Avenue, then right on Ocean View Boulevard, or west through Monterey, 1 block past the Monterey Bay Aquarium. Monday through Saturday, 10:00 A.M. to 6:00 P.M.; Sunday, 11:00 A.M. to 5:00 P.M. More than a half-dozen restaurants and three dozen factory outlet stores, boutiques, and specialty shops. Among the shops are those specializing in clothing, jewelry, kitchenware, crystal, china, gifts, and decorating items. The stores include the Van Heusen Factory Store, Corning Factory Store, Dynasty Imports, Athletic Outlet, The Housewares Store, Come Fly a Kite, The Toy Club, Leni's Antiques & Collectibles, The Wallet Works, and Leather Loft Stores.

MUSEUMS AND AQUARIUM

Maritime Museum of Monterey, 5 Custom House Plaza, Monterey 93940; (831) 375–2553. Downtown Monterey, near Fisherman's Wharf. Tuesday through Sunday, 10:00 A.M. to 5:00 P.M. Extended summer and holiday hours. A large collection of navigational instruments, ship models, scrimshaw, paintings, and nautical hardware and memorabilia.

Monterey Bay Aquarium, 886 Cannery Row, Monterey 93940; (831) 648–4888 or (800) 756–3737. Northwest of downtown, at

Cannery Row. Daily, except Christmas, 10:00 A.M. to 6:00 P.M. More than 6,000 specimens representing nearly 600 species of sea creatures inhabit the tanks at this spectacular $50-million aquarium. Dazzling undersea and above-sea, indoor and outdoor exhibits—nearly one hundred in all. Deep-sea, tidepool, seashore, marsh, and creek exhibits. The Kelp Forest exhibit is an amazing tank three stories high, containing 335,000 gallons of seawater. The Monterey Bay Habitats exhibit is 90 feet long and inhabited by sharks, rays, salmon, and other species. Elsewhere are marine mammals, birds, shellfish, and touch pools. Feeding times are posted and provide exciting shows. Also on the premises are a Cannery Museum, a Marine Mammal Gallery with life-size models of whales and porpoises, a gift shop, and restaurant. Classified *must see.*

Monterey State Historic Park, 210 Oliver Street, Monterey 93940; (831) 649–7118. Downtown, near Fisherman's Wharf. Daily, 10:00 A.M. to 4:00 P.M. Nine historic adobe buildings and museum displays. Maps available at park headquarters next to the Custom House. Custom House, Pacific House, and Cooper Store open most days; others open for guided tours at various times. Check at park headquarters for schedule.

Pacific Grove Museum of Natural History, 165 Forest Avenue, Pacific Grove 93950; (831) 648–3116. West of Highway 1 via Route 68 and Forest Avenue to Central Avenue. Tuesday through Sunday, 10:00 A.M. to 5:00 P.M. Considered the best of its size in the United States. Collection includes more than 400 mounted bird specimens from Monterey County, as well as an interpretive display devoted to monarch butterflies. Traveling exhibits also on display.

Steinbeck's Spirit of Monterey Wax Museum, 700 Cannery Row, Monterey 93940; (831) 375–3770. On the bay, northwest of downtown. Daily, 9:00 A.M. to 9:00 P.M.; winter hours, 10:00 A.M. to 8:00 P.M. More than one hundred life-size and lifelike wax figures in various scenes representing 400 years of California history. Also depictions of Steinbeck's *Cannery Row* scenes and characters.

BEACHES, PARKS, TRAILS, AND WAYSIDES

A string of sandy beaches extends northeasterly from the vicinity of Monterey's Municipal Wharf. There's swimming at Monterey Beach Park, next to the wharf, but at Monterey State Beach, off Del Monte via Park Avenue, the currents and surf are dangerous. West of the Municipal Wharf, Fisherman's Shoreline Park, between Fisherman's Wharf and the Coast Guard Pier, is a pleasant park offering a sidewalk, bike path, and benches as well as a good place for waterfront photography. There are usually pelicans, harbor seals, and sea lions in the area.

The city of Pacific Grove owns the shoreline within the city limits, so the coast along the bay and ocean is just one park after another, with plenty of space to hike, explore tidepools, watch sunsets, and photograph the spectacular scenery.

From Point Cabrillo northwest to Point Pinos, Shoreline, Berwick, Lover's Point, and Perkins parks are on the bay, along the bluffs beside Ocean View Boulevard. Bike paths and hiking trails course through patches of ice plants, which bloom from April through August, adding great swatches of magenta to the already-stunning seascape.

At the tip of the Monterey Peninsula lies the Point Pinos Lighthouse Reservation. The attractive lighthouse, built in 1855, is now the oldest operating light station on the West Coast. The reservation is open to the public from 1:00 to 4:00 P.M. on weekends.

Near Point Pinos, Ocean View Boulevard becomes Sunset Drive, a fitting name for a road flanking the Pacific shoreline. Here Asilomar State Beach offers dunes and tidepools to explore and sandy beaches to hike. Although this is a popular diving area, swimmers should look elsewhere, as the area is subject to dangerous riptides.

WATER SPORTS AND ACTIVITIES

Monterey Bay and nearby waters attract scuba divers from afar and offer excellent diving opportunities. There are dive shops in the area and charter operators catering to divers' needs. The beach on the northwest side of the Coast Guard Pier in Monterey is a popular staging area for divers.

Although fishermen ply the surf east of the Municipal Wharf, most of the fishing on Monterey Bay is from private, party, and charter boats. Anglers towing boats will find launching facilities near the Coast Guard Pier. Party and charter boats are at Fisherman's Wharf.

Aquarius Dive Shop, 2040 Del Monte Avenue, Monterey 93940; (831) 375–1933. Weekdays (closed Tuesdays), 9:00 A.M. to 6:00 P.M.; weekends, 7:00 A.M. to 6:00 P.M. Fully equipped dive shop. Equipment sales, service, and rentals. Professional instruction, guided tours, dive packages, videotaped dives.

Monterey Bay Kayaks, 693 Del Monte Avenue, Monterey 93940; (831) 373–5357. West of Highway 1, in town. Sea-kayak rentals, instructions, and tours. Clinics and classes on such topics as basic skills, the Eskimo roll, kayaking in the surf zone, and rough-water rescues. Tours of Monterey Bay, Carmel Bay, Elkhorn Slough, and Big Sur. Also sunset tours.

Monterey Sport Fishing, 96 Fisherman's Wharf #1, Monterey 93940; (831) 372–2203. Weekdays, check-in at 6:45 A.M.; weekends, 6:00 A.M. Salmon and albacore party trips in season. Bottom-fish trips for lingcod, rockfish, and others. Bait furnished. Licenses, tackle, fish cleaning, and freezing services available. Rod rentals. Half- and full-day charters.

Randy's Fishing Trips, 66 Fisherman's Wharf #1, Monterey 93940; (831) 372–7440. Four boats running deep-sea fishing trips for salmon and albacore. Party trips and private charters. Bait furnished. Tackle, licenses, sack lunches, and fish cleaning available.

RENTALS

Adventures by the Sea, 299 Cannery Row, Monterey 93940; (831) 372–1807. Northwest of downtown. Daily 9:00 A.M. to 6:00 P.M. Rents roller skates, mountain bikes, beach cruisers, four-wheel surreys, and kayaks by the hour, half-day, day, and longer. Free delivery and pickup.

Monterey Moped Adventures, 1250 Del Monte Avenue, Monterey 93940; (831) 373–2696. West of Highway 1, Del Monte Avenue at Sloat Avenue. Rents single- and double-seat mopeds with baskets. Provides free lessons and tour maps.

TRAVEL INFORMATION

Monterey Peninsula Chamber of Commerce, 380 Alvarado Street, P.O. Box 1770, Monterey 93940; (831) 648–5360; www.mpcc.com; e-mail: info@mpcc.com

Pacific Grove Chamber of Commerce, Forest and Central Avenues, P.O. Box 167, Pacific Grove 93950; (831) 373–3304; www.pacificgrove.org

January	Whalefest, Monterey, (831) 784–6464
February	John Steinbeck Cannery Row Birthday Celebration, Monterey, (831) 775–1234
April	Dixieland Monterey, (888) 349–6879
	Monterey Wine Festival, (831) 649–6690
	Wildflower Show, Pacific Grove, (831) 648–5716
	Good Old Days Celebration, Pacific Grove, (831) 373–3304
May	Festival of Winds, (831) 385–3243
	The Great Monterey Squid Festival, (831) 649–6690
June	The Great Cannery Row Sardine Festival, (831) 649–6690
	Monterey Blues Festival, (831) 649–6544
July	Fourth of July Celebration and Fireworks, (831) 646–3427
	Feast of the Lanterns, (831) 373–3304
August	Monterey Historic Automobile Races, (800) 327–7322
September	Triathlon at Pacific Grove, (831) 373–0678
	Monterey Jazz Festival, (831) 373–3366
	Gem and Mineral Show, Monterey, (831) 659–4155
October	Butterfly Parade, Pacific Grove, (831) 646–6540
December	Christmas at the Inns, Pacific Grove, (831) 373–3304

MONTEREY/PACIFIC GROVE

NORTHERN CALIFORNIA

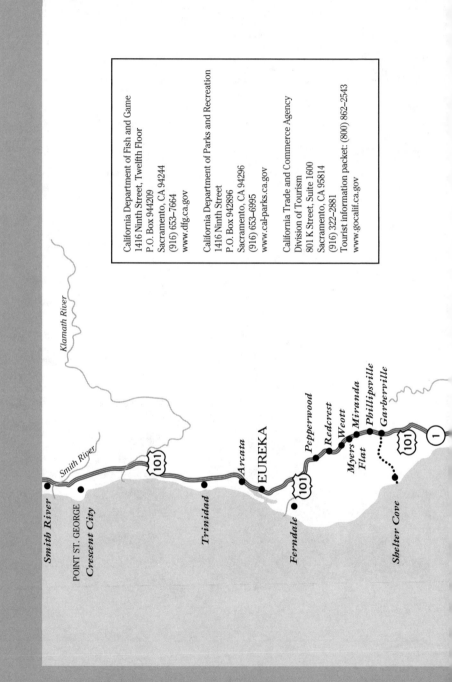

California Department of Fish and Game
1416 Ninth Street, Twelfth Floor
P.O. Box 944209
Sacramento, CA 94244
(916) 653–7664
www.dfg.ca.gov

California Department of Parks and Recreation
1416 Ninth Street
P.O. Box 942896
Sacramento, CA 94296
(916) 653–6995
www.cal-parks.ca.gov

California Trade and Commerce Agency
Division of Tourism
801 K Street, Suite 1600
Sacramento, CA 95814
(916) 322–2881
Tourist information packet: (800) 862–2543
www.gocalif.ca.gov

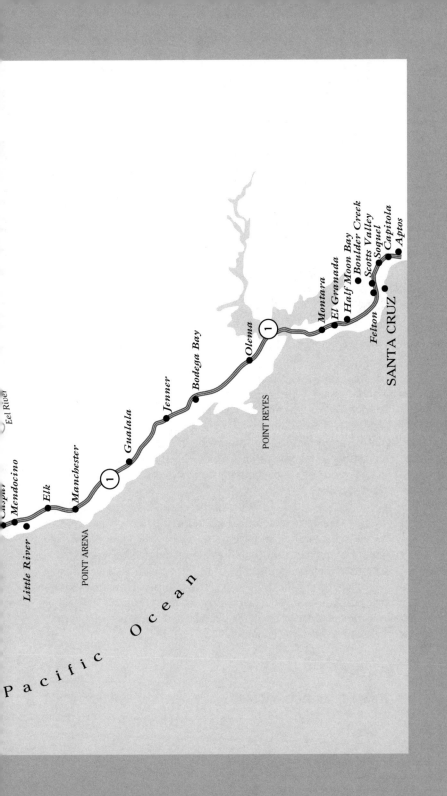

APTOS
Population: 27,000
CAPITOLA
Population: 10,800

Location: *Aptos lies along California Highway 1, 33 miles north of Monterey and 4 miles southeast of Capitola; Capitola, just seaward of Highway 1, is 4 miles east of Santa Cruz.*

At the northern end of the great crescent of Monterey Bay, the Pacific shoreline sweeps westerly, taking Highway 1 with it. Here beaches and surf lie south of the highway, with inland farms and mountains to the north.

Aptos—said to be a Spanish corruption of the Indian word *awotos*, meaning "meeting of the streams"—is the name of an unincorporated village that serves chiefly as a bedroom community for Santa Cruz. With its interesting restaurants, fine bed-and-breakfast inns, and nearby beaches and parks, it's also a pleasant stopover for travelers and destination for vacationers.

Capitola, founded in 1869 by lumber baron Frederick A. Hihn, is purportedly California's oldest seaside resort. By all appearances, it's also the birthplace of the adjective *charming*. It's the kind of clean and perfect little village normally found only in model-railroad layouts.

Compact Capitola is made for walking, so park your vehicle and enjoy strolling along the Esplanade or investigating the many shops and galleries. You can take a sailboat trip or rent a skiff at the Capitola Wharf, or you can swim at any of the sandy beaches that stretch from here east and south along Monterey Bay.

LODGING

Apple Lane Inn, 6265 Soquel Drive, Aptos 95003; (831) 475–6868 or (800) 649–8988. Just north of Highway 1. Five guest rooms with double and queen beds in a lovely restored Victorian farmhouse with private and shared baths. Many antiques and period furnishings and fixtures. Afternoon sherry and full breakfast served in the parlor. Moderate to expensive.

Best Western Seacliff Inn, 7500 Old Dominion Court, Aptos 95003; (831) 688–7300 or (800) 367–2003. Off Highway 1 via Seacliff Beach exit. Has 140 large, comfortably appointed rooms and suites with extra-long double and king beds and cable TV. Each suite has 2 bathrooms and an extra-large whirlpool spa. Heated pool, whirlpool, and putting green. Severino's Restaurant on premises. Cocktail lounge with live entertainment and dancing on weekends. Moderate to expensive.

Mangels House, 570 Aptos Creek Road, P.O. Box 302, Aptos 95003; (831) 688–7982 or (800) 320–7401. North of Highway 1, off Soquel Drive. Six guest rooms, one with a marble fireplace, in the historic Mangels house, built in the 1880s and meticulously restored. Private and shared baths. Complimentary afternoon sherry and full breakfast. Beautiful wooded setting. Expensive.

Pajaro Dunes Rental Agency, Hare, Brewer, & Kelley, Inc., 2661 Beach Road, Watsonville 95076; (831) 722–4671 or (800) 564–1771. Four miles west of Highway 1 via Beach Road, just north of the Pajaro River. Wide range of vacation rentals include condos with 1 to 4 bedrooms, as well as houses and town houses with 2 to 5 bedrooms—all fully furnished and equipped, all on the beach. Security gate. Tennis courts. Expensive to very expensive.

Rio Sands Motel, 116 Aptos Beach Drive, Aptos 95003; (831) 688–3207 or (800) 826–2077. South of Highway 1 via Rio del Mar exit and Rio del Mar Boulevard, then right 1 block on Stephen Road. Queen and king beds or waterbeds in 52 rooms and suites, each with patio or deck, cable TV, and coffeemaker. Heated pool, hot tub, continental breakfast, and barbecue area. Two blocks to the beach. Moderate.

CAMPGROUNDS AND RV PARKS

New Brighton State Beach, 1500 Park Avenue, Capitola 95010; (831) 464–6330 or (800) 444–7275. South of Highway 1, between Aptos and Capitola, via the Park Avenue exit, on a bluff overlooking Monterey Bay. Has 112 campsites with tables and fire pits, but no hookups. Showers and firewood available. Beach access. Moderate.

Santa Cruz KOA Kampground, 1186 San Andreas Road, Watsonville 95076; (831) 722–0551 or 722–2377. South of Aptos off

Highway 1 at Larken Valley Road, then 3 miles south on San Andreas Road. Has 230 full-hookup sites and 21 tent sites. Showers, laundry, tank dump, heated pool, and whirlpools. Store with RV supplies, propane, ice, and gasoline. Video games, basketball, volleyball, and horseshoes. One mile to Manresa State Beach. Moderate to expensive.

Seacliff State Beach, State Park Drive, Aptos 95003; (831) 429–2850 or (800) 444–7275. South of Highway 1 via Seacliff exit. Has 26 premium, full-hookup campsites right on the beach, with tables and fire pits. Showers, easy beach access, nearby fishing pier, snack bar, and bait shop. Expensive.

Sunset State Beach, 201 Sunset Beach Road, Watsonville 95078; (831) 763–7062 or (800) 444–7275. Between Aptos and Watsonville via San Andreas Road. Has 90 campsites with tables and, fire pits, but no hookups. En route campsites also available. Showers, access to dunes and beach, summer campfire programs. Moderate.

FOOD

Cafe Rio, 131 Esplanade, Rio del Mar, Aptos 95003; (831) 688–8917. South of Highway 1 via Rio del Mar Boulevard. Dinner daily; oyster bar and cocktails from 3:00 P.M. daily. Enjoy cocktails with oysters on the half-shell, shrimp or crab cocktail, smoked salmon, steamed mussels or clams, and fresh artichoke or calamari appetizer. Dinners include grilled sanddabs, charbroiled swordfish, broiled or poached salmon, sautéed scallops, broiled halibut, Alaskan king crab, grilled trout, steak, chicken, and rack of lamb. Full bar. Moderate.

Cafe Sparrow, 8042 Soquel Drive, Aptos 95003; (831) 688–6238. East of Highway 1, between Rio Del Mar Boulevard and State Park Drive. Breakfast, lunch, and dinner daily; Sunday brunch. Hearty breakfast offerings include traditional egg dishes, scrambles, and omelets, as well as flapjacks and Sparrow French Toast: cinnamon-raisin bread in spiced batter and topped with toasted almonds. Appetizers and salads include chicken-liver pâté made with herbs and cognac, roasted garlic with melted Brie and croutons, cockles steamed in seasoned white wine and served with drawn butter, pan-fried oysters with lemon-caper crème, goat cheese salad with toast points, and classic Caesar salad for two. French-influenced entrees include vegetarian pasta, stir-fry, ragout, and omelet, as well as chicken breast, rack of lamb, sautéed chicken livers, calamari picatta, and several renditions of filet mignon, cut from Angus beef. House-made desserts include crème caramel, apricot-walnut cake, chocolate truffle cake, warm bread pudding with lemon cream, and pecan-brownie

Capitola Village and Wharf

sundae with caramel sauce. Beer and wine. Moderate.

Shadowbrook Restaurant, 1750 Wharf Road, Capitola 95010; (831) 475–1222. South of Highway 1, Wharf Road at Capitola Road, on Soquel Creek. Daily dinner and weekend brunch. A local favorite since 1947. Appetizers include grilled artichokes, calamari strips, escargots, and baked Brie. Dinners offer choice of artichoke soup, soup of the day, or salad, plus homemade breads and such entrees as scampi, scallops, rack of lamb, veal, steaks, teriyaki brochette of beef, and breast of chicken. Chef's specials served nightly. Full bar, excellent wine list, live entertainment, and dancing. Moderate to expensive.

SHOPPING AND BROWSING

Agriculture is one of the major contributors to the economy of Santa Cruz County. In addition to all the quaint seaside shops and galleries in the vicinity are many roadside stands and farm stores where you can buy the freshest produce and other farm products at unbelievably low prices—imagine, a buck a bag for artichokes. Whether you're stocking a refrigerator, ice chest, or picnic basket, you'll have plenty of opportunities to buy great locally grown products. Boutiques, antiques shops, stores, and art galleries are scattered here and there, between and in Aptos and Capitola. Shop and browse in the sunshine and salt air.

135

Capitola Fine Arts Gallery, 109 Capitola Avenue, Capitola 93010; (831) 464–3838. Featuring many local artists, the gallery is open daily 11:00 A.M. to 5:00 P.M.

The Craft Gallery, 126 San Jose Avenue, Capitola 95010; (831) 475–4466. San Jose Avenue at Capitola Avenue. Daily, 10:00 A.M. to 8:00 P.M. A large selection of handcrafted gift items and souvenirs. Jewelry, jewelry boxes, pottery, stained glass, T-shirts, leather goods, and cards.

BEACHES, PARKS, TRAILS, AND WAYSIDES

From the Santa Cruz County line at the Pajaro River north to Capitola are several long and broad sandy beaches with good public access. Some offer excellent beachcombing, while others are good for swimming, exploring tidepools, or hiking.

San Andreas Road runs roughly parallel to Highway 1, but nearer the beach, and leads to other roads with beach access. Use San Andreas Road to reach Palm Beach (via Beach Road), Sunset State Beach (via Sunset Beach Road), and Manresa State Beach.

Rio del Mar Boulevard and State Park Road, respectively, lead to Rio del Mar Beach and Seacliff State Beach. Between Aptos and Capitola, take the Park Avenue exit to New Brighton State Beach. Park Avenue also leads to Monterey Avenue and the Esplanade at Capitola. The popular City Beach is adjacent.

The Forest of Nisene Marks State Park lies 4 miles north of Soquel Drive, via Aptos Creek Road. Within its boundaries are 10,000 acres of mostly second-growth timber, unpaved roads, picnic areas, and about 30 miles of trails. It's managed as a semiwilderness area and is among Central California's largest state parks.

WATER SPORTS AND ACTIVITIES

Several species of clams reside along the surf of Monterey Bay, from Sunset State Beach to Seacliff State Beach. Manresa State Beach is the most popular spot to dig for pismo clams, and Seacliff Beach is the northern limit for this clam's range. The season for pismo clams runs from September through April.

These are also good surf-fishing beaches, where anglers take a variety of species, including surfperch, flounder, and the occasional shark. The larger creeks entering the bay support runs of coho salmon and steelhead trout.

The old supply ship *Palo Alto* is scuttled at the end of the pier at

Seacliff State Beach, providing habitat for a great assortment of fish, including surfperch, seaperch, halibut, flounder, sole, and white croaker. Offshore, anglers take the same species, as well as salmon, sea bass, and several species of shark.

The Capitola Wharf is another popular place to fish and is a good place to launch a boat or rent one. Anglers are allowed to drive onto the pier to launch and haul out boats and load or unload gear and catch, but they are limited to a twenty-minute stay. Parking is available nearby.

Capitola Boat & Bait, 1400 Wharf Road, Capitola 95010; (831) 462–2208. At the end of the Capitola Wharf. Weekdays, 5:30 A.M. to 6:00 P.M.; weekends, 5:00 A.M. till whenever. Rents 16-foot wooden skiffs with eight-horsepower outboards. Boat-launching facilities. Bait, tackle, licenses, equipment rental, reef maps, food, snacks, ice, and beverages. A good source of information about local fishing and weather and water conditions.

GOLF

Aptos Seascape Golf Course, 610 Clubhouse Drive, Aptos 95003; (831) 688–3213; restaurant, (831) 688–3254. South of Highway 1 via Rio del Mar Boulevard. An eighteen-hole, par-seventy-two course with driving range, pro shop, equipment rentals, and resident pro. Restaurant on premises.

WINERY

Bargetto Winery, 3535 North Main, Soquel 95073; (831) 475–2258. Northeast of Highway 1. Tasting, 10:00 A.M. to 5:00 P.M. daily. Largest winery in the area, established in 1933. Both fruit and varietal wines. White wines include chardonnay, Riesling, and gewürtztraminer. Pinot noir and cabernet sauvignon are red-wine specialties. Tours available.

TRAVEL INFORMATION

Aptos Chamber of Commerce, Redwood Village, 7605–A Old Dominion Court, Aptos 95003; (831) 688–1467; www.aptos chamber.com

Capitola Chamber of Commerce, 716–G Capitola Avenue, Capitola 95010; (831) 475–6522; www.capitolachamber.com; e-mail: capinfo@capitolachamber.com

EVENTS

February   Village Sidewalk Sale, Capitola, (831) 475–6522

April   Easter Egg Hunt at Capitola Beach, (831) 475–6522

May   Capitola Kite Classic, (831) 475–6522
Santa Cruz Blues Festival, Aptos, (831) 479–9814

June   Festival at the Cement Ship, Aptos, (831) 685–4444
Hawaiian Luau, Aptos, (831) 688–7442

July   Wharf to Wharf Race, Capitola, (831) 475–2196
World's Shortest Parade, Aptos, (831) 475–2258

August   Fine Art Festival, Soquel, (831) 475–2258

September   Capitola Begonia Festival, (831) 475–6522
Sand Castle Contest, Capitola, (831) 475–6522
Fishing Derby, Capitola, (831) 475–6522
Rowboat Races, Capitola, (831) 475–6522
Begonia Water Parade, Capitola, (831) 475–6522
Capitola Art and Wine Festival, (831) 475–6522
Women's Longboard Surf Contest, Capitola, (831) 475–6522

October   Village Halloween Parade, Capitola, (831) 475–6522

SANTA CRUZ
Population: 51,731

Location: *On California Highway 1, at the junctures of State Routes 9 and 17, about 70 miles south of San Francisco, 42 miles south of Half Moon Bay, and about 43 miles north of Monterey.*

Santa Cruz has been attracting vacationers and weekend visitors to its rough-hewn coastline, intriguing pocket beaches, and moderate climate since its early days of bayside camps and bathhouses. By the late nineteenth century, it was widely known and highly regarded as a resort community, a reputation it has enjoyed through the twentieth century.

Not even the mighty rumblings of the San Andreas Fault have been able to shake the city's appeal or cause tourism to waver. The same earthquake that tumbled buildings and brought down bridges and freeways in San Francisco on October 17, 1989, caused extensive damage to downtown Santa Cruz, but it left most outlying areas and shoreline attractions and neighborhoods relatively unscathed, or at least reparable.

Santa Cruzans proceeded carefully and thoughtfully with reconstruction of the city's core, where most of the damage occurred. Now, many new shops, boutiques, galleries, and cafes have renewed downtown Santa Cruz's charm and appeal.

Most of the area's natural attractions are along the shore of Monterey Bay and in the forests and foothills of the Santa Cruz Mountains. There are plenty of opportunities for outdoor recreation, many restaurants offering a wide range of cuisines, and a variety of fine accommodations—from graceful old Victorian bed-and-breakfast inns to modern, full-service resorts. The atmosphere is casual and relaxed, and the people are friendly and helpful.

LODGING

The Babbling Brook Inn, 1025 Laurel Street, 95060; (831) 427–2437 or (800) 866–1131. Two blocks south of Highway 1 on Laurel, between California and Walti Streets. Queen and king beds and fireplaces in 13 guest rooms in this secluded inn with French country decor. Set amid lush gardens with trees, creek, and waterfalls. Most rooms have whirlpool baths. Some have decks, some open-beam ceilings, all private baths. Full breakfast; afternoon wine and cheese and teas. Expensive.

Best Western Inn, 126 Plymouth Street, 95060; (831) 425–4717 or (800) 528–1234. South of Highway 1 via Ocean Avenue exit. Queen and king beds in 26 rooms and suites with cable TV and coffeemakers. Suites have whirlpool baths and wet bars. Sauna. Moderate to expensive.

Chateau Victorian, 118 First Street, 95060; (831) 458–9458. South of Highway 1 via Bay Street, then left on West Cliff. One block north of Beach Street, near the boardwalk. Queen beds in 7 rooms with private baths and fireplaces. Complimentary beverages with cheese and crackers each afternoon, continental breakfast each morning. Easy walk to beach, boardwalk, wharf, shops, and restaurants. Moderate to expensive.

The Inn at Pasatiempo, 555 Highway 17, 95060; (831) 423–5000 or (800) 834–2546. North of Highway 1. Cable TV, armoires, quilts, and open-beam ceilings in 54 rooms and suites. Suites have canopy beds, French doors, VCRs, and stocked refrigerators. Pool and whirlpool. Adjacent golf course. Peachwood's Grill & Bar on premises. Room service. Moderate to very expensive.

CAMPGROUNDS AND RV PARKS

Big Basin Redwoods State Park, 21600 Big Basin Way, Boulder Creek 95006; (800) 444–7275; horse-camp reservations, (831) 425–1218. Located 23 miles northeast of Santa Cruz via State Route 9 off Highway 1. Has 147 developed campsites with tables, fire pits, and food lockers. Showers. Six trail camps for backpackers. Horse-trail camp just east of Highway 1, near Waddell Beach. Hiking trails. Moderate.

Henry Cowell Redwoods State Park Campground, 101 North Big Trees Park Road, P.O. Box 53, Felton 95018, (831) 335–4598 or (800) 444–7275. The park is 3 miles north of Santa Cruz via State Route 9. From park headquarters, drive north to Felton, then right on Graham Hill Road to the campground. Has 113 developed campsites with tables and stoves to accommodate RVs to 36 feet. Piped water near all sites, showers, and laundry tubs. Trails for hiking and horseback riding. Moderate.

FOOD

The Crow's Nest Restaurant, 2218 East Cliff Drive, 95060; (831) 476–4560. South of Highway 1, at the small-craft harbor, with a great view of Monterey Bay. Lunch and dinner daily. Luncheon appetizers include chilled artichokes, prawns, and oysters. Luncheon entrees feature crab Louis, enchiladas, seafood thermidor, burgers, steak sandwich, and crab-salad sandwich. Dinner entrees include beef or chicken teriyaki, rack of lamb, sirloin and enchilada, calamari steak, scallops tempura, barbecued prawns, and grilled sole. At the oyster bar and lounge, choose from more than a dozen offerings, such as oyster shooters, shrimp cocktail, stuffed artichokes, stuffed potato skins, and fried calamari. Full bar. Great outdoor deck overlooking the ocean. Live entertainment nightly. Inexpensive to moderate.

Peachwood's Steakhouse, 555 Highway 17, 95060; (831) 426–6333. North of Highway 1, at the Inn at Pasatiempo. Lunch and dinner daily. Enjoy such appetizers as crisp-fried artichoke hearts with tarragon mayonnaise, coconut prawns, or grilled *passilla* peppers filled with Jack cheese. Try the soup of the day or the black bean and smoked sirloin soup with sour cream and salsa. Meal-size salads, big burgers, deli-style sandwiches, and deep-fried catfish. Entrees include chicken, smoked pork tenderloin, baby back ribs, steaks, prime rib, rack of lamb, and rotisserie duckling, all roasted over peachwood for a mildly smoky flavor. Full bar. Moderate.

SHOPPING AND BROWSING

Downtown Santa Cruz is a shopper's delight, where travelers will want to park and stroll along its clean, tree-lined streets and visit the handsome buildings where the city's businesses flourish. All manner of shops and boutiques, specialty stores and art galleries, restaurants and cafes invite visitors to pause, linger, and enjoy the casual hospitality that characterizes this gem of the central California coast.

Spring, summer, and fall, merchants join for seasonal sidewalk sales; in winter they conduct their annual clearance sale. All year long, the Downtown Association sponsors the Antique and Collectibles Faire, from 9:00 A.M. to 4:00 P.M on the second Sunday of every month.

BEACHES, PARKS, TRAILS, AND WAYSIDES

Highway 1 veers inland as it approaches Santa Cruz, and in the center of town it transforms from freeway to city street. Head for the bay to avoid midday and rush-hour congestion.

East Cliff Drive and West Cliff Drive cling to the coastal bluffs and provide many scenic overlooks and access to beaches, tidepools, and other seaside attractions. From Capitola, take Cliff Drive west from the village. Travelers arriving from the south via Highway 1 can take Forty-first Avenue to East Cliff Drive. Those arriving from the north should turn right on Mission Street, then right on Natural Bridges Drive, left on Delaware Avenue, and right on Swanton Boulevard to West Cliff Drive. Bay Street also meets West Cliff, near the Santa Cruz Beach and Boardwalk. It's possible to travel along the coast all the way from Capitola to Natural Bridges State Beach, at the opposite end of Santa Cruz.

Mile-long Santa Cruz Main Beach is probably the area's most popular, especially with swimmers. It's in the heart of the city's bayside recreation area, with the municipal wharf at one end and the boardwalk flanking it.

About a mile west of the Santa Cruz Municipal Wharf is Point Santa Cruz and Lighthouse Field State Beach. The cliffs here overlook a popular surfing area known as Steamer Lane. This is also a good spot for watching whales and sea lions.

The Mark Abbott Memorial Lighthouse stands atop a cliff, with parking nearby. It functions as the Santa Cruz Surfing Museum and is open to the public every day but Tuesday, from noon to 4:00 P.M.

Westward, sheer cliffs are interrupted by pocket beaches, the largest of which is Natural Bridges State Beach. Although it was named after the naturally eroded sandstone bridges in the area, all but one have collapsed. The park is better known now for a eucalyptus grove that is the largest monarch-butterfly wintering area in the nation. A ¾-mile nature trail leads through the grove.

At Henry Crowell Redwoods State Park, north of Santa Cruz on

State Route 9, are 4,000 acres of forest containing Douglas fir, madrone, tanbark oak, coast redwoods, and ponderosa pine. In addition to picnic areas and river bottoms are 15 miles of trails for hikers and equestrians.

Big Basin Redwoods State Park, 23 miles northeast of Santa Cruz via Highways 1 and 9, was established in 1902 and is the oldest in the California system. The 14,000-acre park sprawls from the Santa Cruz Mountains to the coast and has more than 100 miles of hiking and riding trails through the coast redwoods.

WATER SPORTS AND ACTIVITIES

Because of its east-west orientation, the coastline of the Santa Cruz area is ideal for surfing. Pleasure Point Beach—along East Cliff Drive, in Live Oak, between Forty-first and Thirty-second Avenues—is a popular surfing area. Steamer Lane, between Point Santa Cruz and the municipal wharf, is one of the best surfing spots on the California coast.

Several of the larger creeks in the Santa Cruz vicinity support runs of coho salmon and steelhead trout during the fall and winter. The San Lorenzo River gets the biggest runs of any stream south of San Francisco Bay. Fishing is best on the upper river. Some favorite spots are within Henry Cowell Redwoods State Park, north of town, via State Route 9.

Virtually any place that provides parking and beach access offers surf- or rock-fishing opportunities for a variety of species, including surfperch, flounder, and rockfish. The east jetty at the entrance to the small-craft harbor is a good fishing area, reached by way of Twin Lakes State Beach, Seventh Avenue at East Cliff Drive.

The Santa Cruz Municipal Wharf attracts anglers who take bonito, croaker, flounder, halibut, lingcod, and shark. Crabbing is also good here at times.

Charter- and party-boat operators work from the wharf and from the Santa Cruz Small Craft Harbor, Eaton Street at Lake Avenue. For those towing boats, the harbor provides launching facilities, as well as marine service, supplies, and repairs.

Aqua Safari Scuba Center, 6896 Socal Avenue, Santa Cruz 95060; (831) 479–4386. Rents and sells scuba equipment and offers dive tours, boat charters, diving classes, and kayak rentals.

Pacific Yachting & Sailing, 790 Mariner Park Way, Santa Cruz 95062; (831) 423–7245. At the Santa Cruz Yacht Harbor. Sailing

Beach and Boardwalk, Santa Cruz

lessons available: basic, intermediate, and advanced sailing; seamanship; cruising; navigation and piloting; and other courses and instructional vacations, all taught aboard modern 25- to 43-foot yachts.

Shamrock Charters, Inc., Fisherman's Supply, 2210 East Cliff Drive, Santa Cruz 95062; (831) 476–2648. At the Santa Cruz Yacht Harbor. Charter fishing trips for salmon, lingcod, and rockfish. Whale-watching trips in season. Full line of tackle, bait, and fuel available at the tackle shop. Ocean skiffs for rent.

TOURS AND TRIPS

Santa Cruz, Big Trees & Pacific Railway Company, P.O. Box G-1, Felton 95018; (831) 335–4484. Board at Santa Cruz Beach Boardwalk or at Felton, north of Highway 1 via State Route 9. Steam and diesel locomotives pull trains of vintage passenger and open observation cars between Felton and the Santa Cruz Beach Boardwalk. Round-trips take about two hours, not counting layovers. (One-way trip available as well.) Roaring Camp & Big Trees Narrow-Gauge Railroad provides passenger service from Felton on trains pulled by early twentieth-century steam locomotives up the steepest narrow-gauge grades in North America into forests of great coastal redwoods. The round-trip takes about an hour and a quarter.

GOLF

Pasatiempo Golf Club, 18 Clubhouse Road, P.O. Box 535, 95061; (831) 459–9155. A half-mile north of Santa Cruz on State Route 17. An eighteen-hole, par-seventy-one, 6,600-yard course in the hills above Santa Cruz. Ranked in the top 100 courses in America. Driving range, putting greens, pro shop, equipment rentals, golf lessons, restaurant, and bar.

WINERIES

Bonny Doon Vineyard, 10 Pine Flat Road, P.O. Box 8376, 95061; (831) 425–3625. North of Highway 1, west of Santa Cruz. Tasting, 11:00 A.M. to 5:00 P.M. daily. Among the wines produced are chardonnay, grenache, and muscat canelli.

David Bruce Winery, 21439 Bear Creek Road, Los Gatos 95033; (800) 397–9972. North off Highway 1 on State Route 9, then east on Bear Creek Road. Tasting, noon to 5:00 P.M. daily. Specializes in cabernet sauvignon, Pinot noir, and chardonnay. Picnic area.

Hallcrest Vineyards, 379 Felton-Empire Road, Felton 95018; (831) 335–4441. Northwest of Santa Cruz via State Route 9. Tasting, 11:00 A.M. to 5:30 P.M. daily. Specialties include cabernet sauvignon, chardonnay, and Riesling.

OTHER ATTRACTIONS

Santa Cruz Beach Boardwalk, 400 Beach Street, 95060; (831) 423–5590. South of Highway 1 via Bay Street, or follow signs to Santa Cruz Beach. Boardwalk opens 11:00 A.M. daily from Memorial Day through Labor Day; open weekends the rest of the year. Casino Arcade is open daily, except Thanksgiving and Christmas. In operation since 1907, now California's only oceanside amusement park, situated on the beautiful, mile-long Santa Cruz Beach. More than twenty major rides, including a famous carousel and Big Dipper roller coaster, which are National Historic Landmarks. Facilities at adjacent Coconut Grove accommodate many events, including trade shows, concerts, Sunday brunch, and big-band dances. Plenty of places to eat, and gift shops galore.

TRAVEL INFORMATION

Downtown Association of Santa Cruz, 1347 Pacific Avenue, Suite 201, P.O. Box 1384, 95061; (831) 429–8433; www.down townsantacruz.com; e-mail: info@shopsantacruz.com

Santa Cruz County Conference and Visitors Council, 1211 Ocean Street, 95060; (831) 425–1234 or (800) 833–3494; www.scccvc.org

EVENTS

For information about any of the events listed below, or to learn about events recently added to the Santa Cruz calender, write or call the Santa Cruz County Conference and Visitors Council, or visit the Downtown Association's Web site (see above).

February	Clam Chowder Cookoff
April	Ducky Derby at Harvey West Park
May	Great Salsa Taste-off at the Wharf
	Celebrate Santa Cruz: Art, Wine, and Jazz Festival
	Santa Cruz Longboard Club Invitational at Steamers Lane
June	Woodies on the Wharf
July	Shakespeare Santa Cruz
August	Shakespeare Santa Cruz continues
	Cabrillo Music Festival
	Aloha Outrigger Races and Polynesian Festival
September	Shark Festival & Sanctuary Celebration
October	Santa Cruz Fireworks Spectacular
November	Community Tree Lighting
December	Downtown Holiday Parade

HALF MOON BAY

☆

Population: 10,133

Location: *On California Highway 1 at the juncture of Route 92, 42 miles north of Santa Cruz, 95 miles north of Monterey, and 28 miles south of San Francisco.*

Half Moon Bay is the social and economic hub of a collection of small towns and villages clustered along the Pacific and known locally as Coastside. The surrounding marine terraces, creek bottoms, and rolling foothills were inhabited for centuries by Costanoan Indians. Spanish immigrants settled the area in the 1840s, followed by Mexican and Chilean laborers, which accounts for Half Moon Bay's earlier name: Spanishtown.

The first American settlers came after the war with Mexico ended in 1848. During the latter half of the nineteenth century, the area flourished as more immigrants arrived. Rail was laid from San Francisco to just beyond Half Moon Bay, sparking a boom that died with the failure of the railroad, a lingering demise that took from 1906 to 1920.

The Volstead Act of 1919 and consequent Eighteenth Amendment to the U.S. Constitution brought Prohibition to the nation and another boom to the shores of Half Moon Bay. Numerous pocket beaches and coves made ideal landings for the rumrunners. Bordellos and roadhouses served locals and travelers alike, while bootleggers sped nightly along winding coastal and mountain roads, hauling their precious cargo to the San Francisco Bay Area. When Prohibition was revoked in 1933, Half Moon Bay had to settle in and await the next boom.

Rich agricultural lands flank the coast, and the climate is ideal for growing a variety of crops, such as artichokes, brussels sprouts, peas, pumpkins, kiwifruit, and berries. Agriculture is a major contributor to the area economy, with a countywide annual harvest running to $206 million.

Pillar Point Harbor is west of Highway 1, about 4 miles north of Half Moon Bay. In addition to slips and facilities for recreational boaters and anglers, the harbor is also home to a commercial-fishing fleet of more than 200 vessels. The commercial catch includes white croaker, sanddab, several species of sole, rockfish, halibut, salmon, swordfish, Dungeness crab, and red abalone and amounts to more than five million pounds a year.

Today, Half Moon Bay's boom is largely in the form of tourism. Across the county, annual revenues from travel and tourism are approaching $700 million. Many of those dollars are spent along this stretch of the coast, where fine restaurants, superb accommodations, sandy beaches, and other attractions await the traveler.

LODGING

Cypress Inn, 407 Mirada Road, Miramar Beach 94019; (650) 726–6002 or (800) 832–3224. West of Highway 1 via Medio or Magellan, between Half Moon Bay and Pillar Point Harbor. Contemporary bed-and-breakfast inn with 18 rooms, each individually decorated and each with private bath, private whirlpool spa, and private deck with ocean view. On the beach. Afternoon wine and hors d'oeuvres. Full gourmet breakfast. Expensive to very expensive.

Harbor View Inn, 51 Avenue Alhambra, P.O. Box 127, El Granada 94018; (650) 726–2329. Just east of Highway 1, 4 miles north of Half Moon Bay. Double and queen beds in 18 rooms, each with cable TV and a bay-window seat overlooking the harbor and ocean. Complimentary continental breakfast. Comfortable, tastefully decorated rooms at reasonable rates. Inexpensive to moderate.

Mill Rose Inn, 615 Mill Street, 94019; (650) 726–8750 or (800) 900–7673. West of Main Street, south of Half Moon Bay Road (Route 92), and east of Highway 1. Country English elegance at an exquisitely appointed bed-and-breakfast inn with 6 flower-filled rooms and suites, each with private bath, private entrance, fireplace, view of lovely gardens, phones, cable TV, coffeemaker, and well-stocked refrigerator. Queen and king beds. Whirlpool spa. Full champagne breakfast delivered to guests' rooms or served in dining room. Expensive to very expensive.

Old Thyme Inn, 779 Main Street, 94019; (650) 726–1616 or

(800) 720–4277. In town. A Victorian house built in 1899, fully re-stored, with 7 guest rooms, all with private baths. Garden suite has private entrance, whirlpool tub, refrigerator, skylight, TV, VCR, videotapes, and complimentary beverages. Double and queen beds. Complimentary wine and sherry. Full breakfast. Seasonal rates. Moderate to very expensive.

Pigeon Point Lighthouse American Youth Hostel, 210 Pigeon Point Road and Highway 1, Pescadero 94060; (650) 879–0633. Just west of Highway 1, 26 miles north of Santa Cruz, 18½ miles south of Half Moon Bay. Office hours, 7:30 to 9:30 A.M. and 4:30 to 9:30 P.M. Four oceanside bungalows provide lodging for 50 guests. Separate bunkrooms can be reserved for couples or families. Shared bathrooms, kitchens, and living rooms. Recreation and meeting room. Inexpensive.

The Pillar Point Inn, 380 Capistrano Road, P.O. Box 388, Princeton-By-The-Sea 94018; (650) 728–7377 or (800) 400–8281. Four miles north of Half Moon Bay, just west of Highway 1. A bed-and-breakfast inn overlooking the harbor, with 11 rooms, each with private bath, fireplace, featherbed, TV, VCR, and refrigerator. Some have private steam baths. Ocean and harbor views from all rooms. Complimentary afternoon tea. Breakfast served in guests' rooms or in breakfast room. Next to Shore Bird Restaurant. Walk to harbor. Moderate to expensive.

Point Montara Lighthouse American Youth Hostel, Sixteenth Street at Highway 1, Montara 94037; (650) 728–7177. About 23 miles south of San Francisco, about 2 miles north of Pillar Point Harbor, just north of Moss Beach. Office hours, 7:30 to 9:30 A.M. and 4:30 to 9:30 P.M. Eight bedrooms, 2 kitchens, 2 common rooms, shared baths, laundry facilities, and outdoor hot tub. Special rooms for families and couples available by reservation. Rental bikes available. Inexpensive.

CAMPGROUNDS AND RV PARKS

Butano State Park, P.O. Box 9, Pescadero 94060; (650) 879–2040 or (800) 444–7275. Three miles east of Highway 1, 5 miles south of Pescadero on Cloverdale Road, south off Pescadero Road or north off Gazos Creek Road. A 3,200-acre park in the redwoods with 21 drive-in and 19 walk-in campsites. Hiking trails. Summer nature walks and campfire programs. Inexpensive.

Francis Beach Campground, Half Moon Bay State Beach, 95 Kelly Avenue, 94019; (650) 726–8819 or (800) 444–7275. At the foot of Kelly Avenue, west of Highway 1 about ¼-mile south of Route

Point Montara Lighthouse, near Half Moon Bay

92. Has 51 campsites near the beach for tents and RVs. Tables, showers, and beach access.

Pelican Point RV Park, 1001 Miramontes Point Road, P.O. Box 65, 94019; (650) 726–9100. A tree-shaded and grassy park overlooking the ocean, with 76 full-hookup sites. Tables, cable TV, showers, laundry, tank dump, and beach access. Store and gift shop. Ice and propane available. Expensive.

FOOD

The Miramar Beach Restaurant & Bar, 131 Mirada Road, 94019; (650) 726–9053. Just west of Highway 1, at Magellan Avenue and Mirada Road, on the beach. A delightful restaurant with a spectacular ocean view and checkered past, the Miramar was designed and built during Prohibition to function as a roadhouse and speakeasy. Daily lunch and dinner; Sunday champagne brunch. Start with Dungeness crab cakes, Bonzai oysters, Buffalo-style prawns, Castroville artichoke, prawn cocktail, or calamari picante. Try the soup du jour or the creamy seafood chowder, made with crab, shrimp, clams, and a dollop of sherry. Meal-size salads include a seafood Caesar, blackened chicken Caesar, and seafood Louis. Lunch offerings include pasta dishes, fish-and-chips, burgers, and such specialty sandwiches as the Miramar crab melt on toasted sourdough bread or blackened salmon on a sourdough roll. Among the dinner entrees are steaks, rack of lamb, chicken piccata, Coquille St. Jacques, salmon en croute, and more than a half-dozen pasta dishes. Beer, wine, and cocktails. Piano lounge. Moderate.

Moss Beach Distillery, 140 Beach Way, Moss Beach 94038; (650) 728–5595. North of Half Moon Bay, at Beach Way and Ocean Street, west of Highway 1. Lunch and dinner daily. Fresh seafood is done to perfection and served within view of the ocean. Also prime rib, rack of lamb, hardwood-smoked ribs and chicken. Oyster bar and salad bar. Moderate.

Spanishtown Mexican Restaurant & Market, 515 Church Street, 94019; (650) 726–7357. East of Highway 1, west of Main Street, south of Half Moon Bay Road (Route 92). Lunch and dinner daily. Home-style Mexican food. Tacos, enchiladas, burritos, flautas, chimichangas, *chiles rellenos,* fajitas, and more. Combination plates for lunch and dinner. Mexican-style seafood. Inexpensive to moderate.

SHOPPING AND BROWSING

The various communities that make up the Coastside area have a variety of shops and galleries. Half Moon Bay's historic downtown area is a pleasant place to stroll, browse, and shop. But another kind of shopping opportunity awaits travelers to this area—a number of produce stands and "you-pick" farms where you can buy the freshest fruits and vegetables at the lowest prices. Stop by and stock your ice chest or refrigerator, or just pick up some fresh produce for your next hike or picnic or to munch on as you head down the road.

G. Berta's, Half Moon Bay Road, 94019; (650) 726–4922. One mile east of Half Moon Bay on Route 92. Summer, 9:00 A.M. to 6:30 P.M. daily; winter, 10:00 A.M. to 5:00 P.M. daily. Produce stand offering a variety of fruits and vegetables in season, such as peas, green beans, beets, lettuce, carrots, broccoli, cauliflower, leeks, escarole, endive, artichokes, and pumpkins.

Farmer's Daughter, El Granada, 94018. On Highway 1, between El Granada and Moss Beach, 5 miles north of Half Moon Bay. Friday, Saturday, and Sunday, 10:00 A.M. until dark; daily during pumpkin season. Weekend produce stand offering fresh, locally grown peas, corn, potatoes, chard, brussels sprouts, artichokes, fruits, pistachio nuts, pumpkins, and honey.

Phipps Ranch, 2700 Pescadero Road, Pescadero 94060; (650) 879–0787. South of Half Moon Bay, east of Highway 1, just past Stage Road. Summer, 10:00 A.M. to 7:00 P.M. daily; winter, 10:00 A.M.

to 6:00 P.M. daily. Roadside market and nursery with fresh fruits and vegetables available all year; large selection of dried beans, fresh herbs, dried herbs, herbal vinegars, and potpourri. Pick your own berries in summer.

Tom & Pete's Produce and Half Moon Bay Fish Market, Highway 1, 94019; (650) 726–2561. Highway 1 at Route 92. Daily, 9:00 A.M. to 7:00 P.M. Indoor vegetable and fruit stand and adjacent seafood market offering fresh fish and shellfish, including lobsters and crabs, live or cooked.

BEACHES, PARKS, TRAILS, AND WAYSIDES

At the extreme southern end of San Mateo County, west of Highway 1, lies Ano Nuevo Point, the site of a 1,500-acre state reserve known for its abundant wildlife. This is an excellent spot for watching and photographing migratory birds in the spring and fall. Gray whales pass near the point in January and March. And from December through April, huge elephant seals come ashore to give birth and breed, during which time the reserve near the rookery is open only to guided tours, for which reservations are necessary. Information, (650) 879–0227; reservations, (650) 393–6914.

Pigeon Point Lighthouse stands 115 feet tall atop a 35-foot cliff, 18½ miles south of Half Moon Bay. The light began operating in 1872 and is the second tallest lighthouse on the West Coast. Its beacon, automated in 1972, is visible 20 miles out. The lighthouse is open every Sunday for tours at 10:00 and 11:15 A.M. and at 12:30, 1:45, and 3:00 P.M. Saturday tours given summer only, starting in June.

Pescadero Marsh Natural Preserve lies east of Highway 1 off the north side of Pescadero Road and is the largest coastal marsh between San Francisco Bay and Monterey Bay. An interpretive trail along Highway 1 and dirt levees off Pescadero Road offer opportunities for watching and photographing the plentiful bird life.

Half Moon Bay State Beach—encompassing Francis, Venice, and Dunes Beaches—is west of Highway 1 at Half Moon Bay. Francis Beach is at the foot of Kelly Avenue. Venice Boulevard leads west off Highway 1 to Venice Beach. Dunes Beach is at the foot of Young Avenue, west off Highway 1. Hiking, kite flying, horseback riding, and picnicking are among the possible activities.

Point Montara Lighthouse, about 2 miles north of Pillar Point Harbor, is not open for public tours, but the picturesque point with its immaculately kept buildings offers an excellent spot for photography

152

and good seaward views. Although a fog station was established here in 1875, the present lighthouse wasn't built until 1928.

WATER SPORTS AND ACTIVITIES

Miramar Beach, at the foot of Magellan Avenue, west off Highway 1, is a popular surfing area, as are two places farther north. Broad, sandy El Granada Beach runs along Highway 1 near Pillar Point Harbor; surfers like the area near the east breakwater. North of Point Montara Lighthouse, surfing is good at ½-mile-long Montara Beach.

Surf and rock fishing is often good along the coast here, with surfperch, white croaker, starry flounder, and rockfish the species most often taken. South of Half Moon Bay, both Pomponio and San Gregorio state beaches are good spots. Martin's Beach, 6 miles south of Half Moon Bay, is a private beach where a nominal fee is charged. There's good surf fishing here and smelt netting. Rental nets are available.

Half Moon and El Granada state beaches are other favorite surf-fishing areas. The east breakwater at El Granada Beach is a good rock-fishing spot.

Pillar Point Harbor provides boat-launching facilities and other services for anglers. Anglers take rockfish, starry flounder, and other species at Johnson Pier, which is open twenty-four hours a day. Party and charter boats are also moored at the harbor.

Huck Finn Sportfishing, (mailing address) 1016 Bancroft Avenue, 94019; (650) 726–7133. At Pillar Point Harbor, 4 miles north of Half Moon Bay, west of Highway 1 via Capistrano Road. Check in, 5:15 A.M.; departure, 6:15 A.M.; returns between 2:30 and 3:00 P.M. Open-party and charter trips for salmon and rockfish. Also whale-watching trips in season. Bait, tackle, and rental gear available.

BIKE RENTALS

The Bicyclery, 101B Main Street, 94019; (650) 726–6000. In town. Monday through Friday, 9:30 A.M. to 6:30 P.M.; Saturday, 10:00 A.M. to 5:00 P.M.; Sunday, 11:00 A.M. to 5:00 P.M. Rents mountain and touring bikes.

GOLF

Half Moon Bay Golf Links, 2000 Fairway Drive, 94019; (650) 726–4438. Located off Highway 1, 3 miles south of Route 92. Beautiful

153

eighteen-hole course designed by Arnold Palmer. Pro shop, equipment sales and rentals, restaurant, and bar.

WINERY

Obester Winery, 12341 Highway 92, Route 1, Box 2–Q, 94019; (650) 726–9463. Two miles east of Half Moon Bay on Route 92. Tastings daily, 10:00 A.M. to 5:00 P.M. Tasting room in the rolling hills east of Highway 1. Grapes grown in Mendocino County are made into award-winning wines here. Specialties are chardonnay, Riesling, and sauvignon blanc.

OTHER ATTRACTIONS

Sea Horse and Friendly Acres Horse Ranches, P.O. Box 279, 94019; (650) 726–2362 or 726–8550. On Highway 1, 1 mile north of Half Moon Bay. Daily, 8:00 A.M. to 6:00 P.M. More than 200 horses and ponies. Ride the beaches and trails on your own or in a guided group.

TRAVEL INFORMATION

Half Moon Bay Coastside Chamber of Commerce, 520 Kelly Avenue, 94019; (650) 726–8380; www.coastsidelive.com

April	Pacific Coast Dream Machines, Half Moon Bay Airport, (650) 726–2328
May	Pescadero Chamarita Festival, (650) 726–5701
June	Half Moon Bay Chamarita Festival, (650) 726–2729
July	Old Fashioned Fourth of July Parade, Half Moon Bay, (650) 726–7969
	Tours de Fleurs, Coastside, (650) 726–8380
August	Pescadero Arts and Fun Festival, (650) 879–0848
October	Chili Cookoff, Pillar Point Harbor, (650) 726–9071
	The Great Pumpkin Weigh-off, Half Moon Bay, (650) 726–9652
	Half Moon Bay Art & Pumpkin Festival, (650) 726–9652
December	Christmas Tree Lighting, Half Moon Bay, (650) 726–8380
	Harbor Lights Ceremony, Pillar Point Harbor, (650) 726–5723

HALF MOON BAY

BODEGA BAY

Population: 950

POINT ARENA

Population: 440

Location: *Bodega Bay is on California Highway 1, about 60 miles north of San Francisco and about 23 miles west of U.S. 101 at Santa Rosa; Point Arena, also on California Highway 1, lies 63 miles north of Bodega Bay and 35 miles south of Mendocino.*

North of San Francisco Bay along the coast is another California, this one characterized by environmental diversity, a sparse and far-flung population, the absence of freeway noise, and a pace dictated by a tortuous Highway 1. The area from northwestern Marin County, just south of Bodega Bay, to southwestern Mendocino County, in the vicinity of Point Arena, is one of the least developed regions in the state.

The main geologic feature here is the San Andreas Fault, and evidence of upheaval abounds. The famous fault zone begins in south-central California and extends northwesterly from the Salton Sea for about 650 miles, then swings westerly into the ocean near Shelter Cove. The fault lies parallel to and near the coast from south of Bodega Bay northward. Just south of Fort Ross, the fault swings offshore, where the ancient landslide mass has created cliffs that drop 1,000 sheer feet to the surf.

The broad marine terraces and rolling pastureland near Bodega Bay begin to narrow north of the Russian River, with the rocky coastline becoming a series of steep cliffs and tiny pocket beaches. Many sea stacks, offshore rocks, and islets add drama to the seascape and provide havens and rookeries for countless seabirds, seals, and sea lions.

Natural features more than compensate for the lack of man-made attractions along this expanse of fractured coastline, but they also retard

156

the pace of travel. With all its curves, switchbacks, and changes in elevation, Highway 1 allows an average speed of only about 30 miles per hour. So relax and enjoy it.

LODGING

Blackthorne Inn, 266 Vallejo Avenue, P.O. Box 712, Inverness 94937; (415) 663–8621. Located in Iverness Park, 2 miles south of Inverness, off Sir Francis Drake Boulevard, near Point Reyes National Seashore. A bed-and-breakfast inn offering queen beds in 5 guest rooms with balconies. Private and shared baths, huge sundeck, hot tub. Unusual architecture in an interesting inn built of redwood, cedar, and Douglas fir. Full buffet-style breakfast. Expensive.

Bodega Bay Lodge & Spa, 103 Coast Highway 1, 94923; (707) 875–3525 or (800) 368–2468. At the south end of Bodega Bay. King and queen beds in 84 well-appointed rooms and 6 luxurious suites. All rooms have cable TV with on-command movie systems, private balconies or terraces with views, fireplaces, wet bars, stocked refrigerators, and large tile baths. Each suite is 565 square feet and features a comfortably furnished living area with fireplace, king bed with down comforter, two televisions, four telephones, entertainment center, CD stereo, wet bar, refrigerator, whirlpool tub for two, vaulted ceilings, custom lighting and chandeliers, private view terrace, and more. Beach and bay views, ocean-view pool, full-service spa, nightly complimentary wine hour, and guest library. Restaurant on premises. Specials and package deals available. Expensive to very expensive.

The Inn at the Tides, 800 Coast Highway, P.O. Box 640, Bodega Bay 94923; (707) 875–2751. On Highway 1, overlooking the harbor. Twin, queen, and king beds in 86 spacious rooms with remote-control cable TV, refrigerators, and coffeemakers. Robes and daily newspapers provided. Complimentary continental breakfast. Heated indoor/outdoor pool, whirlpool, sauna, fireplaces, and bay view. Lounge on premises. Tides Restaurant serves breakfast, lunch, and dinner. Gourmet dining at the Bay View Room. Package plans available. Expensive.

Jenner Inn and Cottages, Box 69, Jenner 95450; (707) 865–2377 or (800) 732–2377. On Highway 1, 11 miles north of Bodega Bay. Double, queen, and king beds in 13 guest rooms, 3 suites, and 4 cottages with private baths. Kitchens available. River and ocean views, private decks, hot tubs, and private entrances. Furnished with wicker and antiques. No phones or TV. Restaurant on premises.

Highway 1, between Bodega Bay and Point Arena

Wholesome extended continental breakfast. Also, 5 rental cottages available. Expensive.

Point Reyes Seashore Lodge, 10021 Coast Highway 1, P.O. Box 39, Olema 94950; (415) 663–9000. At Olema, about 33 miles south of Bodega Bay. Has 21 rooms, some with fireplaces, most with whirlpool tubs, all with private baths. Three suites also have wet bars, refrigerators, and bedroom lofts with European featherbeds. Continental breakfast. Moderate to expensive.

CAMPGROUNDS AND RV PARKS

Bodega Dunes Campground, Sonoma Coast State Beach, Bodega Bay 94923; (707) 875–3483 or (800) 444–7275. Off Highway 1, about ½-mile north of Bodega Bay. Has 99 developed campsites with tables and fire pits. Showers, tank dump, dunes and beach access, and a 5-mile trail system for hikers and equestrians. More than 10 miles of beach in this 5,000-acre park. Moderate.

Doran County Park, Doran Beach Road, P.O. Box 372, Bodega Bay 94923; (707) 875–3540. West of Highway 1 at the south end of town. Has 138 campsites with tables and fire pits, but no hookups. Tank dump, fishing pier, fish-cleaning facilities, boat ramp, and access to beach and dunes. Moderate.

Manchester Beach KOA Kampground, P.O. Box 266, Manchester 95459; (707) 882–2375. Five miles north of Point Arena, 1 mile north of Manchester, west of Highway 1, via Kinney Road. Has 75 RV and tent sites, full hookups, cable TV, Kamping Kabins, showers, laundry, heated pool, hot tub, store, and campground. Beach access. Expensive.

Salt Point State Park, 25050 Coast Highway 1, Jenner 95450; (707) 847–3221 or (800) 444–7275. Off Highway 1, 20 miles north of Jenner. Has 70 campsites located near the shore with tables, fire pits, and water nearby; on east side of the highway are tables, stoves, and water; but no showers. There are also walk-in sites and hiker/biker sites. Moderate.

Wright's Beach Campground, Sonoma Coast State Beach, Bodega Bay 94923; (707) 875–3483 or (800) 444–7275. Off Highway 1, about 6 miles north of Bodega Bay. Has 30 developed sites, with tables and fire pits, located along the edge of the beach. Ocean view, beach access. Reservations suggested. Moderate.

FOOD

Bay View Room, 800 Coast Highway, P.O. Box 640, Bodega Bay 94923; (707) 875–2751 or (800) 541–7788. At The Inn at the Tides, south end of town. Dinner Wednesday through Sunday. Five-course dinners include such appetizers as crab cakes and pork ribs; choice of chowder, soup, or salad; pasta; such entrees as filet mignon, veal steak, and salmon *en croute;* and sumptuous desserts—Grand Marnier soufflé, double-chocolate almond tart, and poached pear with caramel sauce. Dinner prix fixe or a la carte. Cocktails. Large wine list. Expensive.

The Duck Club Restaurant, 103 Coast Highway 1, 94923; (707) 875–3525. At the Bodega Bay Lodge & Spa, south end of town. Daily breakfast, lunch, and dinner. Breakfast offerings include the traditional egg dishes, omelets, eggs Benedict, Belgian waffles, blueberry buttermilk pancakes, and French toast. For smaller appetites, fresh fruits, cereals, bagels, croissants, and muffins. For lunch or dinner, start with the chef's seafood sampler, duck confit spring rolls, Dungeness crab cakes, or polenta torta. Try the soup of the day or creamy clam chowder. Caesar salads, spinach salad and warm goat cheese, and mixed greens round out the salad offerings. Order a pizza or a burger with fries. The crisp-roasted duck with orange sauce is served with wild rice pilaf and vegetable medley. The marinated pork tenderloin comes with apple-sherry sauce, gnocchi, butternut squash puree, and braised greens with roasted shallots.

Other choices include filet mignon, sea bass with wild mushrooms, seafood pasta, vegetarian plate, daily lamb special, and fresh seafood catch of the day. Desserts include crème brûlée, warm chocolate cake with vanilla ice cream, and Key lime pie. Full bar. Moderate.

MUSEUM

Point Arena Lighthouse & Museum, Point Arena Lighthouse Keepers, 45500 Lighthouse Road, P.O. Box 11, Point Arena 95468; (707) 882-2777. Located 2⅘ miles west of Highway 1, on Point Arena headland. Daily, 11:00 A.M. to 4:30 P.M., except summer weekends and holidays, 10:00 A.M. to 3:30 P.M. Point Arena Lighthouse is open to the public year-round, with guided tours available. Housed in the adjacent fog-signal house, the museum contains photographs and maritime artifacts. The great earthquake of 1906 that destroyed much of San Francisco and the town of Point Arena also toppled the original brick lighthouse that stood here. The present structure was built of steel-reinforced concrete by the Concrete Chimney Company of San Francisco, which accounts for its resemblance to a smokestack.

BEACHES, PARKS, TRAILS, AND WAYSIDES

About 33 miles south of Bodega Bay, at Olema, take Bear Valley Road west to reach the Point Reyes National Seashore, a great natural area with abundant wildlife, a variety of landforms, and both saltwater and freshwater areas, as well as estuarine habitat.

More than 360 species of birds have been recorded here. Sea lions frequent the offshore rocks near Point Reyes, and harbor seals haul out on the beaches. The point is also a good place to watch migrating gray whales. Near Tomales Point, you'll find elk, and anywhere in the area you might encounter the native black-tailed deer or fallow deer, transplanted years ago from the Mediterranean, easily distinguished by their splayed antlers. Some fallow deer are dusky brown, others white as mountain goats.

The seaward beaches are fine for hiking, but stay out of the water there, because the surf is treacherous and the undertow dangerous. Several beaches east of the point are safe for swimming. Be sure to check tide tables before venturing onto any of the beaches, to avoid being stranded—or worse.

Visitor centers are on Bear Valley Road, on Drake's Bay, and at the Point Reyes Lighthouse. There you'll find maps, guides, and books to help you enjoy your visit.

North from Olema and Point Reyes Station, Highway 1 parallels mile-wide Tomales Bay for much of its 13-mile length. This shallow bay is a drowned rift valley that lies along the San Andreas Fault. Its great diversity of bottom sediments, sand, and gravel encourages the growth of hundreds of species of invertebrates and shellfish, which in turn attract shorebirds, waterfowl, and fish.

At the northern end of Bodega Bay, Bodega Head is a popular spot for whale watching and for panoramic views of the Pacific. To reach it, take Bay Flat Road west off Highway 1, then Westside Road to road's end.

From Bodega Head north, Sonoma Coast State Beach stretches past Jenner to Russian Gulch. This 16-mile expanse of sand and gravel beaches, rocky bluffs, tidepools, and trails is accessible to hikers, beach-combers, picnickers, and others at more than a dozen points along Highway 1.

This area attracts more than 300 species of birds, among them several endangered species, such as peregrine falcon, California brown pelican, and snowy plover. The marshes near the mouth of Salmon Creek, 2½ miles north of Bodega Bay, are particularly good for observing migrating and wintering waterfowl, including the magnificent tundra swan, which is normally found farther inland. The shallow Russian River estuary also attracts a great number of shorebirds and waterfowl.

Fort Ross State Historic Park, 11 miles north of Jenner, is where early nineteenth-century Russian fur traders erected fortifications and dwellings—and nearly exterminated every sea otter on the north coast. Only one of the original buildings remains standing, but replica structures within a stockade provide an idea of what life was like here in the 1830s.

Seven miles of shoreline at the 4,000-acre Salt Point State Park include sheltered coves beneath sandstone cliffs where there are many tidepools to explore. Hiking and horseback trails along the bluffs lead to some excellent vantage points for observing the abundant bird life and migrating gray whales.

Adjacent Kruse Rhododendron State Reserve comprises 317 acres of second-growth forest with 5 miles of hiking trails through stands of redwood, Douglas fir, and, of course, rhododendrons.

On the east side of Highway 1, 3½ miles south of Gualala, is an interesting but different kind of wayside—a small, nondenominational chapel that is a pleasant wonder of art and architecture. Built in 1985 mainly of redwood, the unusual structure has teak doors, a cedar roof with copper crown, and walls made of local stone. It's a good place to take five and admire the work of local artisans.

In the vicinity of the Gualala River, which parallels Highway 1 near the ever-growing community of Gualala, bald eagles spend the winter months. Egrets, herons, loons, ospreys, and other shorebirds, seabirds, and waterfowl also frequent the area, as do such mammals as raccoons and river otters.

The Garcia River estuary, adjacent to the Point Arena headland, attracts a variety of migratory shorebirds and waterfowl, including both diver ducks and puddle ducks, as well as tundra swans.

A mile north of Manchester, take Kinney Road west of Highway 1 to reach Manchester State Beach. Here you'll find access to a fine beach and nearby dunes. The beach extends south almost to the Garcia River and north to Alder Creek.

WATER SPORTS AND ACTIVITIES

Surf and rock anglers find plenty of places to fish here, with surfperch, greenling, rockfish, and flounder the main quarry. The estuaries of rivers and large creeks also offer fishing for salmon and steelhead trout.

Shallow Tomales Bay offers good fishing for surfperch, seaperch, flounder, and sanddab. This is also a popular place with crabbers. The mudflats give up gaper, hard-shell, and littleneck clams.

Bodega Bay is another favorite fishing area, with the catch consisting mainly of rockfish, greenling, and surfperch. Crabbers harvest both Dungeness and rock crabs, and diggers take gaper and hard-shell clams on the mudflats. Offshore, fishing is for salmon, bottom fish, and albacore.

North of Bodega Bay to the Point Arena area, the Russian, Gualala, Garcia, and Navarro Rivers support sizable runs of coho salmon and steelhead trout in the fall and winter. The lower reaches of these rivers also offer fishing for a number of saltwater species.

The Boat House, 1445 Highway 1, Bodega Bay 94923; (707) 875–3495. At the harbor. Open-party and charter trips for salmon and rockfish. Bait included. Rod rental, tackle, and licenses available. Whale-watching cruises January through April.

GOLF

Bodega Harbour Golf Links, 21301 Heron Drive, P.O. Box 368, 94923; (707) 875–3538. South of town and just off Highway 1, via South Harbor Way. An eighteen-hole, par-seventy, 6,220-

yard, Scottish-style course with pro shop, clubhouse, driving range, practice greens, and club and cart rental.

TRAVEL INFORMATION

Bodega Bay Chamber of Commerce, 850 Highway 1, Bodega Bay 94923; (707) 875–3422; www.bodegabay.com

Point Reyes National Seashore, Point Reyes 94956; (415) 663–1092; www.nps.gov/pore

EVENTS

February	Crab Cioppino Feed, Bodega Bay, (707) 875–3616
April	Risotto and Sausage Dinner, Bodega Bay, (707) 875–3866
	Bodega Bay Allied Arts Show and Sale, (707) 875–3866
	Bodega Bay Fisherman's Festival and Blessing of the Fleet, (707) 875–3866
	Fish Fest Kite Fly, (707) 875–3777
May	Memorial Weekend Barbecue and Disco, Jenner, (707) 875–3866
	Memorial Day Kite Fly, Salmon Creek Beach, (707) 875–3866
July	Fireworks on the Bay, Bodega Bay, (707) 875–3422
	Bash on the Bay, Bodega Bay, (707) 875–3866
August	Bodega Bay Big Event, (707) 875–3866
	Seafood, Art, and Wine Festival, Bodega Bay, (707) 875–3866
September	Bodega Bay Allied Arts Show, (707) 875–3866
	Jenner Whale of a Gala, (707) 875–3866
	Sailboat Regatta and Shark Feed, Bodega Bay, (707) 875–3866
November	Taste of Bodega, Crab Cioppino, (707) 875–3866
	Bodega Christmas Craft Fair, (707) 875–3866

☆ MENDOCINO

Population: 1,100

Location: *On California Highway 1, 10 miles south of Fort Bragg, 2 miles north of Little River, 5 miles north of Albion, 7 miles north of the Route 128 junction, and about 150 miles north of San Francisco.*

Rocky coastal bluffs rise 50 feet above the surf to a marine terrace where the nineteenth-century buildings of Mendocino stand amidst a scattering of pine and cypress trees. Even to the casual observer, the quaint seaside village is at once reminiscent of another era, another place, from the Eastlake Victorians surrounded by picket fences to the sharply spired steeple of the old Presbyterian church, now a State Historical Landmark.

If the place looks more down east than out west, rest assured others have made the same observation. In fact, millions who have never been to the northern coast of California know the town as Cabot Cove, Maine, the fictional hometown of Jessica Fletcher, the supersleuth played by Angela Lansbury on the television series *Murder She Wrote*. Jessica's lovely Victorian home turns out to be one of Mendocino's many fine bed-and-breakfast inns.

Mendocino, founded in the early 1850s, was first known as Meiggsville, after Harry Meiggs, a San Francisco entrepreneur who built the first redwood mill here. Early settlers came from the eastern United States by ship around Cape Horn and built houses and commercial buildings similar to those they had left behind. When the timber industry declined in the 1930s and local mills shut down, Mendocino languished. In the 1950s it began attracting the attention of artists who moved here and transformed the old lumber town into an artists' colony. Today, evidence of the residents' creativity and craftsmanship is everywhere in this town.

Two miles south of Mendocino is the town of Little River, site of the Little River Inn; the inn and, basically, the town were created by shipbuilder and lumberman Silas Coombs. Caspar is a tiny village located west of Highway 1 and 3 miles north of Mendocino. Like Mendocino, many of the early settlers in Caspar and Little River came from New England, and the architecture of the inn and of several of the older homes in Caspar is similar in style to that found in Mendocino. Caspar and Little River are great sites for diving, hiking, feeling the beauty and serenity of the Mendocino coast, and experiencing a spectacular sunset over the ocean.

Mendocino, along with neighboring Caspar and Little River, has more than its share of quaint and comfortable accommodations, fine restaurants, shops, and galleries. It's a pleasure to poke around in the compact downtown area, browsing through a gallery one moment, breathing crisp salt air the next, then checking out a neighboring shop, eatery, or watering hole.

LODGING

Agate Cove Inn, 11201 North Lansing Street, P.O. Box 1150, 95460; (707) 937–0551 or (800) 527–3111; www.agatecove.com. West of Highway 1 via Lansing Street exit, on the north end of town. An 1860's farmhouse and cottages with a total of 10 rooms, some with fireplaces, some with private decks. Private baths, queen and king beds, and comforters. Ocean view. Full country breakfast served. Moderate to very expensive.

Blair House Inn, 45110 Little Lake Street, P.O. Box 1608, 95460; (707) 937–1800 or (800) 699–9296. West of Highway 1 via Little Lake Road. A Victorian bed-and-breakfast inn built in 1888, offering 4 guest rooms. Private and shared baths. Rooms with fireplaces and ocean views available. Exterior familiar to millions of TV viewers as the home of Jessica Fletcher on *Murder She Wrote*. Moderate to expensive.

Little River Inn, 7750 North Highway 1, Drawer B, Little River 95456; (707) 937–5942 or (800) 466–5683. On Highway 1, 2 miles south of Mendocino. Built in 1853. Has 55 lodge rooms and cottages, some with kitchens, some with fireplaces. Breakfast and dinner served daily in the dining room, where seafood and steaks are house specialties. Full bar and renowned weekend brunch. Regulation nine-hole golf course and lighted tennis courts on premises. Moderate to expensive.

Village of Mendocino

MacCallum House Inn, 45020 Albion Street, P.O. Box 206, 95460; (707) 937–0289 or (800) 609–0492. West of Highway 1, downtown, between Lansing and Kasten. King and queen beds in 19 rooms or suites, all with private baths, in a stunning old Victorian built in 1882. Unique structures, including a barn, gazebo, and water tower. Claw foot tubs for two. Restaurant and Grey Whale Bar on premises. Continental breakfast. Moderate to expensive.

Mendocino Hotel & Garden Suites, 45080 Main Street, P.O. Box 587, 95460; (707) 937–0511 or (800) 548–0513. West of Highway 1, downtown. Twin, double, queen, and king beds in 50 rooms and suites with private and shared baths, some with fireplaces, some with balconies. Built in 1878 and decorated with Victorian antiques. Room service. Dining rooms and lounges on premises. Moderate to expensive.

Mendo Coast Reservations, 1000 Main Street, Mendocino 95460; (707) 937–1000. Arranges for rental of private homes in and around Mendocino. Moderate to expensive.

CAMPGROUNDS AND RV PARKS

Caspar Beach RV Campground, 14441 Point Cabrillo Drive, P.O. Box 189, 95460; (707) 964–3306. West of Highway 1, 2 miles north of Mendocino, via exit for Russian Gulch State Park. Has 114 sites with tables and stoves. Full and partial hookups and cable TV available. Showers, laundry, tank dump, fish-cleaning facilities, horseshoe pits, video arcade, and convenience store. Expensive.

Russian Gulch State Park, Mendocino District, P.O. Box 440, 95460; (707) 937–4296 or (800) 444–7275. Two miles north of Mendocino, west side of Highway 1. Has 30 developed sites with tables, fire pits, and food lockers for tents, trailers, and motor homes. Also a horse camp with 4 tent sites. Hiking and biking trails, nature trails, and showers. Moderate.

Schooner's Landing RV Park & Marina, P.O. Box 218, Albion 95410; (707) 937–5707. Five miles south of Mendocino, 2 miles north of Route 128, east off Highway 1, near the mouth of the Albion River. A fishing camp with 27 full-hookup sites, 4 sites with water and electricity, 3 tent sites. Boat launch, boat docks, trailer storage, fish-cleaning facilities, showers, and tank dump. Moderate.

Van Damme State Park, Mendocino District, P.O. Box 440, 95460; (707) 937–5804 or (800) 444–7275. On Highway 1 at Little River, 3 miles south of Mendocino. Has 74 developed and 10 hike-in campsites with tables and fire pits and 24 en-route sites at the beach parking lot. Showers, hiking and nature trails, beach, and beautiful wooded setting. Moderate.

FOOD

Bay View Cafe, 45040 Main Street, Mendocino 95460; (707) 937–4197. West of Highway 1. Breakfast, lunch, and dinner daily. Breakfast includes *huevos* California, various omelets, eggs Benedict or Florentine, blintzes, and crepes. Great seafood salads, burgers, and deli-style sandwiches. Seafood hors d'oeuvres, seafood crepes with Mornay sauce, charbroiled chinook salmon steaks, roast duckling, pasta dishes, and steaks. Excellent view. Full bar. Moderate.

Hill House Inn, 10701 Palatte Drive, P.O. Box 625, Mendocino 95460; (707) 937–0554. West of Highway 1 via Little Lake Road exit, then right 1 block on Lansing. Dinner daily. Mostly Italian cuisine. Appetizers include escargot, coquille St. Jacques, and veal pâté. Clam chowder, shrimp bisque, and soup of the day. Entrees include chicken, quail, filet mignon with artichoke hearts, and veal dishes. Full bar. Appetizers served in the lounge, downstairs. Moderate to expensive.

The Ledford House, 3000 North Highway 1, Albion 95469; (707) 937–0282. Just south of Mendocino. Dinner daily. Delicious appetizers include Pacific oysters on the half-shell, black mussels baked with Italian sausage, and grilled asparagus tart. Among the entrees are New York steak, rack of lamb, pepper-encrusted ahi tuna, braised halibut, and roasted half duckling with strawberry-rhubarb sauce. Moderate.

Little River Restaurant, 7901 North Highway 1, Little River 95456; (707) 937–5942. Dinner daily. Start with such appetizers as Brie baked in phyllo pastry, clams steamed in wine with garlic and herbs, baked escargot with whipped garlic butter, or sautéed prawns with beurre blanc sauce. Then choose from such entrees as New York steak with crushed peppercorns and cabernet sauce, filet mignon with Marsala-butter sauce, roasted pork tenderloin with ginger-scallion sauce, roasted quail with hazelnut-port sauce, or roasted duck with apricot-vermouth sauce. Seafood selections include sautéed petrale sole, Pacific red snapper (rockfish), and scampi. All dinners include soup, salad, vegetables, potato, and freshly baked bread. Beer and wine. Moderate to expensive.

MacCallum House Restaurant, 45020 Albion Street, P.O. Box 500, 95460; (707) 937–5763. West of Highway 1, downtown, between Lansing and Kasten Streets. Dinner daily. From the cafe menu choose a double burger with caramelized onions and white cheddar on a poppyseed bun, grilled day-boat scallop and asparagus salad, potato gnocchi with wild mushroom-sherry sauce, or the nightly hand-rolled pasta special. From the dinner menu try such appetizers as steamed mussels in coconut-ginger broth with lemongrass or oysters on the half-shell in champagne-shiitake mushroom glaze with black pepper brioche and alder-smoked salmon roe. Main courses include roast thyme-scented chicken, roast duck leg confit, grilled loin lamb chops, grilled steak, Chilean sea bass, and north coast rockfish—all served with tantalizing accompaniments. Desserts include a tangerine soufflé, chocolate brownie mousse, and an assortment of house-made ice creams. Full bar. Moderate to expensive.

Mendocino Cookie Company, 10450 Lansing Street, P.O. Box 630, Mendocino 95460; (707) 937–4843. West of Highway 1. Weekdays and Saturday, 7:30 A.M. to 7:00 P.M.; Sunday, 10:30 A.M. to 4:00 P.M. A great assortment of delicious cookies, such as old-fashioned oatmeal-raisin, peanut butter, and white-chocolate chip. Espresso, cappuccino, and other coffees. Gourmet ice cream. Inexpensive to moderate.

SHOPPING AND BROWSING

Highlight Gallery, 45052 Main Street, P.O. Box 1515, Mendocino 95460; (707) 937–3132. West of Highway 1, between Lansing and Kasten. Daily, 10:00 A.M. to 5:00 P.M. One of the best galleries on the north coast with many fine wooden items and exquisite furniture—all handcrafted. An excellent collection of paintings, ceramics, sculpture, jewelry, scrimshaw, and gift items. A large and pleasing gallery.

The Irish Shop, 45050 Main Street, P.O. Box 1636, Mendocino 95460; (707) 937–3133. West of Highway 1, between Kasten and Lansing. Sunday through Friday, 9:30 A.M. to 5:30 P.M.; Saturday, 9:30 A.M. to 6:00 P.M. Woolen clothing, sweaters, ties, coats, hats, scarves, and water-repellent Icelandic clothing. Jewelry, china, jellies, mustards, and more.

Out of This World, 100 Main Street, Mendocino 95460; (707) 937–3335 or (800) 485–6884. Albion at Lansing Street. Daily, 10:00 A.M. to 6:00 P.M. An unusual and interesting shop selling telescopes, microscopes, binoculars, celestial and terrestrial maps, celestial mobiles, and many other items related to astronomy and science fiction.

Papa Birds, 45040 Albion Street, P.O. Box 2380, Mendocino 95460; (707) 937–2730. West of Highway 1. Daily, 10:00 A.M. to 5:00 P.M. An interesting specialty shop for anyone who likes and wants to care for wild birds. Handmade birdhouses and feeders, books, and gift items.

William Zimmer Gallery, 45101 Ukiah Street, Mendocino 95460; (707) 937–5121. At Kasten and Ukiah Streets. Wonderful collection of hand-blown, playful and unique martini glasses, handcrafted wood furniture and watercolors and oil paintings by the finest local and California artists. Open 10:30 A.M. to 5:00 P.M.

BEACHES, PARKS, TRAILS, AND WAYSIDES

Van Damme State Park has a small sandy beach at the mouth of the Little River. Nature trails in the park lead through pygmy forests of dwarf cypress no more than 1 foot tall and pines of 6 feet or so that are more than fifty years old. Despite the nearly perfect tree-growing climate here, poor soils have retarded the growth of these trees.

In Mendocino, take Lansing Street north to Heeser Drive, turn left, and drive to Mendocino Headlands State Park, where you can hike or bike along bluff-top trails overlooking the spectacular seascape.

North of Mendocino, 1½ miles beyond Caspar, is Jughandle State Reserve. Here you'll find about 5 miles of nature trails, a beach, and a series of terraces called an "ecological staircase." The terraces were formed during the Pleistocene period as sea levels fluctuated.

GOLF AND TENNIS

Little River Inn Golf & Tennis Club, 7751 North Highway 1, Drawer B, Little River 95456; (707) 937–5667. Nine-hole golf course and lighted tennis courts. Pro shop, resident pro, driving range, putting green, motel, and restaurant.

OTHER ATTRACTIONS

Mendocino Theater Company, Helen Schoeni Theatre, 45200 Little Lake Road, P.O. Box 800, Mendocino 95460; (707) 937–4477. Performances Thursday through Sunday, 8:00 P.M. sharp. A variety of stage productions offered throughout the year.

TRAVEL INFORMATION

Fort Bragg–Mendocino Coast Chamber of Commerce, 332 North Main Street, P.O. Box 1141, Fort Bragg 95437; (707) 961–6300; www.mendocino.org

EVENTS

January	Crab & Wine Days Festival, (707) 462–7417 or (800) 726–2780
March	Mendocino Whale Festival, (707) 961–6300
May	Historic House & Building Tour, Mendocino, (707) 937–5791
	Arts & Crafts Market, Little River, (707) 937–5791
June	Mendocino Coast Garden Tour, Mendocino, (707) 937–5818 or (800) 653–3328
	Mendocino Village Walking Tour, (707) 937–5818 or (800) 653–3328
July	July Fourth Parade, Mendocino, (800) 726–2780
	Mendocino Music Festival, (707) 937–2044
	Summer Art Fair, Mendocino, (707) 937–5818
October	Halloween Party, Mendocino, (707) 961–6300
November	Mendocino Coast Mushroom Festival, (707) 462–7417
December	Candlelight Inn Tours, Mendocino, (800) 726–2780

FORT BRAGG

Population: 6,200

Location: *On California Highway 1, 42 miles southwest of Leggett, 135 miles south of Eureka, 44 miles north of Point Arena, and 180 miles north of San Francisco.*

A t the business end of the Mendocino Coast stands Fort Bragg, the largest north coast city between San Francisco and Eureka. The area was settled in the mid-nineteenth century, shortly after the Mendocino Indian Reservation was created in 1856. The following year, the U.S. Army established a post near the reservation and named it after Colonel Braxton Bragg, who later rose to the rank of general in the Confederate army. The fort was abandoned in 1864, and the reservation followed suit in 1867.

After the Indians were moved to various California reservations, the area was opened to settlement and incorporated as a city in 1889. The building of the Union Lumber Company in the 1880s and the subsequent establishment of a steamship company and railroad did much to secure Fort Bragg's position as the economic hub of the Mendocino Coast, a role it retains today.

The Noyo Harbor, near the mouth of the Noyo River, is home port to the largest commercial-fishing fleet between Eureka and San Francisco. The fleet harvests rockfish (marketed as snapper or rockcod), sablefish (marketed as black cod), salmon, sole, shrimp, Dungeness crab, and sea urchin.

The harbor is a busy, bustling place with several good seafood restaurants and fish markets. A parking area near the jetty provides a vantage for watching boat traffic and photographing the activities. One

171

of the best places to watch and photograph the harbor is from one of the balconies at the Harbor Lite Lodge, at the north end of the bridge.

LODGING

Grey Whale Inn, 615 North Main Street, 95437; (707) 964–0640 or (800) 382–7244. On Highway 1, downtown. Twin, double, queen, and king beds in 14 rooms with private baths, some with ocean views. A beautiful old inn near shops and restaurants. Recreation room with TV, VCR, and billiards. Fireside Rendezvous Room with many books and magazines. Buffet-style breakfast with homemade baked goods. Moderate to expensive.

Harbor Lite Lodge, 120 North Harbor Drive, 95437; (707) 964–0221 or (800) 643–2700. Just east of Highway 1, overlooking the harbor. Satellite TV in 79 rooms with queen and king beds. Some ocean-view rooms with private balconies that overlook the harbor. Watch the fishing fleet come and go. From November through March, watch migrating gray whales. Moderate.

Howard Creek Ranch Bed & Breakfast Inn, 40501 North Highway 1, P.O. Box 121, Westport 95488; (707) 964–6725. Three miles north of Westport on Highway 1, north of Fort Bragg. Fourteen rooms, suites, and cabins, some with kitchens, some with fireplaces, some with ocean view, and most with private baths, on a ranch settled in 1867. Ranch house was built in 1871. Furnished with antiques and collectibles. Wood-heated hot tub, sauna, and pool. Massage available by appointment. Cottages available. Moderate to expensive.

The Surrey Inn, 888 South Main Street, 95437; (707) 964–4003. On Highway 1, just north of the harbor. Cable TV in 53 rooms with queen beds. Some rooms have ocean view. Restaurant on premises serves breakfast, lunch, and dinner. Inexpensive to moderate.

CAMPGROUNDS AND RV PARKS

MacKerricher State Park, Mendocino District, P.O. Box 440, Mendocino 95460; (707) 964–9112 or (800) 444–7275. On Highway 1, 3 miles north of Fort Bragg. Has 150 developed sites and 11 walk-in sites with tables, fire rings, and food lockers. Showers, tank dump, beach, hiking trails, and a freshwater lake with a trail around it for bird-watching and fishing. Moderate.

Pomo Campground, 17999 Tregoning Lane, 95437; (707) 964–3373. On Highway 1, 1½ miles south of Route 20 junction. Has

110 campsites with tables, fire rings, full hookups, and cable TV. Showers, laundry, tank dump, fish-cleaning station, horseshoe pits, and convenience store. Propane and firewood available. Moderate.

Wages Creek Beach Campground, 37700 North Highway 1, Westport 95488; (707) 964–2964. On Highway 1, ½-mile north of Westport. Has 175 campsites, but no hookups. Showers, tank dump, and beach access. Warm, potable water; dogs allowed, and you can camp by the creek or on the beach. Moderate.

Woodside RV Park & Campground, 17900 North Highway 1, 95437; (707) 964–3684. Two miles south of Fort Bragg on Highway 1. A nine-acre wooded park with 104 campsites, full hookups, partial hookups, cable TV, showers, tank dump, horseshoe pits, fish-cleaning table, beach access, and minimarket. Moderate.

FOOD

Egghead's Restaurant, 326 North Main Street, 95437; (707) 964–5005. On Highway 1, downtown. Breakfast and lunch daily. In addition to pancakes, French toast, waffles, and other breakfast favorites, a selection of more than forty omelets with such fillings as cream cheese, Jack cheese, cheddar, sour cream, bell pepper, green chilis, onions, black olives, sprouts, spinach, mushrooms, avocado, zucchini, Polish sausage, ham, bacon, ground beef, and crab in a variety of combinations. Also deli-style sandwiches and half-pound burgers. Moderate.

North Coast Brewing Company, 444 North Main Street, 95437; (707) 964–3400. On Highway 1, downtown. Lunch and dinner daily. Large salads, nachos, deli-style sandwiches, burgers, grilled sausages, chili, Cajun black beans and dirty rice, and fish-and-chips. Ten varieties of beer are brewed here, among which are Scrimshaw (pale pilsner style), Red Seal Ale (copper-red pale ale), and Old No. 38 (a dry, full-bodied stout). Moderate.

North Coast Sports Cafe, 118 East Redwood Avenue, 95437; (707) 964–1517. Downtown, just east of Main Street (Highway 1). Lunch and dinner daily; Sunday brunch. Menu includes salad, beef, ham, chicken, and fresh local seafood. Homemade soups. Freshly baked rolls and muffins. Beer and wine. Moderate.

The Restaurant, 418 North Main Street, 95437; (707) 964–9800. On Highway 1, downtown. Lunch Thursday and Friday; dinner Thursday through Tuesday; Sunday brunch. Lunch includes cobb salad, wilted-spinach salad, luncheon salads, soups, burgers, and deli-style sandwiches. Among dinner appetizers are cornmeal-fried oysters, warm smoked duck sausage salad, and spring rolls. Dinner features beef stir-fry, roast rack of lamb, roast quail, poached halibut, calamari, and sautéed scallops. Beer and wine. Moderate.

SHOPPING AND BROWSING

For the Shell of It Et Cetera, 344 North Main Street, 95437; (707) 961–0461. On Highway 1, downtown. Daily, 9:00 A.M. to 6:00 P.M. Not just a shell shop, but much more. Jewelry, baskets, ceramics, folk art, marine art, collectibles, Christmas ornaments, gift items, and, of course, lots of shells.

Tangents, 368 North Main Street, 95437; (707) 964–3884. At the corner of Laurel. Open daily from 10:00 A.M. to 5:30 P.M. This store has a unique collection of original art and cards, ethnic crafts, clothing, furniture, and jewelry from all over the world, as well as creations of local artists and writers.

MUSEUM

Guest House Museum, 343 North Main Street, 95437; (707) 961–2840. On Highway 1, downtown. Wednesday through Sunday, 10:00 A.M. to 4:00 P.M. A three-story Victorian structure built of redwood in 1892 as the residence of T. L. Johnson, whose brother C. R. Johnson founded the Union Lumber Company. In 1912, the building became a guest house for lodging customers and others associated with the lumber company. Inside are photos of and artifacts from early Fort Bragg and the Mendocino Coast logging days. Outside are steam donkeys, locomotives, and other vintage logging equipment.

BEACHES, PARKS, TRAILS, AND WAYSIDES

Two miles south of Fort Bragg, on the west side of the highway, you'll find Mendocino Coast Botanical Gardens, a 47-acre park with thousands of native and introduced plants, including trees and shrubs, roses, camellias, succulents, ivies, heathers, and rhododendrons. Trails lead past dwarf and hybrid species as well.

MacKerricher State Park, 3 miles north of Fort Bragg, is a 1,600-acre park containing dunes, wetlands, and 10 miles of coastline. Horse and hiking trails lead to a great variety of flora and fauna for study and photography.

Highway 1 bridge over Noyo River, Fort Bragg

WATER SPORTS AND ACTIVITIES

Noyo River estuary is popular with anglers who take surfperch, starry flounder, and various bottom species, as well as salmon and steelhead.

At MacKerricher State Park, north of Fort Bragg, Lake Cleone is regularly stocked with rainbow trout. Surf anglers work the rocky shore near Laguna Beach for cabezon, lingcod, and rockfish. This is also both a good spot for dipping smelt and an access area for abalone divers.

Lady Irma II, 780 North Harbor Drive, P.O. Box 103, 95437; (707) 964–3854. At Noyo Harbor. Charter fishing and party-boat trips for salmon and rock cod. Two five-hour trips daily, from 6:30 A.M. to noon and from 1:00 to 6:00 P.M. Two-hour whale-watching trips from December through April.

Noyo Fishing Center, 32450 North Harbor Drive, 95437; (707) 964–7609. At Noyo Harbor. A well-stocked bait and tackle shop offering a complete line of fishing tackle and bait, as well as one-day licenses and tags. Also books charter and party-boat trips.

Patty **Charter Fishing,** 34250 North Harbor Drive, P.O. Box 2596, 95437; Noyo Fishing Center, (707) 964–0669; www.blue dragoncharters.qpg.com. At Noyo Harbor. A fast, 26-foot party boat that fishes five for salmon and bottom fish. Half- and full-day trips; entire boat can also be chartered for half or full day. Specializes in light-tackle fishing. Tackle furnished, or bring your own.

Sub-Surface Progression, 18600 North Highway 1, 95437; (707) 964–3793. This establishment sells and rents wet suits, tanks, and diving equipment and organizes trips for abalone diving.

TOURS AND TRIPS

California Western Railroad, P.O. Box 907, 95437; (707) 964–6371; recorded information, (415) 399–1194; www.skunk train.com. West off Main Street (Highway 1) at the foot of Laurel Avenue or Pine Street. Train trips through the redwoods in passenger cars and open-observation cars pulled by diesel or steam locomotives, or in self-powered motorcars known as "skunks," so called because they were originally powered by gas engines that emitted unpleasant fumes. Trips are between Fort Bragg and Willits at U.S. 101, and between Fort Bragg and Northspar, which is halfway to Willits. On the 40-mile trip to Willits, trains cross thirty bridges and trestles and pass through two deep-mountain tunnels. Spectacular mountain and forest scenery. One of Fort Bragg's biggest attractions and certainly *a must* for every rail buff.

OTHER ATTRACTIONS

The Fort Bragg Footlighters, Footlighters Little Theatre, 248 East Laurel Street, P.O. Box 575, 95437; (707) 964–8050. East of Main Street (Highway 1), downtown. Wednesday and Saturday, 8:00 P.M., from Memorial Day weekend through Labor Day weekend. Original comedy and melodrama in the tradition of the 1890s.

Gloriana Opera Company, 721 North Franklin Street, between Bush and Spruce, downtown; 95437; (707) 964–7469. Musical theater and opera, performed by local talents, many of whom are professional and world-renowned musicians and opera singers.

Lari Shea's Ricochet Ridge Ranch, 24201 North Highway 1, 95437; (707) 964–7669. North of town. Horseback riding on the beach or in the redwoods. Western or English tack.

TRAVEL INFORMATION

Fort Bragg–Mendocino Coast Chamber of Commerce, 332 North Main Street, P.O. Box 1141, 95437; (707) 961–6300; www. mendocino.com

January	Crab & Wine Days Festival, (707) 462–7417 or (800) 726–2780
March	Fort Bragg Whale Festival, (707) 961–6300
May	Mendocino Coast Furniture Makers Exhibition, (707) 541–0220
	Prime Time Rhododendron Tours, Fort Bragg, (707) 964–4352
	Fort Bragg Rhododendron Show, (707) 964–0994
	Mendocino Coast Kite Festival, Fort Bragg, (707) 937–0971
	Great Rubber Ducky Race, Westport, (707) 964–2872
	Heirloom Day, Fort Bragg, (707) 961–0902
	Fort Bragg Quilt Show, (707) 961–9446
June	Music! Music! Music!, Fort Bragg, (707) 964–7652
July	World's Largest Salmon Barbecue, Fort Bragg, (707) 964–2781
	Fireworks Extravaganza, Fort Bragg, (707) 961–6300
August	Kaleidoscope Street Fair, Fort Bragg, (707) 964–0807
	Shoreline Riders Rodeo, Fort Bragg, (707) 964–6941
	Art in the Gardens, Fort Bragg, (707) 964–4352
	Historic Skunk Train Mail Run, (707) 964–9535
September	Paul Bunyon Days, Fort Bragg, (707) 961–6300
	Winesong! At The Mendocino Coast Botanical Gardens, (707) 961–4688
	Portuguese Festa, Fort Bragg, (707) 964–9217
October	Halloween Train, Fort Brag, (800) 777–5865
November	Mendocino Coast Mushroom Festival, (707) 462–7417
December	Craft Show & Sale, Fort Bragg, (707) 964–0807

FORT BRAGG

GARBERVILLE

Population: 2,200

SHELTER COVE

Population: 350

Location: *Garberville is on U.S. 101, 68 miles south of Eureka, 24 miles north of Leggett, and 200 miles north of San Francisco; Shelter Cove is on the coast, about 24 miles west of Garberville.*

Rugged terrain forces highway travelers well inland in this part of northern California, but local roads and thoroughfares carry them through country that rivals the coast for scenic splendor. Magnificent redwoods are the attraction here, and from Garberville north are some of the greatest stands of these trees remaining on the planet.

Although U.S. 101 cuts through the redwoods as it heads north and becomes one of the most scenic stretches of freeway in the state, remnants of the old Coast Highway remain intact and afford the traveler a much more pleasant and intimate relationship with these magnificent trees. Known as the Avenue of the Giants, this two-lane, paved road begins at Sylvandale (via the Phillipsville exit), about 6 miles north of Garberville, and meanders northward for 33 miles, much of the way along the banks of the Eel River and the South Fork of the Eel. It stays fairly near the freeway and in fact crosses over or under it several times. A number of freeway exits lead to the avenue, so it's possible to enjoy this scenic route in sections.

Between Sylvandale to the south and Stafford at the north end of the Avenue of the Giants lie the small communities of Phillipsville, Miranda, Myers Flat, Weott, Redcrest, and Pepperwood, separated from one another by roughly 6 miles. In addition to the state parks and many groves along the avenue are small motels and lodges, camp-

178

grounds and RV parks, several restaurants, convenience stores, and gift shops.

Garberville makes an excellent headquarters for exploring the redwoods north and south. Those who require frequent doses of salt air can drive over the hump to Shelter Cove for a quick fix. A two-lane paved road leads west from Redway over the mountains to Shelter Cove, King Range National Conservation Area, and what's known as California's "Lost Coast." Although the road is narrow and curvy, often steep, and full of switchbacks through the mountains, it is a year-round road, suitable for travel trailers, motor homes, and vehicles towing boats. But it's not a route for people in a hurry. Those in cars, vans, or pickup trucks not towing anything should plan at least forty-five minutes for the one-way trip, not counting stops.

Shelter Cove is a tiny community on a grassy marine terrace overlooking the Pacific. North and south of it are steep mountains sloping sharply to the sea. Mariners have used the natural harbor here for many years. Today, it mainly attracts commercial and sport fishermen. There are overnight accommodations, an RV park, marina, and several restaurants in town and primitive camping areas in the King Range.

LODGING

Benbow Inn, 445 Lake Benbow Drive, Garberville 95542; (707) 923–2124. Just west of U.S. 101, 2 miles south of Garberville. Cable TV in 55 rooms in a beautiful inn opened in 1926 and recently restored and remodeled. Some rooms with fireplaces, some with VCRs. Elegant, with many amenities and nice touches, such as complimentary English tea and scones every afternoon, mulled wine on chilly afternoons, and hors d'oeuvres from 5:00 to 7:00 P.M. in the lounge. A basketful of mystery novels in each room, along with coffee, tea, and sherry. Nearby tennis courts, stables, golf course, and exercise trail. Dining room on premises. Expensive.

Best Western Humboldt House Inn, 701 Redwood Drive, Garberville 95442; (707) 923–2771 or (800) 528–1234. East of U.S. 101, downtown. Queen and king beds in 54 rooms with cable TV, most rooms offering private balconies or patios. Heated pool, whirlpool, and laundry facilities. Continental breakfast. Easy walk to shops and restaurants. Moderate.

Dean Creek Resort Motel, 4112 Redwood Drive, P.O. Box 157, Redway 95560; (877) 923–2555. East of U.S. 101, 3 miles north of Garberville. Queen beds in 9 rooms and suites with cable TV. Kitchen units available. Whirlpool. Moderate.

Redcrest Resort, 26459 Avenue of the Giants, P.O. Box 235, Redcrest 95569; (707) 722–4208. On the Avenue of the Giants, between Weott and Pepperwood, north of Garberville. Double and king beds in 12 cottages with kitchens. Laundry facilities on premises. Inexpensive to moderate.

Shelter Cove Beachcomber Inn, 412 Machi Road, Shelter Cove, 95589; (707) 986–7551 or (800) 718–4789. Queen and twin beds in 6 units, each with private entrance and private bath. Three have fireplace woodstoves; all have TV, coffeemakers, and either full or minikitchens. Ocean-view deck, easy beach access. Picnic tables and barbecue areas. Inexpensive to moderate.

Shelter Cove Motor Inn, 205 Wave Drive, Shelter Cove, 95589; (707) 986–7521 or (888) 570–9676. King and queen beds in 16 rooms and suites with Direct TV and VCR, microwave ovens, refrigerators, coffeemakers, and hair dryers. Private balconies with ocean view. Laundry facilities and barbecue available. Moderate.

Sherwood Forest Motel, 814 Redwood Drive, Garberville 95442; (707) 923–2721. East of U.S. 101, downtown. Queen beds, cable TV, and cable movies in 32 rooms and suites. Heated pool, hot tub, and barbecue area. Cribs and roll-aways available. Easy walk to shops and restaurants. Inexpensive to moderate.

Whispering Pines Lodge, 6582 Avenue of the Giants, P.O. Box 246, Miranda 95553; (707) 943–3182 or (800) 626–6835. On the Avenue of the Giants, north of Garberville. Queen beds in 17 rooms and suites with satellite TV. Kitchens available. Set amid three acres of redwoods. Heated pool, table tennis, horseshoes, shuffleboard, and badminton. Picnic tables and barbecue grills. Recreation room with pool table, games, books, and fireplace. Moderate.

CAMPGROUNDS AND RV PARKS

Albee Creek Campground, Humboldt Redwoods State Park, P.O. Box 100, Weott 95571; (707) 946–2409 or (800) 444–7275. Five miles west of U.S. 101 and Avenue of the Giants, on Bull Creek Flats Road. Has 39 developed campsites with tables, stoves, and food lockers. Piped water and showers. Sites available on first-come, first-served basis. Closed October to mid-May. Moderate.

Benbow Lake State Recreation Area, 1600 U.S. Highway 101, Garberville, 95442; (707) 923–3288, summer; (707) 247–3318, winter; (800) 444–7275, reservations. Has 76 developed campsites with tables and fire rings. Showers. Open spring and summer. Moderate.

Benbow Inn, Garberville

Burlington Campgrounds, Humboldt Redwoods State Park, P.O. Box 100, Weott 95571; (707) 946–2409 or (800) 444–7275. On the Avenue of the Giants, near park headquarters. Has 56 developed campsites with tables, stoves, and food lockers. Piped water, showers, laundry tubs, and tank dump. Moderate.

Dean Creek Resort RV Park, 4112 Redwood Drive, P.O. Box 157, Redway 95560; (707) 923–2555. East of U.S. 101, 3 miles north of Garberville. Has 60 campsites—some with full hookups, some with water and electricity, and 6 with no hookups. Cable TV, tables, stoves, showers, laundry, tank dump, whirlpool, and sauna. Store with ice, propane, and firewood available. Moderate.

Giant Redwoods RV & Camp, 455 Boy Scout Camp Road, P.O. Box 222, Myers Flat 95554; (707) 943–3198. On the Avenue of the Giants and the Eel River, north of Garberville. Has 82 campsites— 14 with full hookups, 43 with water and electricity, and 25 with no hookups. Drive-through sites available. Tables, showers, laundry, tank dump. Camping in the redwoods. Store on premises. Propane and ice available. Moderate.

Hidden Springs Campground, Humboldt Redwoods State Park, P.O. Box 100, Weott 95571; (707) 946–2409 or (800) 444–7275. East of U.S. 101, on the Avenue of the Giants, near Myers Flat. Has 154 developed campsites with tables, stoves, and food lockers. Piped water, showers, and laundry tubs. Closed mid-October to mid-May. Moderate.

Redcrest Resort, 26459 Avenue of the Giants, P.O. Box 235, Redcrest 95569; (707) 722–4208. On the Avenue of the Giants, between Weott and Pepperwood, north of Garberville. Has 19 campsites—9 with full hookups, 1 with water and electricity, and 19 with no hookups. Showers, laundry, and store on premises. Moderate.

Richardson Grove State Park, 1600 Highway 101, Garberville 95542; (707) 247–3318, 946–2311, or (800) 444–7275. Has 169 developed campsites with tables, fire rings, and food lockers. Showers and tank dump. Reservations accepted during spring and summer; open October through April on a first-come, first-served basis. Moderate.

Shelter Cove Campground, 492 Machi Road, Whitehorn 95589; (707) 986–7474. Across the road from the marina. Has 105 campsites—52 with full hookups, 53 with no hookups. Showers, laundry, tank dump, deli, and store with propane available. Moderate.

Trailer Life's Benbow Valley RV Resort, 7000 Benbow Drive, Garberville 95542; (707) 923–2777. Just east of U.S. 101, 2 miles south of Garberville. Has 112 full-hookup sites with cable TV. All roads and pads paved. Pull-through sites available. Grassy sites with trees, set in beautiful rolling hills. Showers, laundry, and heated pool. Recreation room and nine-hole golf course. Convenience store with ice and propane available. Moderate.

FOOD

Benbow Inn, 445 Lake Benbow Drive, Garberville 95542; (800) 355–3301. Located 2 miles south of Garberville, this Tudor-style inn serves some of the very best food in southern Humboldt County; exquisite appetizers. The food is California style with a French twist. Open daily for lunch and dinner; patio dining. Moderate to expensive.

Sicilito's Casa De Linda, 445 Conger Street, Garberville 95442; (707) 923–2814. Behind the Humboldt House Inn, downtown. Lunch and dinner daily in summer, dinner only in winter. Mexican and Italian-American food. Mexican appetizers include nachos or guacamole and chips. Such dinners as steak ranchero, Vera Cruz–style fish, enchiladas, *chiles rellenos,* burritos, tostadas, tacos, and combinations. Pizza, Italian sandwiches, and pasta with shrimp, scallops, or chicken. Beer and wine. Carryout service available, with free delivery in Garberville and Redway. Inexpensive to moderate.

The Waterwheel Restaurant & Gift Shop, 924 Redwood Drive, Garberville 95442; (707) 923–2031. East of U.S. 101, downtown. Breakfast, lunch, and dinner daily. Hearty breakfasts with large portions, served all day. Eggs with bacon, sausage, ham, steak, half-pound hamburger steak, or corned-beef hash come with biscuits, gravy, and potatoes. Soups, chowder, salads, French dip, burgers, and other sandwiches, as well as spaghetti and ravioli. Dinner entrees include sole Monterey, scampi, calamari, honey-raisin ham, chicken, steaks, and pasta dishes. Mexican food Thursday and Friday. Domestic and imported beers and wines. Inexpensive to moderate.

SHOPPING AND BROWSING

Ancient Redwood Resort, 28101 Avenue of the Giants, P.O. Box 254, Redcrest 95569; (707) 722–4396. North end of the Avenue of the Giants. Daily, 9:00 A.M. to 5:00 P.M.; extended hours in summer. Large selection of redwood carvings, toys, kitchen items, desk accessories, clocks, mirrors, furniture, slabs, table bases, wood signs, and more.

BEACHES, PARKS, TRAILS, AND WAYSIDES

Shelter Cove has several sandy beach areas, as well as rocky shoreline with tidepools. In all, more than 4 miles of beach are accessible and open to the public. The beaches provide good places for hiking and beachcombing, and the bluffs in the Shelter Cove area offer excellent vantage points for whale watching.

Nearby King Range National Conservation Area reaches as much as 6 miles inland and extends along 35 miles of coastline. It contains 47,000 acres of paved, graveled, and dirt roads, some of them impassable during wet winter months. Hiking and backpacking are popular along beaches and bluffs and on mountain trails. A guide with map is available from the Bureau of Land Management in Ukiah or Arcata. Hiking can be very difficult along the mountain trails between November and April, due to frequent floods and landslides.

Seven miles south of Garberville, on U.S. 101, lies Richardson Grove State Park, comprising more than 1,000 acres of forest and river bottoms. Hikers and nature enthusiasts enjoy miles of trails. Guided hikes and interpretive programs are conducted in the summer.

Two miles south of Garberville is Benbow Lake State Recreation Area. A dam on the South Fork of the Eel River creates a summer lake where swimming is popular. A park along the sandy riverbank near the Benbow Inn provides access and has picnic tables. There are hiking trails and summer interpretive activities, including nature hikes, canoe hikes on the lake, and paddleboat rentals.

Along the length of the Avenue of the Giants are many redwood groves with trails, picnic areas, and some phenomenal specimens of the mighty coast redwood. For much of the length of the avenue and well west of the road is the huge Humboldt Redwoods State Park. At more than 51,000 acres, it ranks third in size among California's state parks, and it continues to grow, thanks to the efforts of the Save-the-Redwoods League. Within the park proper are more than 100 miles of hiking and backpacking trails and six trail camps.

WATER SPORTS AND ACTIVITIES

A summer fishery draws a few anglers to the banks of the Eel River and its South Fork, but the water is warm and low then, with the catch consisting of small trout and rough fish. Summer river activities are mainly swimming and floating the river in inner tubes.

Fall and winter rains signal the anadromous salmon and steelhead, which move up the rivers to spawn. Both coho (silver) and chinook (king) salmon use the Eel River system and draw many anglers each year. Steelhead trout also enter the river system in the fall, and some are still present as late as March and April.

Saltwater recreation will require a trip to Shelter Cove, where surfing, diving, fishing, and crabbing are popular. Surf anglers take surfperch and several species of bottom fish. Offshore, people troll for salmon and jig for lingcod, rockfish, cabezon, and other bottom fish.

***Annika* Sport Fishing,** Shelter Cove, 95589; (707) 986–7836 or (916) 686–1507. The 28-foot *Annika* accommodates up to 4 anglers on half-day and full-day trips for salmon, halibut, lingcod, and rockfish. Bait and tackle furnished. Also offers whale-watching trips.

GOLF

Benbow Valley Golf Course, 7000 Benbow Drive, Garberville 95442; (707) 923–2777. Just east of U.S. 101, 2 miles south of Garberville, at Benbow Valley RV Resort. A nine-hole, par-thirty-five course with pro shop, cart and club rental.

Shelter Cove Golf Links, 1555 Upper Pacific Drive, Shelter Cove, 95589; (707) 986–7000. Next to the airport. A nine-hole, par-thirty-three, 2,465-yard course with great ocean views. Pro shop, clubhouse, club and cart rental. Missing Links Pub serves food and beverages.

OTHER ATTRACTIONS

The Chimney Tree, 1111 Avenue of the Giants, P.O. Box 86, Phillipsville 95559; (707) 923–2265. One mile south of Phillipsville, 8 miles north of Garberville on Avenue of the Giants. Daily, 8:00 A.M. to 8:00 P.M. In 1914, an unextinguished campfire near this redwood set fire to the great tree and burned inside it for days, hollowing out its interior. Later, a severe storm blew off the top of the tree. Not only did the mighty redwood survive, but for years it also provided shelter to hunters, whose campfire smoke rose through the tree and out the top—hence the name. At one time the tree was further hollowed out and shelves were installed when it was used as a gift shop. The amazing tree has healed itself and sprouted much new growth. When last measured, in 1978, it stood 78 feet tall, more than 14 feet in diameter, and more than 50 feet in circumference. Gift shop and restaurant on premises.

TRAVEL INFORMATION

Arcata Resource Area, Bureau of Land Management, 1125 Sixteenth Street, P.O. Box 1112, Arcata 95521; (707) 822–7648; www.shastacascade.org/blm/arcata/arcata.htm

Garberville/Redway Chamber of Commerce, 773 Redwood Drive, P.O. Box 445, Garberville 95442; (707) 923–2613 or (800) 923–2613; www.garberville.org; e-mail: info@garberville.org

Shelter Cove Information Bureau, 412 Machi Road, Shelter Cove 95489; (707) 986–7474

Redwood Empire Association, 2801 Leavenworth Street, Second Floor, San Francisco, 94133; (888) 678–8506; www.redwood empire.com; e-mail: reavisit@aol.com

Save-the-Redwoods League, 114 Sansome Street, San Francisco 94104; (415) 362–2352; www.savetheredwoods.org

Ukiah District Office, Bureau of Land Management, 555 Leslie Street, Ukiah 95482; (707) 462–3873

EVENTS

May	Antique Fair, Benbow, (707) 923–2613
	Cinco de Mayo Celebration, Garberville, (707) 923–2613
June	Summer Arts Fair and Music Festival, Benbow Lake State Recreation Area, (707) 923–3368
	Jazz on the Lake, Benbow Lake State Recreation Area, (707) 923–4599
	Garberville Rodeo, (707) 923–2119
July	Shakespeare Festival, Benbow Lake State Recreation Area, (800) 923–2613
	Reggae on the River, Benbow Lake State Recreation Area, (707) 923–1060
September	Labor Day Arts and Crafts Fair, Shelter Cove, (707) 986–7474
October	Humboldt Redwood Marathon, Humboldt Redwoods State Park, (707) 946–2311
December	Winter Arts Fair, Redway, (707) 923–3368

FERNDALE

Population: 1,500

Location: *17 miles southwest of Eureka, 5 miles southwest of U.S. 101 via Route 211.*

Take the Ferndale exit off U.S. 101, and the short drive becomes a trip in a time machine to a quaint Victorian village in the heart of a rich farming area sometime in the nineteenth century. Founded in 1852, Ferndale became the hub of a prosperous dairy-farming community, with many ornate Victorian mansions, known then as the "Butterfat Palaces."

The Victorians are still standing, either meticulously preserved or painstakingly restored, and several now function as bed-and-breakfast inns. Churches, the public library, and various business establishments also seem frozen in time. The face of Main Street has gone nearly unchanged. There are even a general store that still sells penny candy, a blacksmith shop where you can buy handmade weather vanes, and a bank that looks the way it did when a dollar was a dollar.

Something else carefully preserved is the town's sense of humor. You'll find it expressed in many ways, such as the whimsical names of some of the businesses, or the zany works and collections of Hobart Brown at Hobart Galleries, or Stan Bennett's wild and wonderful "motion sculpture."

Even the village's best-known annual event takes on a proportion of humor and level of high jinks unrivaled anywhere. What started simply with one of Hobart Brown's nutty inventions—a modified tricycle called the "pentacycle"—that was then challenged by the nutty inventions of other artists and artisans to a race down Main Street has grown considerably over the years. The World Championship Great Arcata to

187

Ferndale Cross-Country Kinetic Sculpture Race now takes three days to run and covers 38 miles of land, sand, mud, water, bog, and marsh—all in homemade, people-powered contraptions. The major networks and several national magazines have covered the event, and there's no telling what it might eventually grow into.

Ferndale is a pleasant place to visit, as much for its friendly and witty inhabitants as for its idyllic beauty. The entire village has been designated a State Historical Landmark.

LODGING

The Fern Motel, 332 Ocean Avenue, P.O. Box 121, 95536; (707) 786–5000. Queen beds in 8 rooms and suites with cable TV and refrigerators; suites also have full kitchens. Laundry facilities on premises. Easy walk to all in-town attractions. Moderate.

The Gingerbread Mansion Inn, 400 Berding Street, 95536; (707) 786–4000 or (800) 952–4136. One block southeast of Main Street. Nine rooms and suites in one of the most elegant Victorian mansions in coastal California. Not just private baths here, but the Fountain Suite has his-and-her claw-foot tubs on a raised platform by the fireplace. Many amenities, such as bathrobes, hand-dipped chocolates at bedside, complimentary afternoon tea, and morning coffee tray. Four parlors and English garden. Lavish full breakfast served in formal dining room. Bicycles available. One block to Main Street shops and galleries. Expensive to extremely expensive.

The Shaw House Inn, 703 Main Street, P.O. Box 1125, 95536; (707) 786–9958. Built in 1854 in the Carpenter gothic style of architecture, the first structure in Ferndale, now on the National Register of Historic Places. Five rooms and 1 suite with private baths. Double and queen beds. Furnished with antiques, memorabilia, and original art. A short walk to all the village attractions. Continental breakfast. Moderate to expensive.

CAMPGROUNDS AND RV PARKS

Humboldt County Fairgrounds Campground, (707) 786–9511. Van Ness Avenue at Fifth Street, $\frac{3}{10}$ mile north of Main Street, via Van Ness. Has 100 grassy sites with hookups and tank dump. Near town. Inexpensive.

Gingerbread Mansion, Ferndale

FOOD

Curly's Grill, 460 Ocean Street, 95536; (707) 786–9696. Downtown. Specializes in grilled foods and California cuisine with an Asian accent. Local art adorns the walls. Good food in pleasant surroundings. Moderate.

SHOPPING AND BROWSING

Foggy Bottoms Antiques, 563 Main Street, Suite 3, P.O. Box 998, 95536; (707) 786–9188. Monday through Saturday, 10:00 A.M. to 5:00 P.M.; Sunday, 10:00 A.M. to 4:00 P.M. Antiques and collectibles include a good selection of jewelry, glass, porcelain, and furniture.

Golden Gait Mercantile, 421 Main Street, 95536; (707) 786–4891. Monday through Saturday, 10:00 A.M. to 5:00 P.M.; Sunday, noon to 5:00 P.M. Step back more than a few decades as you walk across creaky wooden floors past the counter where the penny candy is sold. A great old general store offering antiques, collectibles, and modern goods, such as kitchenware and cookware. A good browse.

Hobart Galleries, 393 Main Street, 95536; (707) 725–3851. Main Street at Brown Street. Monday through Saturday, 11:00 A.M. to 5:16 P.M.; Sunday, noon to 5:16 P.M. Closed Monday in winter. Objets d'art—from semiserious to outrageous. A fascinating place to browse and buy. This is a *must stop,* and if you comport yourself with all due dignity, you might be invited to see the upstairs museum. If you're not invited, save yourself the embarrassment of asking why. This is a small town, and word spreads fast.

MUSEUM

Ferndale Museum, 155 Shaw Avenue, P.O. Box 431, 95536; (707) 786–4466. Just west of Main Street at Third and Shaw. June through September, 11:00 A.M. to 4:00 P.M. on Tuesday through Saturday and 1:00 to 4:00 P.M. on Sunday; October through May, 11:00 A.M. to 4:00 P.M. on Wednesday through Saturday and 1:00 to 4:00 P.M. on Sunday; closed in January. A fine country museum with a surprising array of tools, farm implements, antiques, and artifacts. Many items are set up in specific kinds of rooms: kitchen, dining room, bedroom, parlor, and such. Many changing displays as well. Also on premises is an operating Bosch-Omori seismograph with an interesting history.

BEACHES, PARKS, TRAILS, AND WAYSIDES

A half-mile east of Main Street via Ocean Avenue and Bluff Street is Russ Park, where trails lead through a forest of Sitka spruce and fir. Guided nature hikes are conducted Saturday morning, spring and summer, from 9:00 to 11:00 A.M.

Take Ocean Avenue west, instead, and it becomes Centerville Beach Road, which will take you past magnificent Fern Cottage to Centerville Beach, about 5 miles from town. There's a county park with meager facilities. Activities include surf fishing, beachcombing, and hiking on the beach and in the dunes. Currents are dangerous, so don't swim here.

Just south of the beach parking lot stands a white concrete cross that commemorates the loss of thirty-eight lives when the side-wheel steamer *Northerner* went down off the beach in 1860 after striking an uncharted reef.

Farther south, Wildcat Road rises into rugged but lush and beautiful ranchlands where sheep and cattle graze. This is the northern extreme of California's "Lost Coast." Seaward views are spectacular, with whale watching an added bonus.

OTHER ATTRACTIONS

Fern Cottage, 2121 Centerville Road, P.O. Box 36, 95536; (707) 786–4835 or 786–4735. About 3 miles west of Ferndale on Centerville Beach Road. The magnificent Russ family home, open for tours. Write or call for days and times.

TRAVEL INFORMATION

Ferndale Chamber of Commerce, P.O. Box 325, 95536; (707) 786–4477; www.victorianferndale.org/chamber

EVENTS

April	Spring Concert, (707) 786–4477
May	Cinco de Mayo Folkloric Festival, (707) 786–9668
	World Championship Great Arcata to Ferndale Cross–Country Kinetic Sculpture Race, (707) 786–4477
	Memorial Day Parade, (707) 786–4477
June	Portuguese Holy Ghost Celebration, (707) 786–9640
	Scandinavian Mid Summer Festival, (707) 444–8444
	Pet Parade, (707) 786–4477
	Garden Tour, (707) 786–4477
August	Humboldt County Fair and Horse Races, (707) 786–9511
September	Tastes of Ferndale and Friends, (707) 786–4477
October	Octoberfest, (707) 786–4477
December	Lighting America's Tallest Living Christmas Tree, (707) 786–4477
	Portuguese Linguica & Beans Dinner, (707) 786–4477
	Hospitality Night Open House, (707) 786–4477
	Lighted Tractor Parade, (707) 786–4477

EUREKA

Population: 27,750

Location: *On U.S. 101, 80 miles south of Crescent City, 65 miles north of Garberville, 287 miles north of San Francisco, and 150 miles west of Redding.*

That a California town called Eureka could trace its history to the gold rush and the era of the forty-niners shouldn't surprise anyone, but the growth and success of this city had less to do with gold dust than with sawdust. The town of Arcata, 8 miles to the north, was in fact nearer the goldfields in the Trinity Mountains and was outgrowing Eureka in the early 1850s. But when mine activity waned in 1856, it was Eureka, with its deepwater port, that was destined to become the largest city on Humboldt Bay.

Lumber is the area's major industry, as it always has been. When the city was incorporated in 1856, there were already seven sawmills operating here. Even then Eureka had the capability of turning out two million board feet of lumber a month, southbound by schooner for booming and lumber-starved San Francisco.

As the bay area developed and the forest-products industry flourished, Eureka grew into the largest coastal California city north of San Francisco, situated on the second-largest deepwater port in the state.

The 500 boats of the Humboldt Bay commercial-fishing fleet annually land the largest catch on the California coast. The cold, nutrient-rich Pacific waters beyond the harbor entrance give up chinook and coho salmon, halibut, rockfish (marketed as snapper and cod), albacore, lingcod, perch, sole, Dungeness crab, and shrimp. Most of the same species are included in the sport catch.

Eureka's most popular attraction is the original town site, known as Old Town. To get there, turn toward the bay from U.S. 101 (Fourth Street southbound, Fifth Street northbound) between C and M Streets. Old Town lies along First, Second, and Third Streets, where you will find various types of Victorian architecture well represented: Queen Anne, Eastlake, Italianate, Greek Revival, and Stick Style.

Second Street is the heart of Old Town, at the head of which stands the district's doyenne, the grande dame of venerable Victorians—the Carson Mansion. Built of redwood in the mid-1850s by lumber baron William McKendrie Carson, this three-story structure combines a variety of architectural styles and displays an abundance of adornments. Although now a private men's club and closed to the public, the mansion is easily photographed from M or Second Streets.

Carson also built the beautiful pink-and-white Queen Anne across the street. It was a wedding gift for his eldest son, J. Milton Carson.

Old Town also houses some of the area's best restaurants and most interesting shops and galleries. Maps and guides are available at the chamber of commerce visitor center.

LODGING

Best Western Thunderbird Motor Inn and Executive Suites, 232 West Fifth Street, 95501; (707) 443–2234 or (800) 528–1234. On U.S. 101, in town, near Old Town. Queen and king beds in 115 rooms and suites with cable TV and cable movies. Heated pool, whirlpool, electronic-game room, and coffee shop on premises. Moderate to expensive.

Carter House Country Inn, 1033 Third Street, 95501; (707) 445–1390. One of the most handsome Victorian structures in Old Town, based on designs by Samuel and Joseph Newsom, architects who also designed the Carson Mansion. Six guest rooms and a large suite with private and shared baths. Full breakfast served, considered among the best in the state. Limousine service in a 1958 Bentley available to and from airport. Moderate to very expensive.

An Elegant Victorian Mansion, 1406 C Street, 95501; (707) 444–3144 or 442–5594. C Street at Fourteenth Street, near Old Town. A beautifully preserved and restored architectural treasure, this fine old Victorian functions as a bed-and-breakfast inn where elegance is the watchword and guests are pampered. Three guest rooms with 3 shared baths, 1 suite with private bath. Opulent French breakfast includes fresh-brewed coffee, assorted teas, juice, fresh fruits, and homemade breads, followed by a main course that changes daily. Views of

193

city, bay, and mountains. Sauna and laundry facilities on premises. Secured parking behind locked gates. Moderate to expensive.

The Eureka Inn, 518 Seventh Street, 95501; (707) 442–6441 or (800) 862–4906. At Seventh and F Streets. An English Tudor–style inn built in 1922, now a National Historic Landmark. Has 110 rooms and suites. Luxury suites have fireplaces and whirlpool spas. Heated pool, whirlpool, and 2 saunas. Restaurant, coffee shop, cocktail lounge, and pub on premises. Limousine and concierge service available. Moderate to very expensive.

Hotel Carter, 301 L Street, 95501; (707) 444–8062. Third Street at L Street, in Old Town. Double and queen beds in 20 rooms in a wonderfully modern hotel fashioned after the old Cairo Hotel. Rooms are furnished with antique pine but contain modern amenities as well—cable TV, private baths, some in-room whirlpools. Continental breakfast available. Superb restaurant on premises serves dinner nightly. Bay view. Moderate to expensive.

Old Town Bed & Breakfast Inn, 1521 Third Street, 95501; (707) 445–3951. Third Street at P Street, 1 block from the Carson Mansion. Twin, double, queen, and king beds in 5 rooms with private and shared baths in a Greek Revival–Victorian house built in 1871 and once the residence of the William Carson family. Evening social hour and full breakfast. Moderate.

CAMPGROUNDS AND RV PARKS

E-Z Landing RV Park & Marina, King Salmon Resort, 1875 Buhne Drive, 95501; (707) 442–1118. Four miles south of Eureka, 1 mile west of U.S. 101, via King Salmon Avenue. Has 45 full-hookup sites with cable TV for trailers and motor homes; 20 drive-through sites available. Fishing tackle, docks, boat rentals, and full-service marina on premises. Moderate.

Johnny's RV Park & Marina, King Salmon Resort, 1821 Buhne Drive, 95501; (707) 442–2284. Four miles south of Eureka, 1 mile west of U.S. 101, via King Salmon Avenue. Has 53 sites with full hookups. Showers and laundry facilities. Full-service marina on premises. Moderate.

KOA Kampground, 4050 North Highway 101, 95501; (707) 822–4243. Four miles north of Eureka. Has 165 full-hookup sites and 29 grassy tent sites with tables and grills. Kamping Kabins, showers, laundry facilities, hot tub, grocery store, recreation room, and snack bar. Propane and ice available. Moderate.

Carson Mansion, Eureka

FOOD

Samoa Cookhouse, 79 Lookhouse Lane, Samoa 95564; (707) 442–1659. West of U.S. 101 via the Samoa Bridge (Route 255), then left on Samoa Road, and left again at the first road. Breakfast, lunch, and dinner daily. The last of the great lumber-camp cookhouses, where fresh, wholesome food is served camp style. The menu varies according to availability, but always includes the freshest meats, vegetables, fruits, and butter. Homemade bread, pastries, and pies. Meals are made to satisfy loggers' appetites. Nobody leaves hungry. This is an eating experience you won't want to miss. Moderate.

The Sea Grill, 316 E Street, 95501; (707) 443–7187. In Old Town. Lunch, Tuesday through Friday; dinner, Monday through Saturday. French dip, burgers, and such seafood sandwiches as grilled crab and Jack cheese on sourdough, grilled shrimp and cheddar on sourdough, and calamari steak on French roll. For dinner, try the Cajun-style cod, beer-batter prawns, orange roughy amandine, scallops, clams, oysters, or combination plate. Full bar. Moderate.

SHOPPING AND BROWSING

Abraxas Jewelry & Leather, 425 Third Street, 95501; (707) 443–4638. In Old Town, next to the Ritz. Monday through Saturday,

10:00 A.M. to 5:30 P.M. Gold and silver jewelry, large selection of earrings, custom leather goods, pottery, craft items, jewelry boxes, and leaded glass.

American Indian Art & Gift Shop, 241 F Street, 95501; (707) 445–8451. In Old Town. Monday through Saturday, 10:00 A.M. to 5:00 P.M. A large selection of Indian arts and crafts. Exquisite baskets, fine silver and turquoise jewelry and accessories, moccasins, and beadwork.

Antiques & Goodies, 1128 Third Street, 95501; (707) 442–0445. Upper end of Old Town, next to Hotel Carter. Monday through Saturday, 10:00 A.M. to 5:00 P.M.; Sunday, 10:00 A.M. to 2:00 P.M. A large and interesting shop with 5,000 square feet of fine Old World antiques, oak furniture, crockery, china, cloisonné, paintings, and prints.

The Irish Shop, 334 Second Street, 95501; (707) 443–8343. In Old Town. Monday through Thursday, 9:30 A.M. to 6:00 P.M.; Sunday, 11:00 A.M. to 6:00 P.M. Friday and Saturday, 9:30 A.M. to 8:00 P.M. Specializes in imports from Ireland, Scotland, and Iceland. Beautiful handmade sweaters, Irish hats and caps, gloves, ties, blouses, sport coats, and scarves. Walking sticks, jewelry, china, and gift items.

Old Town Art Gallery, 233 F Street, 95501; (707) 445–2315. In Old Town. Monday through Saturday, 8:30 A.M. to 5:00 P.M.; Sunday, 11:00 A.M. to 5:00 P.M. A lovely gallery with good selection and variety. Landscapes, seascapes, and wildlife art. Stained glass, sculpture, pottery, drawings, old paintings, acrylics, watercolors, batiks, and craft items.

Restoration Hardware, 417 Second Street, 95501; (707) 443–3152. In Old Town. Monday through Friday, 10:00 A.M. to 7:00 P.M.; Saturday, 10:00 A.M. to 6:00 P.M.; Sunday, 11:00 A.M. to 5:00 P.M. Victorian fixtures of all kinds—door, garden, plumbing, lighting, and electrical. Clocks, lamps, artwork, mailboxes, sundials, and bathroom accessories. A great shop for the fixer-upper or for anyone looking for unusual gifts.

MUSEUMS

Clarke Memorial Museum, 240 Third Street, 95501; (707) 443–1947. In Old Town. At Third and E Streets. Tuesday through Saturday, noon to 4:00 P.M. Built in 1911–12 to house the Bank of Eureka, the beautiful Italian Renaissance structure that now functions as a museum is itself a valuable piece of local history. Excellent collection of American Indian artifacts—especially fine baskets. More than

1,200 Indian artifacts on display. Firearms, glassware, nineteenth-century paintings, models, and exhibits of logging, lumber, shipbuilding, and maritime trades. Pioneer memorabilia, Victorian furniture, textiles, and decorative pieces.

Humboldt Bay Maritime Museum, 423 First Street, 95501; (707) 444-9440. Behind the Carson Mansion. Daily, 11:00 A.M. to 4:00 P.M. Artifacts depicting the maritime history of Humboldt Bay. Models of ships and boats, plus many photographs of the Humboldt Bay area. An interesting little museum.

BEACHES, PARKS, TRAILS, AND WAYSIDES

The vicinity of Eureka and Humboldt Bay isn't famous for broad beaches, lush green parks, and abundant hiking trails; areas to the north and south are better choices for such outdoor attractions. The region does, however, offer ocean beaches and dunes along the North Spit, as well as areas for camping and picnicking there. To reach the spit, take the Samoa Bridge, Route 255, west from Eureka to Samoa, and turn left on New Navy Base Road.

As industrialized as the north arm of Humboldt Bay is, much of the south arm is a wildlife refuge, where egrets, herons, waterfowl, and shorebirds are seasonally abundant. Fields Landing and King Salmon Resort, south of Eureka, provide access to the south bay.

In town, the Eureka Mooring Basin, at Commercial and First Streets, is where most of the local fishing boats and pleasure craft are moored. This is a good place for a picnic and for watching harbor traffic, birds, seals, and sea lions.

WATER SPORTS AND ACTIVITIES

Boaters and anglers who tow boats will find several launching facilities in and near Eureka. There's a one-lane concrete ramp at the Eureka Mooring Basin, at First and Commercial Streets. At the foot of Railroad Avenue in Fields Landing, south of town, is a two-lane concrete ramp on the bay. Nearby King Salmon Resort has two full-service marinas with hoists.

Much of the sportfishing activities center on the King Salmon Resort. The beach and breakwaters here serve as popular fishing spots, the catch consisting mainly of surfperch and various bottom species.

Offshore fishing is seasonally good for coho and chinook salmon, and bottom fishing is excellent much of the year, weather and water conditions permitting.

Crabbers take Dungeness, red, and rock crabs from the bay. On minus tides, clam diggers ply the mudflats for gaper, littleneck, and hard-shell clams.

Bucksport Sporting Goods, 3650 South Broadway, 95501; (707) 442–1832. On U.S. 101, south end of town. Monday through Saturday, 9:00 A.M. to 5:30 P.M. A fine sport shop with a large selection of top-quality outdoor clothing, fishing tackle, crab pots, and more. Sells fishing licenses.

E-Z Landing RV Park & Marina, King Salmon Resort, 1875 Buhne Drive, 95501; (707) 442–1118. On Humboldt Bay, 4 miles south of Eureka, west of U.S. 101, via King Salmon Avenue. Electric boat launch for vessels to two tons and 22 feet. Marine gas and oil, bait, tackle, and rental boats and motors.

Johnny's RV Park & Marina, King Salmon Resort, 1821 Buhne Drive, 95501; (707) 442–2284. On Humboldt Bay, 4 miles south of Eureka, west of U.S. 101, via King Salmon Avenue. Electric boat launch, boat repairs, marine supplies, and boat rentals.

Sailfish, 1821 Buhne Drive, P.O. Box 6393, 95501; (707) 442–6682. At King Salmon Resort, 4 miles south of Eureka, west of U.S. 101, via King Salmon Avenue. Check in and board at 5:30 A.M. and 12:30 P.M.; departs at 6:00 A.M. and 1:00 P.M. Salmon and bottom-fish trips. Specializes in light-tackle fishing. Bait, fish bags, fish cleaning, and hot beverages provided.

TOURS AND TRIPS

Humboldt Bay Harbor Cruise. Enjoy narrated cruises aboard the beautiful M/V *Madaket,* launched in 1910 and owned by the Humboldt Bay Maritime Museum. Daily sight-seeing cruises depart at 1:00, 2:00, 4:00, and 5:30 P.M. Friday and Saturday dinner cruises leave at 7:30 P.M. Sunday brunch cruises sail at 11:00 A.M. All departures from the foot of C Street in Old Town.

GOLF

Eureka Municipal Golf Course, 4750 Fairway Drive, 95501; (707) 443–4808. Follow F Street to the south end of town, where F Street turns into Fairway Drive. An exceptionally beautiful eighteen-hole public course. Driving range, pro shop, resident pro, cart and club rentals.

WEATHER AND TIDE INFORMATION

National Weather Service; recorded message, (707) 443–7062

TRAVEL INFORMATION

Eureka Chamber of Commerce, 2112 Broadway, 95501; (707) 442–3738 or (800) 356–6381; www.eurekachamber.com; e-mail: eurekacc@northerncoast.com

EVENTS

March	Daffodil Show, Fortuna, (707) 725–2281
April	Redwood Coast Dixieland Jazz Fest, (707) 445–3378
	Rhododendron Festival, (707) 442–3738
May	Avenue of the Giants Marathon, (707) 443–1226
June	U.S. Coast Guard Days, (707) 443–5097
	Redwood Acres Fair & Rodeo, (707) 445–3037
July	The Sea Hunt Archery Tournament, (707) 839–7600
	Humboldt Bay Fourth of July Festival, (707) 442–9054
	Blues by the Bay Music Festival, (707) 443–3378
September	Festival on the Bay, (707) 445–3801
November	Gem & Mineral Show, (707) 445–3037
	Holiday Craft Bazaar, (707) 443–2874
December	Truckers Christmas Convoy, (707) 442–5744

ARCATA

Population: 16,300

TRINIDAD

Population: 367

Location: *Arcata is on U.S. 101, 8 miles north of Eureka; Trinidad lies west of U.S. 101, 13 miles north of Arcata, 19 miles south of Orick, and 59 miles south of Crescent City.*

Arcata began in the early 1850s as a supply depot for the gold mines in the Trinity Mountains. It was the county's first seat of government, a post Eureka took over in 1856. As mining activity decreased, agriculture and logging gained importance in and near Arcata.

Like its neighbor across the bay, Arcata has dozens of Victorian houses, mansions, and other structures, many of which are well preserved and lovingly cared for. The downtown area is built around a plaza. In the hills above downtown is the campus of Humboldt State University.

Every town with an eye on tourism claims to be a county's, region's, or state's "best-kept secret." The phrase is so often used it's a cliché and so often abused it's usually a lie. But it might just fit Trinidad, a tiny town and teacup harbor just far enough north of San Francisco and south of Portland that most people "driving the Pacific Coast" seem to drive right by.

Don't make the same mistake. Take the Trinidad exit and visit the spotless town and nearby beaches and headlands. Fish out of the harbor aboard your own boat or one of the charter craft. Stay at one of the beautiful bed-and-breakfast inns or bargain-priced motels. If you're camping, pitch a tent or plug in the RV at one of several campgrounds and RV parks.

LODGING

Bishop Pine Lodge, 1481 Patrick's Point Drive, Trinidad 95570; (707) 677–3314. West of U.S. 101 on Main Street, via Trinidad exit, then north 2 miles on Patrick's Point Drive. Double, queen, and king beds in 13 1-, 2-, and 3-bedroom cottages with cable TV and cable movies, most with fully equipped kitchens. Two rooms share outdoor hot tub. Two deluxe suites have kitchen, microwave, refrigerator, and phones with bathroom extensions. Hair dryers in all units. Barbecue area. Cribs, roll-aways, and waterbeds available. Moderate.

The Lady Anne Victorian Inn, 902 Fourteenth Street, Arcata 95521; (707) 822–2797. West of U.S. 101, Fourteenth at I Street. Five rooms in a Victorian mansion built in 1888, furnished with antiques. Shared and private baths. Music room. Bicycles available. Full breakfast. Walking distance to several restaurants. Near the university. Moderate to expensive.

The Lost Whale Bed & Breakfast Inn, 3452 Patrick's Point Drive, Trinidad 95570; (707) 677–3425. West of U.S. 101 via Seawood Drive exit or Patrick's Point Drive exit. Four ocean-view rooms with private baths and 2 with shared bath in a contemporary inn offering one of the best views on the coast. The building is uniquely designed and set up with families in mind, featuring sleeping lofts for kids and a two-story playhouse; baby-sitting provided. Private path to private beach. Afternoon cappuccino, sherry, and homemade pastries. Full breakfast served in bright and cheerful dining area. Lots of deck space and a big backyard. Moderate to expensive.

Trinidad Bay Bed & Breakfast, 560 Edwards Street, P.O. Box 849, Trinidad 95570; (707) 677–0840. West of U.S. 101, Edwards at Trinity, overlooking harbor and lighthouse. Twin and queen beds in 4 rooms with private baths in a Cape Cod house affording ocean and harbor view. Walk to shops, restaurants, and beaches. Continental breakfast. Moderate to expensive.

Trinidad Inn, 1170 Patrick's Point Drive, Trinidad 95570; (707) 677–3349. West of U.S. 101, 2 miles north of town. One of those sleeper bargains (no pun intended), with 7 spotless rooms and suites, tastefully decorated. Large honeymoon suite with wicker furniture and lots of white and muted pastels. Family suite on 2 floors sleeps 6 to 8 persons. Kitchen units available. Cable TV, queen beds. Quiet, wooded setting. Inexpensive to moderate.

Trinidad Harbor and Memorial Lighthouse

CAMPGROUNDS AND RV PARKS

Mad River Rapids RV Park, 3501 Janes Road, Arcata 95521; (707) 822–7275. West of U.S. 101 via Guintoli Lane, just north of Arcata. Has 92 full-hookup sites with cable TV. Barbecue grills, showers, laundry, tank dump, VCR equipment and movie rentals, heated pool, hot tub, horseshoe pits, video arcade, pool tables, table tennis, and basketball court. Grocery store and snack bar. Moderate.

Midway RV Park, P.O. Box 830, Trinidad, 95570; (707) 677–3934. West of U.S. 101 via Trinidad exit and Main Street, then north ½-mile on Patrick's Point Drive. Has 72 full-hookup sites with cable TV and tables. Showers, tank dump, recreation room, fish-cleaning facilities, smokehouse, canning facilities, and boat and RV storage. Moderate.

Patrick's Point State Park, 4150 Patrick's Point Drive, Trinidad 95570; (707) 677–3570 or (800) 444–7275. West of U.S. 101, 5 miles north of Trinidad. Has 124 developed campsites with tables, stoves, and cupboards. Piped water and showers. Trails to the beach. Summer camp-fire program. Moderate.

Sounds of the Sea RV Park, 3443 Patrick's Point Drive, Trinidad 95570; (707) 677–3271. One mile south of Patrick's Point. Has 52 full-hookup sites with tables, some with ocean view. Showers, laundry, horseshoes, volleyball, and croquet. Store with ice and camping supplies. Moderate.

FOOD

Humboldt Brewery, 856 Tenth Street, Arcata 95521; (707) 826–2739. West of U.S. 101, downtown. Monday through Wednesday, 11:30 A.M. to midnight; Thursday through Saturday, 11:30 A.M. to 2:00 A.M.; Sunday, 2:00 to 10:00 P.M. Pub food includes spicy or mild Buffalo chicken wings, Cajun chicken sandwiches, Cajun burgers, bacon cheeseburgers, "chainsaw" chili cheeseburgers, beer-batter fish-and-chips, and pasta dishes. Fine English-style brews are Gold Rush Ale, Red Nectar Ale, Storm Cellar Porter, and award-winning Oatmeal Stout. Good food and great brew, but college-student waiters inspire little hope for the planet's future. Moderate.

Katy's Smokehouse, 740 Edwards Street, Trinidad 95570; (707) 677–0151. In town, above the harbor. Daily, 9:00 A.M. to 6:00 P.M. A small seafood market offering whatever is locally fresh and in season, as well as what can be shipped in fresh, including halibut, lingcod, salmon, rockfish, perch, oysters, prawns, shrimp, crab, and lobster. Smoked treats include salmon, salmon jerky, albacore, and halibut. Canned products also available. Gift packs shipped anywhere.

Los Bagels, 1061 I Street, Arcata 95521; (707) 822–3150. West of U.S. 101, downtown. Monday, Wednesday, Thursday, and Friday, 7:00 A.M. to 6:00 P.M.; Saturday, 7:00 A.M. to 5:00 P.M.; Sunday, 8:00 A.M. to 3:00 P.M. Fresh bagels, croissants, and muffins. Sandwiches, lox, smoked fish, and freshly brewed coffee. Inexpensive to moderate.

Seascape Restaurant, P.O. Box 1007, Trinidad 95570; (707) 677–3762. West of U.S. 101, on Bay Street, at the boat basin. Daily breakfast, lunch, and dinner; weekend brunch. Summers, open until 10:00 P.M.; October through April, open until 8:30 P.M. Traditional breakfast and lunch menu but also a large selection of three-egg seafood omelets, clam chowder, seafood bisque, salads, and seafood Louis. Dinners include steaks and such seafoods as halibut, salmon, scallops, prawns, oysters, calamari, lobster tails, and lobster thermidor. Beer and wine. Moderate.

Wildflower Cafe & Bakery, 1604 G Street, Arcata 95521; (707) 822–0360. West of U.S. 101, Sixteenth Street and G Street. Monday through Saturday, breakfast, lunch, and dinner. Vegetarian cuisine includes such bakery goodies as raisin-date bars, poppyseed muffins, and apple-bran muffins. Among breakfast offerings are omelets, pancakes, and waffles with fruit and yogurt. Lunch features homemade soups, quiche, steamed-vegetable salad, and Mexican beans and cheese. Dinner includes mushroom stroganoff, chow mein, sweet-and-sour vegetables, and a daily special. Inexpensive to moderate.

MUSEUM AND AQUARIUM

Humboldt State University Marine Lab Aquarium, P.O. Box 690, Trinidad 95570; (707) 826–4479. Corner of Edwards and Ewing, in town, near the harbor. Monday through Friday 8:00 A.M. to 5:00 P.M., Saturday and Sunday 10:00 A.M. to 5:00 P.M. (weekend hours during school sessions only). Aquarium, touch tank, and tidepool exhibits open to the public.

Humboldt State University Natural History Museum, Arcata 95521; (707) 826–4479. West of U.S. 101, G Street at Thirteenth Street. Tuesday through Saturday, 10:00 A.M. to 5:00 P.M. Among the exhibits at this museum, which opened in 1989, are nearly 2,000 fossils dating back more than 200 million years, as well as fossils from Europe, Africa, and North America providing information about the planet's oceans as far back as 500 million years. An impressive collection superbly displayed.

BEACHES, PARKS, TRAILS, AND WAYSIDES

The Arcata Marsh and Wildlife Sanctuary stands as an example of what people can do to improve the environment when they put their minds to it. South of downtown, via I Street, is an area of some seventy-five acres that until 1979 was what one report euphemistically referred to as "degraded salt marsh." Area residents called it the city dump. Next to it was the sewage-treatment plant. A delightful combination.

Not only did the city clean up the mess, but in the process it also created a beautiful natural area that includes a lake, three marshes, hiking trails, and picnic areas. The lake is stocked with rainbow trout, and salmon are reared in a mixture of bay water and treated wastewater at the treatment plant's oxidation ponds. The lush vegetation also attracts more than 150 species of birds and waterfowl. To make watching and photographing easier, the city has built all-weather blinds along the shores.

If the place sounds unbelievable, see it for yourself. As one resident asked, "How many cities do you know of where people take their sack lunches to the local sewage-treatment plant?"

In the vicinity of Trinidad are a number of beaches offering a variety of activities. Take Scenic Drive south off Main Street for 3 miles to the broad and sandy Moonstone Beach. On the way are several smaller pocket beaches and tidepool areas. North of Main Street, off Trinity

Street, is Trinidad State Beach. Agate Beach is at Patrick's Point State Park, 5 miles north of Trinidad.

These are some of the best beaches in California for hiking, beachcombing, and photography. Some stretches are littered with driftwood; others give up agates, jasper, and jade. Offshore rocks, sea stacks, and islets punctuate the seascape and add elements of interest and drama to photographs. They also harbor seabirds by the tens of thousands.

WATER SPORTS AND ACTIVITIES

Beaches and rocky areas north and south of Trinidad offer excellent opportunities for surfperch fishing and smelt dipping. Sandy beaches and tidal flats are popular, too, for clam digging. Moonstone Beach provides a good surfing area.

The Mad River, just north of Arcata, and Little River, 4 miles south of Trinidad, get seasonal runs of salmon and steelhead. Sea-run cutthroat trout also enter the Little River in late summer. The estuaries of both rivers offer angling for surfperch and other saltwater species.

Trinidad's natural harbor and pier are favored by anglers. Offshore, fishing is good for salmon and bottom fish. Near-shore waters also give up rockfish, lingcod, cabezon, and Dungeness crab.

Bob's Boat Basin, Trinidad 95570; (707) 677–3625. At the pier, on the harbor. Bait, tackle, snacks, beverages, and boat rentals (16-foot skiffs). Boats up to 24 feet launched. Charters booked. Source of information on local fishing.

TRAVEL INFORMATION

Arcata Chamber of Commerce, 432 Heindon, Arcata 95521; (707) 822–3619 or (800) 553–6569; www.arcata.com/chamber

Greater Trinidad Chamber of Commerce, P.O. Box 356, Trinidad 95570; (707) 677–0591

EVENTS

March	Humboldt State University Pow Wow, Arcata, (707) 826–4994
	First Nations Feast, Arcata, (707) 826–4994
April	Annual Dinner Auction, Arcata, (707) 822–6918
May	Bebop & Brew, Arcata, (707) 826–2267
	Mother's Day Garden Tour Home & Garden, Trinidad, (707) 677–0467
	World Championship Great Arcata to Ferndale Cross-Country Kinetic Sculpture Race, (707) 443–5167
June	Trinidad Fish Festival, (707) 677–1610
	Humboldt Folklife Festival, (707) 826–9043
July	Fourth of July Jubilee, Arcata, (707) 822–3619
August	Humboldt County Fair, Ferndale, (707) 786–9511

CRESCENT CITY

Population: 8,300

Location: On U.S. 101, 20 miles south of the California–Oregon state line, 19 miles north of Klamath, and 78 miles north of Eureka.

During the California gold rush, the towns of Klamath and Crescent City burgeoned simultaneously when mining brought thousands to the nearby mountains and beaches in 1850. The Klamath River bar, however, proved too treacherous for the San Francisco schooners to cross, so Crescent City, with its excellent natural harbor, became the supply depot for the mining camps.

The Crescent City Light Station, generally referred to as the Battery Point Lighthouse, began guiding mariners into Crescent Bay on December 10, 1856. It's located at the west end of the town and harbor, on an islet near Battery Point. Although it ceased operating in 1965, it now functions as a museum that's open during the summer months only. The islet, however, is open to the public all year, though it can be reached only at low tide. Offering a good spot for photography or a picnic on any sunny day, the islet commands an excellent view of the harbor and coastline north and south. It also provides a good vantage for watching whales and winter storms.

Crescent City's first lumber mill was built in 1853, and timber eventually became the area's main industry, followed by commercial fishing, agriculture, and tourism. What draws visitors to this part of northern California today is what attracted the early settlers: the ocean, a safe harbor with no bar to cross, the state's two top rivers for salmon and steelhead fishing, and the magnificent coastal redwood trees.

207

LODGING

Bayview Inn, 310 Highway 101 South, 95531; (707) 465–2050 or (800) 446–0583. South end of town, west side of U.S. 101. Queen and king beds in 67 rooms with cable TV, cable movies, and coffeemakers. Rooms with whirlpool spas available. Laundry facilities on premises. Inexpensive to moderate.

Best Western Ship Ashore Motel, 12370 Highway 101 North, P.O. Box 75, Smith River 95567; (707) 487–3141 or (800) 528–1234. Located 17 miles north of Crescent City, at the mouth of the Smith River. Cable TV and cable movies in 50 rooms and suites. Kitchen and hot-tub suites available. Riverfront units and ocean-view rooms available. Coffee shop, restaurant, lounge, and gift shop on premises. Boat rentals and guide service. Moderate.

Curly Redwood Lodge, 701 Highway 101 South, 95531; (707) 464–2137. South end of town, opposite the waterfront. Queen beds in 36 rooms and family units with cable TV. The lodge was built from a single redwood tree that, when sawed, yielded 57,000 board feet of lumber. Walking distance to waterfront, shops, and restaurants. Inexpensive to moderate.

Redwood Hostel, 14480 Highway 101, Klamath 95548; (707) 482–8265. The only youth hostel located right in the redwoods, amidst hiking trails and offering spectacular views of the ocean. Shared cooking facilities and laundry. Inexpensive.

CAMPGROUNDS AND RV PARKS

Crescent City Redwoods KOA Kampground, 4241 Highway 101 North, 95531; (707) 464–5744. Five miles north of town. Has 94 campsites, half with full hookups. Cable TV, showers, laundry, tank dump, snack bar, groceries, ice, beer and wine, souvenirs, redwood and myrtlewood items, propane, firewood, volleyball, badminton, horseshoes, tether ball, and nature trails—all on ten wooded acres. Kamping Kabins available. Moderate.

Del Norte Coast Redwoods State Park, 1375 Elk Valley Road, 95531; (707) 464–6101, extension 5120, or (800) 444–7275. On U.S. 101, 7 miles south of Crescent City. Open year-round, unless closed due to slides or flooding. Has 145 campsites with tables and fire pits. Showers, tank dump, inland and coastal hiking and nature trails. More than 6,000 acres. Beach access. Moderate.

Salmon Harbor Resort, 200 Salmon Harbor Road, Smith River 95567; (707) 487–3341. About 18 miles north of Crescent City, at the mouth of the Smith River. Has 90 full-hookup sites and 10 with water and electricity. Showers and laundry facilities. Beer, wine, ice, and propane available. Recreation room, playground, boat ramp, and dock. Riverfront sites available. Inexpensive to moderate.

Ship Ashore Resort, 12370 Highway 101 North, Smith River 95567; (707) 487-3141. About 17 miles north of Crescent City, on the Smith River. Look for the 160-foot yacht parked at roadside. Has 200 full-hookup and 12 tent sites. Cable TV, showers, hot tub, laundry facilities, recreation room, gift shop, general store, and boat dock. Restaurant and cocktail lounge on premises. Boat rentals and guide service available. Tackle shop. Moderate.

Sunset Harbor RV Park, 205 King Street, 95531; (707) 464-3423. About 1 block east of U.S. 101 at the south end of town. Has 75 full-hookup sites with tables and cable TV. Tent area, showers, laundry facilities, minimart, beer, wine, ice, and supplies. Near the waterfront. Moderate.

Village Camper Inn, 1543 Parkway Drive, 95531; (707) 464-3544. About ¼-mile east of U.S. 101 via Washington Boulevard exit, north of town. Has 135 full-hookup sites with cable TV and 15 tent sites. Showers, laundry facilities, and tank dump. Wooded setting with playground and horseshoe pits. Moderate.

FOOD

China Hut, 928 Ninth Street, 95531; (707) 464-4921. West of U.S. 101, in town. Lunch and dinner daily. Chinese and American cuisine with specialties in Cantonese and Mandarin dishes. American menu includes steaks, chicken, veal, seafood, and a dozen different sandwiches. Among the appetizers are egg rolls, fried wonton, pot stickers, and barbecued pork. Chop suey, chow mein, sweet-and-sour dishes, egg foo yung, and various combination and family dinners offered. Cantonese specialties include *mar far* chicken, curry shrimp or chicken, scallop *chow yuk,* and chicken with black-bean sauce. Mandarin offerings include Peking spareribs, beef with scallions, and Szechuan shrimp, chicken, or pork. Inexpensive to moderate.

Harbor View Grotto Restaurant & Lounge, 150 Starfish Way, Crescent City 95531; (707) 464-3815. West of U.S. 101 at the boat basin. Lunch and dinner daily. Lunch: salads, burgers, oyster stew, clam chowder, fish and shellfish sandwiches and platters. Dinner: large selection of seafood, chicken, steaks, prime rib. Crab, prawns, scallops, oysters, lobster, salmon, halibut, and more—all deep-fried in pure vegetable oil. Cocktails, beer, and wine. Moderate.

Crescent City Harbor

MUSEUMS

Del Norte County Historical Society Main Museum, 577 H Street, 95531; (707) 464–3922. West of U.S. 101 at Sixth and H Streets. April through September, 10:00 A.M. to 4:00 P.M. Monday through Saturday. Historical society collections and exhibits of pioneer artifacts in the former jail and hall of records, built in 1926. On display also is the first-order Fresnel lens from the St. George Reef Lighthouse.

Lighthouse Museum, P.O. Box 396, 95531; (707) 464–3089. Battery Point Lighthouse at the foot of A Street, west of U.S. 101. April through September, 10:00 A.M. to 4:00 P.M. Wednesday through Sunday, tides permitting. Lighthouse built in 1856 on a near-shore island, accessible at low tide.

BEACHES, PARKS, TRAILS, AND WAYSIDES

Nine miles northeast of Crescent City—via Route 199, east off U.S. 101—Jedediah Smith Redwoods State Park lies along the Smith River, amid some of the most spectacular redwood groves in the state. The park offers fishing, boating, picnicking, camping, hiking, sightseeing, and innumerable photographic opportunities.

North of Crescent City and west of U.S. 101, via Morehead Road and Lake Earl Drive to Kellogg Road, Kellogg Beach offers beach recreation and picnicking. The sandy beach spreads before dunes and marshes to the tumbling surf.

The Lake Earl Wildlife Area lies west of U.S. 101 and north of town. From Crescent City, take Lake Earl Drive north to Old Mill Road, turn left, and proceed 1½ miles to the area headquarters. There are few roads and no trails in this 5,000-acre reserve, but there's plenty of room to roam through the stabilized dunes and along the shoreline of Lake Talawa and Lake Earl.

Although fishing is good here, especially in the channel connecting the two lakes, the main attraction for many visitors is the abundant and varied bird life. More than 250 species have been recorded, some extremely rare or endangered. In addition to numerous residents present all year, great flocks of migrants swell the bird population seasonally.

Shorebirds—including black turnstones, dowitchers, godwits, and sandpipers—pour into the reserve in early fall, followed soon by the puddle ducks, such as teal, pintail, mallard, and widgeon. Great flocks of diver ducks follow with the season's first storms, adding bluebill, redhead, canvasback, and others to the colorful gathering.

Rare Aleutian Canada geese arrive in small flocks until they number about 6,000—the world's entire population of this endangered species. Tundra and trumpeter swans, white as wedding dresses, join the gathering flocks.

Among the eighty species of songbirds that have been counted here are chickadees, finches, flycatchers, juncos, larks, robins, sparrows, thrushes, vireos, warblers, and wrens.

With birds, mice, and ground squirrels in such great numbers, raptors are also well represented here. Bald and golden eagles, red-tailed and rough-legged hawks, kestrels, merlins, and black-shouldered kites hunt here by day, while owls take the night shift. Listen, too, for the high-pitched whistle of the osprey as it soars and hunts for fish.

Lake Earl is also a good place to encounter black-tailed deer and smaller mammals, such as rabbits and raccoons. Frequenting the shoreline and marshy areas are river otter, beaver, and muskrat.

Point St. George Public Access is at the end of Radio Road, west of U.S. 101, via Washington Boulevard or Pebble Beach Drive. Here you'll find a trail leading from a large parking area to the beach, where you can explore tidepools, hike, beach-comb, or just enjoy the scenery. The St. George Light, standing about 6 miles offshore, is visible here.

At the west end of town, Pebble Beach Drive parallels Pebble Beach, where you'll find a number of parking areas and easy beach access. This is a wonderfully scenic area, a photographer's delight. The beach is also popular with beachcombers and is a good place to search for agates and other semiprecious gemstones.

Along the northern shore of Crescent Bay lies Beach Front Park, a large, attractive park with play areas, grassy lawn, trees, benches, and picnic tables. There's plenty of parking along the bay and easy bay access. To reach the park, take Front Street west off U.S. 101 to the park entrance. Howe Drive parallels the bayshore for the length of the park.

Crescent Beach and Enderts Beach are west of U.S. 101, via Enderts Beach Road, 2 miles south of town. Both areas offer picnicking, and Enderts Beach has primitive campsites. The rocky beaches are good for examining tidepools.

Four miles south of Crescent City is the 6,000-acre Del Norte Coast Redwoods State Park. Trail systems lead to beaches and into the redwoods. Both sandy beaches and rocky shoreline are here to enjoy.

Del Norte State Park is part of Redwood National Park, established in 1968 and enlarged in 1978 and headquartered at Crescent City. From its northern boundary southward along the coast for 50 miles, Redwood National Park comprises three state parks, virgin old-growth forests, new-growth forests, herds of wild elk, and great stands of the planet's tallest trees: coast redwoods. Within the park boundaries are beaches, overlooks, fishing-access points, a beautiful coastal drive, and miles of hiking and nature trails.

WATER SPORTS AND ACTIVITIES

The Klamath and Smith Rivers head the list of top-producing streams in California, the former hosting the state's largest salmon and steelhead runs, the latter yielding the biggest salmonids, including steelhead exceeding twenty pounds and chinook salmon weighing more than fifty pounds. Both rivers and their tributaries also offer excellent fishing for sea-run cutthroat trout.

Both coho and chinook salmon move into the Klamath in mid-July, providing angling opportunities in the lower river and at the river mouth until November. Chinook action on the lower and middle Smith occurs from September through December. Steelheading on both rivers runs from August through October. The best angling for sea-run cutthroat takes place in September and October. Native rainbow and cutthroat angling in the upper rivers and their tributaries is good through the summer and into early autumn. Sturgeon are taken from the lower Klamath from midsummer through early autumn.

Angling in the salt chuck focuses on chinook and coho salmon during the summer months. Local bottom fishes include lingcod, cabezon, and various species of rockfish (known locally as snapper), and angling for them is year-round. Seaperch and surfperch are also available all year and at times are abundant.

Saltwater salmon angling is predominantly an offshore sport. The harbor provides excellent launching facilities for those who tow boats and charter services for those who don't.

Bottom-fish angling is also good offshore, but it is available to the shore-bound angler as well. The best bets are rocky coastal areas north and south of town, along the breakwaters, and from the public pier near Battery Point, in town.

Anglers take seaperch and surfperch from the pier and breakwaters on the harbor. Perch fishing is also good near the river mouths and from the beaches. A favorite spot is Kellogg Beach, about 10 miles north of town, near Fort Dick.

Another area that provides excellent angling can't be strictly classified as either fresh or salt water. Lake Earl, commonly referred to as a freshwater lagoon, is fed by Jordan Creek and numerous groundwater sources. During the winter storm season, however, the ocean sometimes breaches the dunes and floods the area, turning the water brackish. Although fifteen species of fish populate the lagoon, the best angling is for large sea-run cutthroat of three to five pounds. Shore access is almost nonexistent, and shallow water and state regulations call for small, shallow-draft boats with outboards not exceeding 10 horsepower; electric motors are ideal here. All motors are prohibited during duck-hunting season. Launch ramps can be found at the ends of Buzzini Road and Lakeview Drive, each off Lake Earl Drive.

Shellfish, too, are present in the vicinity. Crabbers take tasty Dungeness crab in the harbor area from docks and piers, from December through July. North and south of town, sandy beaches provide good digging for razor, gaper, hard-shell, and littleneck clams. Mussels are found in rocky areas on minus tides.

A mussel quarantine—prohibiting all harvesting—is in effect each year from May 1 through October 31, because mussels can be toxic then. Clams are often affected, too, so the state issues a warning during that same period to clean clams thoroughly and discard any dark parts—this is no time for steamers. Because of dwindling stocks, razor clams are further regulated. Beaches south of Battery Point are open for razor-clam digging during even-numbered years, and north of the point during odd-numbered years.

Sailing, surfing, and sailboarding are also popular in the area, and the rivers attract rafters and kayakers.

GOLF

Del Norte Golf Club, 130 Club Drive, Hiouchi 95531; (707) 458–3214. Nine miles northeast of Crescent City via North Bank Road (Route 197) at Smith River. A par-seventy-one course amid the redwoods, open to the public. Pro shop, snack bar, and cocktail lounge. Club and cart rentals.

Kings Valley Golf Course, 3030 Lesina Road, 95531; (707) 464–2886. Five miles north of Crescent City, then east off U.S. 101 via Elk Valley Cross Road to Lesina Road. A nine-hole, par-twenty-eight, executive course with driving range, putting green, pro shop, and snack bar. Club and cart rentals. Restaurant and lounge on premises.

TRAVEL INFORMATION

Crescent City/Del Norte County Chamber of Commerce Visitor Center, 1001 Front Street, P.O. Box 246, 95531; (707) 464–3174; www.delnorte.org

U.S. Department of the Interior, National Park Service, Redwood National Park, 1111 Second Street, 95531; (707) 464–6106; www.nps.gov/redw/home.html

EVENTS

March	Aleutian Goose Festival, (707) 465–0888
June	Bay Blues Festival, (707) 464–1336
July	Art Show & Sale, (707) 464–9133
	Fourth of July Celebration, (707) 464–3174
	Cele-Bear-Ation—Annual Weekend in Bear Country, (707) 465–3013
August	Del Norte County Fair, (707) 464–9556
	Fuchsia Show & Sale, (707) 464–3827
	Klamath Salmon Festival, (707) 444–0433
	Crescent City Triathlon, (707) 464–6636
September	Crescent City Kite Festival, (541) 476–7208
	Jefferson State Bike Tour, (707) 464–8344
October	Noll Longboard Classic, (707) 465–4400
	Sea Cruise Classic Car Show, (707) 464–3174
November	Country Christmas in the Redwoods, (707) 482–2551
December	Holiday Fair, (707) 464–9556
	Festival of the Trees, (707) 482–4201

INDEX

ABOUT THE EDITOR

Donna Peck has been traveling the length and breadth of California as a writer and journalist for fifteen years. In addition to updating guidebooks for Globe Pequot Press, she writes online at Bay Area Traveler and in print for HarperCollins' ACCESS guides, *San Francisco Magazine,* and *In-Room CityGuide.*